Jugendzentrum erhält 15 000 Euro

Hamburg Am gestrigen Dienstag kam Herr Marquardt von der Stadtverwaltung zum Jugendzentrum ESCAPE, um die Teilnahme an dem Wettbewerb: ‚Deine Vision von der Zukunft Europas' zu würdigen. Die Jugendlichen dieses Jugendzentrums hatten ihre Vision in das Zentrum ihres Theaterstücks „My Way" gestellt. Dies präsentierten sie in Brüssel und schafften es so auf den dritten Platz. Dafür hat die Stadt Hamburg 15.000,00 € vergeben, die sie gestern feierlich überreichte.

Herr Mende, der Sozialarbeiter in dem Jugendzentrum sagte, er habe von Anfang an hinter der Idee des Theaterstücks gestanden und die Jugendlichen intensiv auch mit professioneller Hilfe von Schauspielern unterstützt.

Die bunt gemischte Gruppe der Jugendlichen will das Geld zur Renovierung und Erweiterung ihres Jugendzentrums nutzen und ihre Vision von Europa durch interkulturelle Seminare und Veranstaltungen leben. stw

When Justin arrived home from the clubhouse he emailed Chris because he wanted to tell him all the interesting news about ESCAPE.

ESCAPE

Senden | Chat | Anhang | Adressen | Schriften | Farben | Als Entwurf sichern

An: Chris@yahoo.ca

Kopie:

Betreff: ESCAPE

Account: Justin@yahoo.ca Signatur: Keine

Hi Chris,

My evening at the clubhouse was great fun. The clubhouse isn't like ours back home in Canada but very good. It's an old building and needs a lot of renovation work.

Mr Mende is the youth worker at the clubhouse and he and some of the members entered a competition about 'Your vision of Europe in the future'. This was a competition held by the City of Hamburg and the winners went to Brussels to discuss their vision with members of the European Parliament. ESCAPE didn't win, but the cool thing is that the City Council awarded us money to renovate our clubhouse and build a workshop extension. It's not a very big amount, so we have to do a lot ourselves and both Lucy and I are now part of this team.

We're meeting again later this week to discuss and decide on the next steps for our plans.

We've met Patrick, a good friend of Sebastian. I think Lucy rather likes him. I still can't speak a lot of German and I don't understand everything, but Sebastian explains and translates for me. He's a good guy.

I'll keep you updated but must go to bed now.

Justin

Struktur des Buches

TO DO Situationen, die auf den nächsten 4 Seiten behandelt werden.

PHRASES Satzbausteine, die bei der Kommunikation hilfreich sind.

HOW TO ... Erklärungen, Lerntipps, Methoden, ...

Die Lupe hebt Besonderheiten der englischen Sprache hervor.

VOCAB Wichtige Vokabeln, die auf der Doppelseite verwendet werden.

1. Aufgaben

HIerzu gibt es einen Höhrverstehentext auf der Audio-CD.

Beispielhafte Antworten

Verwendete grammatikalische Strukturen sind im Anhang näher erläutert.

Englisch

für gewerblich-technische Ausbildungsberufe

von
Stefanie Kunde
Elbie Picker
Klaus Rischbode

westermann

Englisch
für gewerblich-technische Ausbildungsberufe

1. Auflage, 2010
Druck 1, Herstellungsjahr 2010

Redaktion: Simone Wind, Holger Alex
Satz und Layout: Jesse Konzept & Text GmbH, Hannover
Umschlaggestaltung: boje5 Grafik & Werbung, Braunschweig
Druck und Bindung: westermann druck GmbH, Braunschweig

ISBN 978-3-14-**245010**-0

Vorwort

In der sich zunehmend internationalisierenden Arbeitswelt ist Englisch eine unverzichtbare Grundlage für eine erfolgreiche Kommunikation. Mitarbeiter aus vielen verschiedenen Ländern kommen auf deutsche Baustellen, umgekehrt ist deutsches Know-how, insbesondere im technischen Bereich, auch im Ausland gefragt. Wenn die Verständigung in der Landessprache nicht möglich ist, erfolgt die Kommunikation häufig auf Englisch.

Englisch wird an der Berufsschule berufsbezogen unterrichtet. Mit dem vorliegenden Lehrwerk kann dies im Unterricht umgesetzt werden. Sprachliche Kenntnisse und kommunikative Fertigkeiten werden in beruflichen (und privaten) Zusammenhängen vermittelt. Der Aufbau ist prozessorientiert: Im Mittelpunkt steht die Renovierung des Jugendklubs „ESCAPE“.

Für den (Berufs-)Alltag relevante sprachliche Strukturen werden in verschiedenen Units geübt. Die erforderliche englische Grammatik wird am Ende des Lehrwerks auf besondere Art dargestellt: Die Mitglieder des Jugendklubs „ESCAPE“ erklären sie anhand konkreter Situationen.

Das Lehrwerk führt den Lernenden von der Niveaustufe A2 (Basic User) zu B1 (Independent User). In jeder Unit werden die vier Kompetenzbereiche (Reception, Production, Mediation, Interaction) trainiert.

Am Ende jeder Doppelseite finden sich Übersetzungen neu eingeführter oder schwieriger Vokabeln, sodass aufwendiges Nachschlagen entfällt. In der Vokabelliste am Ende des Buches sind alle wichtigen englischen Vokabeln mit ihrer deutschen Übersetzung aufgeführt.

Die Inhalte des Lehrwerks sind für viele verschiedene Alltags- und Berufssituationen relevant und sprechen die Lernenden in allen gewerblich-technischen Berufen an.

Zu diesem Buch werden Zusatzmaterialien erscheinen. Bitte informieren Sie sich unter www.westermann.de

Wir wünschen Ihnen viel Spaß und Erfolg bei der Arbeit mit diesem Lehrwerk.

Autoren und Verlag

Contents

Setting the scene

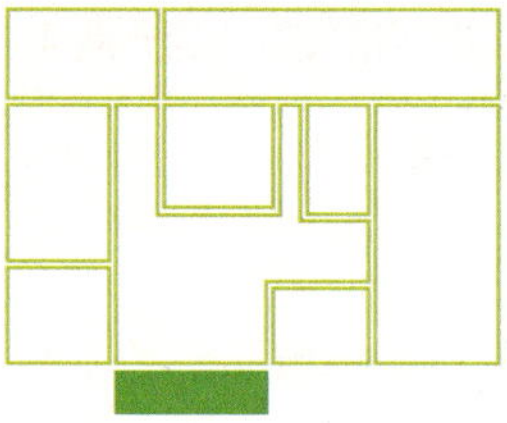

1. Front Door

1.1 ■ Greetings and introductions
■ Say goodbye 6

1.2 ■ Talk about hobbies and interests
■ Explain where things are 10

1.3 ■ Mediate between people
■ Identify parts of a house 14

1.4 ■ Talk about times and dates 18

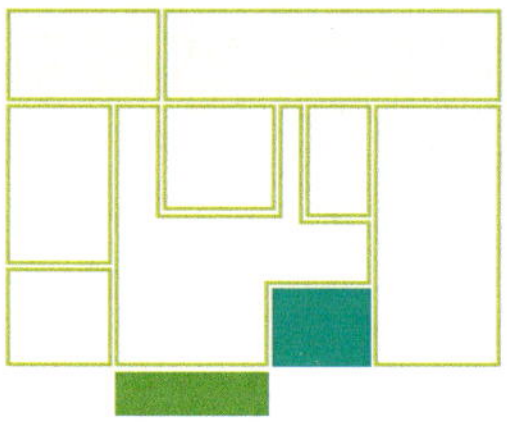

2. Kitchen

2.1 ■ Talk about sizes and dimensions
■ Measure things
■ Repair a blocked drain 22

2.2 ■ Get to know different kinds of food
■ Talk about meals and dishes 26

2.3 ■ Talk about daily routines and and duties
■ How to be polite
■ Talk about dishes one likes/dislikes .. 30

2.4 ■ How to ask questions
■ talk about general feelings 34

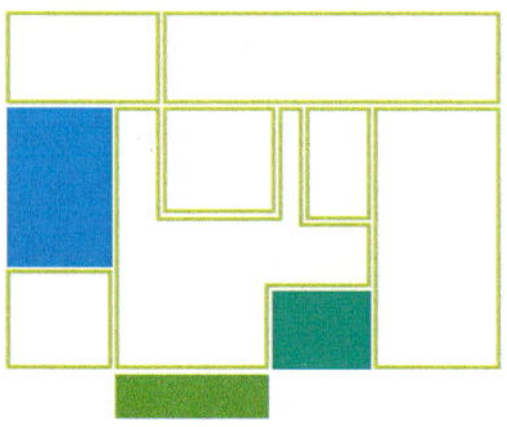

3. Workshop

3.1 ■ Use the present tense
■ Explain jobs on a building site 38

3.2 ■ Label tools
■ Look up vocabulary 42

3.3 ■ Understand instructions
■ Give instructions 46

3.4 ■ Express frequency
■ Talk about maintenance and repair
■ Describe problems at work 50

4. Billard Room

4.1 ■ Record vocabulary
■ Calculate quantities
■ Measure objects 54

4.2 ■ Say where things are
■ Describe packaging
■ Use much and many 58

4.3 ■ Talk about colours
■ Safety signs and colours 62

4.4 ■ Talk about the environment 66

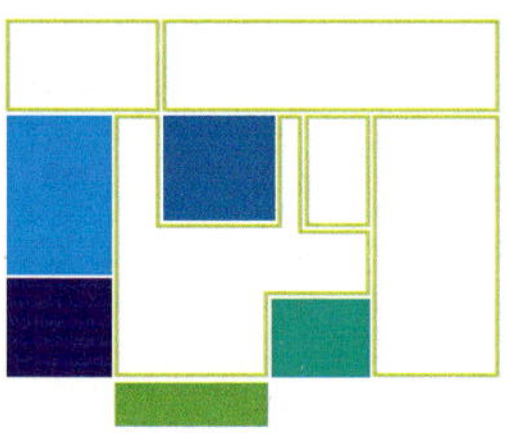

5. Office

5.1 ■ Talk about office equipment
■ Use the internet
■ Read an email address correctly 70

5.2 ■ How to speak on the telephone...... 74

5.3 ■ Write a simple enquiry
■ Write an offer 78

5.4 ■ Talk about things in the past 82

6. Extension

6.1 ■ Arrange a delivery
■ Arrange a meeting
■ Describing the way 86

6.2 ■ Explain mandatory signs
■ Give safety instructions 90

6.3 ■ Describe processes
■ Use sequence words 94

6.4 ■ Describe goods
■ Compare things and people 98

7. Lounge

7.1 ■ Apply for a job
■ Write a CV 102

7.2 ■ Write a covering letter 106

7.3 ■ Prepare for a job interview
■ Talk about likes and dislikes 110

7.4 ■ Talk about famous football clubs
■ Present yourself 114

8. First Aid Room

8.1 ■ Make emergency calls 118

8.2 ■ Parts of the body
■ Describe health problems 122

8.3 ■ Learn about a first aid kit
■ Deal with minor injuries 126

8.4 ■ Deal with stress
■ Find out how you learn best 130

9. Garden

9.1 ■ Talk about technical parts of a lawn mower
■ Fill a petrol can
■ Deal with problems with a lawn mower 134

9.2 ■ Talk about parts of a tree
■ Distinguish between different wood grains and paving materials
■ Form nouns 138

9.3 ■ Describe different paving materials and their uses
■ Describe how to build a fish pond 142

9.4 ■ Describe how to lift heavy objects safely
■ Become a member in a fitness club
■ Train at a fitness club 146

10. Big Hall

10.1 ■ Arrive in a foreign city
■ Go through immigration/passport control
■ Talk about holidays 150

10.2 ■ Talk about idols
■ Understand general information
■ Use the passive
■ Use some and any 154

10.3 ■ Give an opinion
■ Agree and disagree 158

10.4 ■ Plan a party
■ Talk about music
■ Discuss own past and furture 162

Grammar 166
Important irregular verbs 184
Appendix 186
Wordlist (German → English) 194

1. Front Door

1.1

TO DO

- Greetings and introductions
- Say goodbye

New kid on the block

Monday morning, maths lesson.

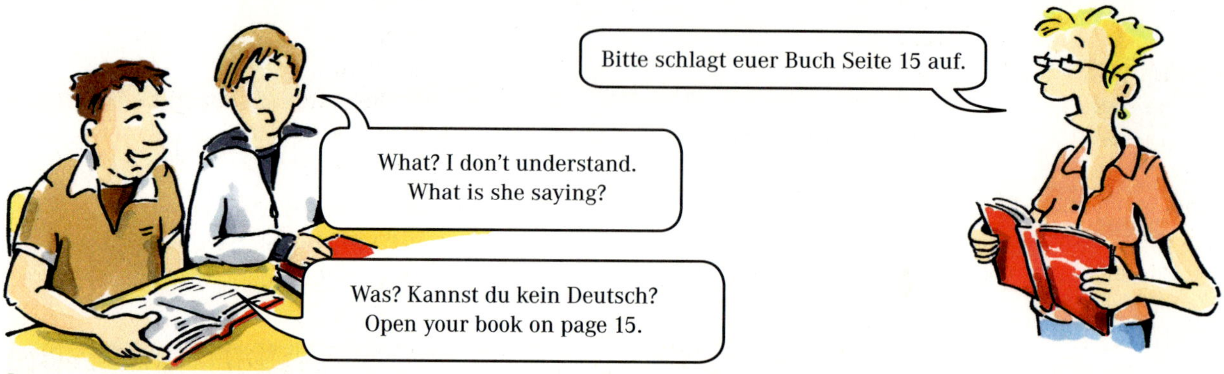

In the break

Between lessons the two boys have a chance to chat.

PHRASES

Greetings and introductions

Hello/Hi
Good morning. / afternoon. / evening.

What's your name?
My name's ...

Where are you from?
I'm from ...

This is (Lucy).
Nice to meet you.
Nice to meet you, too.

Saying goodbye

Goodbye
Bye
See you later. / soon. / tomorrow. / at the clubhouse tonight. / then. / at 6 o'clock.

1. **Imagine you have to introduce yourself to a stranger.**
Choose one of the roles below and practise your introduction with a partner.
Use the dialogue between Sebastian and Justin as a guide.

Sven	Anna	Behros	Carla	you
Poland	Sweden	Iran	Portugal	....
■ better jobs in Germany	■ mum followed her dad	■ moved away for a better life ■ no future for family in Iran	■ gap year	■ ...

take a **gap year** for example
- to travel
- to work as an au pair
- to do social services

2. **Find out about your class mates:**
- **Which countries do they come from?**
- **What nationality are they?**
- **Which languages do they speak?**

VOCAB

to imagine something sich etwas vorstellen	**a stranger** ein Fremder
to introduce a person eine Person vorstellen	**gap year** ein Jahr „Auszeit"

1. Front Door

In the canteen

It's lunch time and Justin and Sebastian are in the canteen.

Sebi: Hey, look at that girl with the red hair.
Justin: That's my sister, Lucy.

friend
Im Englischen nennt man jemanden seinen Freund, auch wenn man ihn gerade erst kennengelernt hat. Ein guter Freund wäre ein „best friend".

Later at home, Justin checks his emails and writes about his vocational school to his friend, Christopher, in Canada.

my first day

Senden Chat Anhang Adressen Schriften Farben Als Entwurf sichern

An: Chris@yahoo.ca

Cc:

Betreff: my first day

Hi Chris,
How are you? Did you **pass** the maths test that was so difficult?
Did the Edmonton Oilers win? There is a good ice-hockey team in Hamburg, the Hamburg Freezers. Do you know them? They are seventh in the **league**. I want to go to one of their **league games**.
How is school? School here is great, but it starts so early, eight o'clock!
My classmates are friendly and very helpful, especially as I don't understand everything. Sebastian, one of my school friends, helps me a lot.
I really enjoy the technical drawing lesson where we learn how to **draw to scale**. The teacher is great. He makes a lot of jokes but I don't understand them all.
There is a clubhouse near us where the young people meet. Lucy and I are going there tonight with Sebastian. I'll tell you about it next time I write.
Keep in touch.
Justin

3. **Read Justin´s email to Chris.**

a) Identify all simple present forms in the email.

page 167

b) Why do we use the simple present form?

4. **Write an email about your vocational school.**
What do / don't you like?
Write about your school friends, teachers, subjects, …

VOCAB

to colour färben	**league** Liga, **league game** Ligaspiel
vocational school Berufsschule	**to draw to scale** maßstabsgerecht zeichnen
to pass a test hier: einen Test bestehen	**subject** (Schul-) Fach

1.2

TO DO

- Talk about hobbies and interests
- Explain where things are

Meeting at the club

Sebastian, Justin and Lucy arrive at the clubhouse and meet Patrick.

1. Read the bubbles and complete the table with the information from the bubbles.

Name	Place of birth	Age	Interests and Hobbies	Favourite Music
Sebastian	Hamburg	17	music, computers	hip-hop
Justin				

2. page 167

Find a partner and ask and answer questions about the friends.

A: What is Sebastian's favourite music?
B: His favourite music is hip-hop.
A: What are his hobbies?
B: He likes music and computers.
A: How old is he?
B: He's 17.

PHRASES

Talking about hobbies and interests

I	love like	soaps talk shows music programmes tennis fashion sport books
	watch play read listen to	films football magazines music

3. **What are your interests?**
Form sentences about your hobbies and interests with the help of the above phrases.

4. **Listen to 4 people talking about themselves. Note down**

3

a) who they are and
b) what their hobbies and interests are.

Complete the table.

Who are the people?	What are their hobbies and interests?
Jona: from Toronto, Canada	

VOCAB

usually gewöhnlich **together** zusammen **favourite** Lieblings… **actor** Schauspieler	**gym** Sporthalle, Fitnessstudio **fashion magazine** Modezeitschrift **to complete something** etwas vervollständigen **table** Tabelle

1.2

1. Front Door

ESCAPE to the clubhouse

They enter the clubhouse and Sebi tells them more about the name.

This is our clubhouse.
The name „Escape“
stands for
Everyone
Should
Contribute
And
Participate
Enthusiastically
Come inside and
I'll show you around.

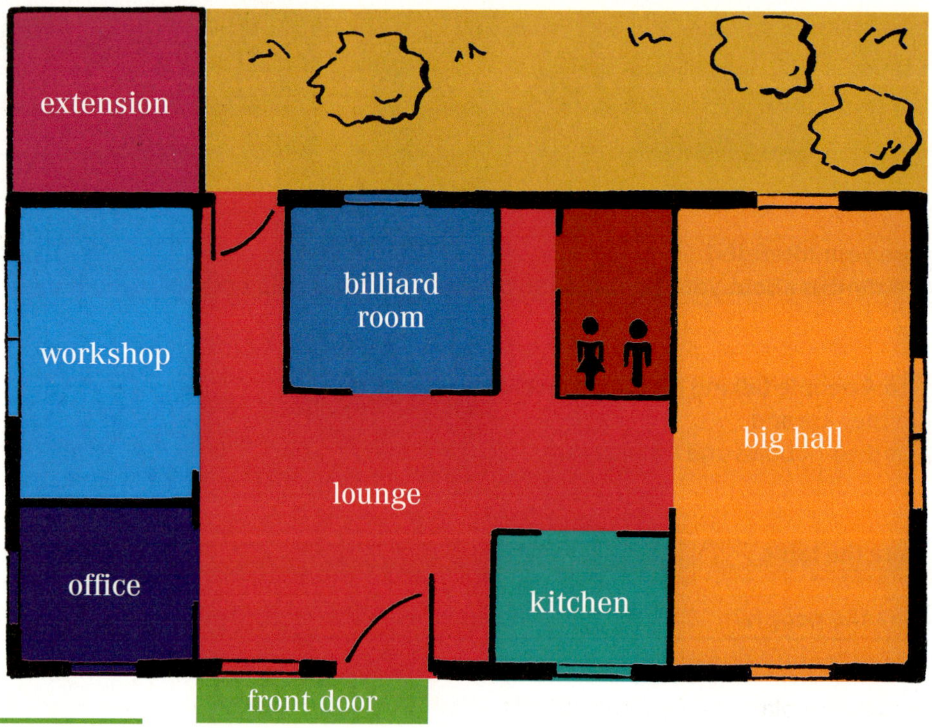

- 1. front door
- 2. kitchen
- 3. workshop
- 4. billiard room
- 5. office
- 6. **extension** for car repairs
- 7. **lounge**
- 8. first aid room/ toilets
- 9. garden
- 10. big hall

5.

Look at the plan of the clubhouse.
Listen to the conversation and follow Lucy, Sebastian and Justin on their tour through the clubhouse.

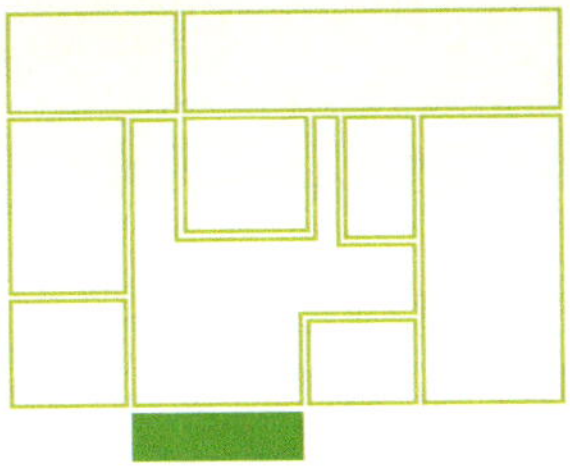

VOCAB — **Where is it?**

6. Look at the pictures above and the floor plan of ESCAPE (page 12).
Tell your partner where these places are.

place	preposition
front door	between
garden	next to
big hall	on the left
billiard room	on the right
kitchen	in front of
office	behind
toilets	in the centre of
lounge	
workshop	
back door	

7. Draw the floor plan of your flat/house. Describe the layout to your partner.

VOCAB

escape hier: Zuflucht **to contribute** beitragen **enthusiastically** mit Begeisterung	**extension** Anbau **lounge** hier: Aufenthaltsraum

1. Front Door

1.3

TO DO

- Mediate between people
- Identify parts of a house

The meeting in the big hall

Sebastian, Lucy and Justin join the others in the big hall for the meeting. They are talking about the renovation and the extension of the building because they want to have a new workshop for car and motorbike repairs.

HOW TO ... Mediate between people

Mit Mediation ist die Vermittlung zwischen zwei Sprachen gemeint. Hierbei kann es sich um schriftliche Texte oder Gespräche handeln. Ziel einer Mediation ist es, die wesentlichen Informationen in die andere Sprache zu übertragen. Im Gegensatz zur Übersetzung geht es nicht um eine „Wort-für-Wort-Übersetzung", sondern darum, die wesentlichen Inhalte eines Textes oder Gespräches zu erfassen und diese in der anderen Sprache zu vermitteln.

1. **Justin and Lucy didn't understand much in the meeting. Help Sebastian to explain what each of them can do themselves. Are the following statements true, false or not mentioned?**

a) **Victor, the plumber**

- I can't install the water pipes.
- I can connect the sink.
- I want to install the heating.

b) **Olga, the metalworker**

- I can make a railing.
- I can't install burglar bars.

c) **Lucy, the painter**

- I can help with the painting.
- I want to paint walls and ceilings without help.

d) **Hakan, the car mechanic**

- I can install a car hoist.
- I want to buy a car hoist.
- I would like to buy tools.

e) **Mr Mende, the youth worker**

- I can organize the electricity.
- I want to help the electrician.

f) **Anna, the gardener**

- I can lie down in the garden.
- I can lay out the garden.
- I can't plaster the walls.

2. **What can Sebastian and his friends do themselves? Make a list.**

VOCAB

I don't get anything Ich verstehe nichts	**railing** Geländer
true wahr	**burglar bars** Fenstergitter
false falsch	**car hoist** Hebebühne
not mentioned nicht erwähnt	**tool** Werkzeug
to install installieren, einsetzen, anbauen	**to lay out** anlegen
sink Waschbecken	**to plaster** verputzen

1. Front Door

Parts of a house

After the meeting Sebastian, Justin and Lucy are still talking about the renovation and what they can do themselves. Justin explains how he helped his father to renovate their home in Canada.

3.

Justin and Lucy lived in a house in Canada.
Listen to Justin and Lucy describing their house to Sebastian.
Find the mistake.

Outside the house

- chimney
- driveway
- front door
- front steps
- garage
- gate
- gutter
- hedge
- lawn
- roof
- wall
- window
- wooden porch

4.

What are the different parts of a house?
Translate them and match them with the numbers in the picture.

Parts of the house
1 gutter – Dachrinne
2

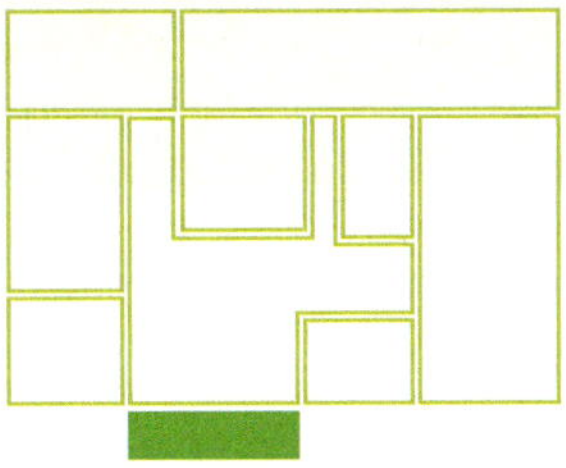

5. Now describe Justin´s house to a partner. "The house has a brown front door."

VOCAB — **Colours**

blue	red	yellow	green	orange	purple	brown	grey	black	white

light hell **dark** dunkel **bright** strahlend, leuchtend

Live like the stars on Pinetree Drive, Miami Beach, South Florida
For sale: Bargain price $ 13,900,000.00

This **two-storey** impressive Mediterranean-style **residence** is **set well back** from the road in the spacious grounds of prestigious Pinetree Drive. This magnificant estate, with its **acres** of ground and **private ocean access** with dock for private yachts, **captures** the elegance of the past, but still provides **state-of-the-art** luxury; ideal for the modern couple of today who enjoy entertaining and socializing with friends and business partners.
Entry to the **waterfront property** is secured through **ornate iron gates** with a high brick wall to prevent **intrusion**. A security system with **CCTV** monitoring is installed.
True to the Mediterranean style, the house with its 5 bedrooms, 7 full bathrooms and 3 showers is designed around a **courtyard** including a **marble patio**, **gazebo**, outdoor kitchen with BBQ and swimming pool. In addition to the main house, there are **self-contained detached** staff quarters as well as a detached **double-storey** guest house with kitchenette, living room and bathroom. The house has a circular marble driveway with a beautiful fountain near the entrance. Further **interior features** are marble floors, central air conditioning, **central heating**, **intercom system**, fireplace, wine cellar, mahogany kitchen with **granite kitchen counters** and **impact-resistance** windows and doors.

For further information please contact Jo Carr under the number: (786) 349-8992, Homes Galore, the **real estate agency** you can trust.

6. Tell your classmates in German about the home for sale. (Mediation)

VOCAB

two storey / double-storey zweistöckiges Haus	**courtyard** Hof
residence Wohnhaus	**marble patio** Marmorterrasse
set well back zurückgesetzt	**gazebo** Pavillion
an acre ein Morgen	**self-contained** abgeschlossen
private ocean access privater Strandzugang	**detached** alleinstehend
to capture einfangen	**interior features** Innenausstattung
state-of-the-art modern(ste)	**central heating** Zentralheizung
waterfront property Grundstück am Wasser	**intercom system** Gegensprechanlage
ornate iron gates prunkvolle Eisentore	**granite kitchen counter** Granit-Küchentresen
intrusion Einbruch	**impact-resistance** Schlagfestigkeit
CCTV (= closed circuit television) Videoüberwachung	**real estate agency** Immobilienmakler

1.4

TO DO

- Talk about time and dates

Opening hours

Sebi and Justin are standing in front of the clubhouse.

So, Justin, this is our clubhouse or **rather** we want to make it our clubhouse.

Huh! It's very **shabby** and **dilapidated**. It needs a lot of repairing and renovating. Somebody has broken into the house; the door is open!

Yes, I know. But we have already got 15,000 € from the city council. So, we can **restore** it. At the moment, the most important thing is that nobody can get in. Mr Mende told me that he'll **take care** of the **lock**.

Oh, that's good. But the door has to be **replaced**, it looks completely **rotten**.

Oh no. We'll **sand it down** and paint it and then it will look as good as new again.

And, does everybody get a key? Or ...

No, we have special **opening hours**. You see, Mr Mende, our youth worker, is always here Monday, Tuesday and Wednesday from 5 pm to 8 pm and at the weekends on Saturdays from 4 pm to 10 pm and on Sundays from 4 pm to 8 pm. Let me write the opening hours down for you:

PHRASES

Nur zur vollen Stunde benutzt man ***o'clock:***	
Es ist 4 Uhr.	It's four **o'clock**.
Es ist viertel nach 4.	It's **a quarter past** four.
Es ist 10 Minuten nach 4.	It's ten **past** four. (It's four ten.)
Es ist viertel vor 5.	It's **a quarter to** five.
Es ist 20 Minuten vor 5.	It's twenty **to** five. (It's four forty.)
Im Englischen spricht man von der halben Stunde nach der vollen Stunde.	
Es ist halb 5.	It's **half past** four. (It's four thirty.)
Sind die Minuten nicht durch 5 teilbar, wird „minutes" ausgesprochen.	
Es ist 4 Minuten nach 8.	It's four **minutes past** eight.
Es ist 12 Minuten vor 5.	It's twelve **minutes to** five.

What time is it?

Die 24-Stunden-Uhr wird im Englischen nur für z. B. Fahrpläne genutzt.

a.m. (ante meridiem = vor dem Mittag)
p.m. (post meridiem = nach dem Mittag)

Es ist 4 Uhr morgens.
It's 4 o'clock **in the morning**.
It's 4 **a.m.**

Es ist 10 Uhr abends.
It's 10 o'clock **in the evening**.
It's 10 **p.m.**

More Examples:
12.00 p.m. = midday (noon)
12.00 a.m. = midnight
7.57 = nearly eight o'clock
8.02 = just after eight

1. Listen to the three dialogues. Which time belongs to which dialogue?
16:00 – 2:00 – 8:05 – 16:30 – 8:00 – 20:00 – 8:45

7

2. Error spotting: Is there anything wrong with the following times? If yes, what?

a) It's a quarter to five.
b) It's half past 12. ➔ Es ist halb 1.
c) It's twelve to eight.
d) It's a quarter past seven o'clock.
e) It's four past seven.
f) It's nine.
g) It's quarter past two.
h) Es ist 11 Uhr morgens. ➔ It's 11 a.m.

Justin: Is the clubhouse open next Friday?
Sebi: You mean, because it's the 1st of May? No, it's not. The clubhouse is closed on all **public holidays**, like Christmas, Easter, 1st of May, **Pentecost**, 3rd of October ...
Justin: What's the 3rd of October?
Sebi: It's **German Unity Day**. This day **marks** the unification of the **former** East Germany and West Germany. Germany was **divided** after the Second World War.
Justin: I see. Are there any more public holidays?
Sebi: Well, you can see them on a calendar. They are usually marked in red.
Justin: Of course, sure. But what happens **during** the school holidays? Is Mr Mende also here or is the clubhouse closed then?
Sebi: **That depends**. The clubhouse is usually open during the school holidays in spring and autumn. In December it is closed between Christmas and New Year. During the summer holidays the clubhouse is usually closed for one month. This year it'll be closed in July. That's when Mr Mende goes on holiday.
Justin: All right, that's easy to remember...

3. List all puplic holidays mentioned in the dialogue above together with the date. If the date is not given find it out with the use of a calendar.

VOCAB

rather eher
shabby schäbig
dilapidated heruntergekommen
to restore restaurieren
to take care of something sich um etwas kümmern
lock Schloss
to replace austauschen
rotten verfallen, morsch
to sand something down etwas abschmirgeln

opening hours Öffnungszeiten
public holidays Feiertage
Pentecost Pfingsten
German Unity Day Tag der deutschen Einheit
to mark markieren
former ehemalig
to divide teilen
during während
that depends es kommt darauf an

PHRASES

Im Englischen wird bei der Angabe des Datums kein Punkt gesetzt.

Dates and Months

Es gibt mehrere Möglichkeiten, das Datum zu schreiben:

1st January 20XX,	1 January 20XX,	the first of January	(British English)
January 1st 20XX,	January 1, 20XX,	January first	(American English)

Die Zahl im Datum wird wie folgt abgekürzt:

1st	first	der erste (Januar)	16th	sixteenth
2nd	second		17th	seventeenth
3rd	third		18th	eighteenth
4th	fourth		19th	nineteenth
5th	fifth		20th	twentieth
6th	sixth		21st	twenty-first
7th	seventh		22nd	twenty-second
8th	eighth		23rd	twenty-third
9th	ninth		24th	twenty-fourth
10th	tenth		25th	twenty-fifth
11th	eleventh		26th	twenty-sixth
12th	twelfth		27th	twenty-seventh
13th	thirteenth		28th	twenty-eighth
14th	fourteenth		29th	twenty-ninth
15th	fifteenth		30th	thirtieth
			31st	thirty-first

Monatsnamen werden im Englischen immer groß geschrieben.

January – February – March – April – May – June
July – August – September – October – November – December

4. **Write the following dates in words (British English):**
04.11.1903 – 24.12.2022 – 03.03.2019 – 21.08.1978
01.01.1990 – 02.09.1998 – 14.02.2009 – 07.12.2044

5. **Write down the birthdays of some of your friends and family members. Dictate them to a classmate. Now check: Are they written correctly?**

6. **Using a calendar name the dates of the German public holidays.**

7. **Read Justin's email and then reply to it. Include these points:**
a) Talk about your difficult time in maths because Justin isn't there to help you.
b) Ask about Justin's German.
c) Ask about Justin's job as a joiner.
d) Ask about Lucy and her **relationship** to Sebastian.
e) Tell him about your **work experience**.
f) You are happy that Justin invited you to visit him in Hamburg.

An: Chris@yahoo.ca
Cc:
Betreff: the German way of life

Hi Chris,
How are you? I'm o.k. but still a little bit **confused** about the German way of life. People are sometimes very formal to each other. For example, they always use "Sie" at work or when they don't know each other well.
This is very formal, but our new friends really help Lucy and me a lot to get along.
Today, Sebastian showed us around the clubhouse. Nearly all the rooms have to be **redecorated**, or something has to be repaired. They also want to **extend** it to have a place to repair cars and motorcycles. Really a lot of work, but Sebastian and Patrick are very motivated and want to **tackle** it. It is really great to be with them, we have a lot of fun. Hope you can come to visit us some time and meet all these great guys.
CU Justin

VOCAB

to include einschließen	**to redecorate** renovieren
relationship Beziehung	**to extend** erweitern
work experience Praktikum	**to tackle something** etwas angehen
confused verwirrt	**something worth celebrating** das sollte gefeiert werden

2. Kitchen

2.1

TO DO

- Talk about sizes and dimensions
- Measure things
- Repair a blocked drain

A new dishwasher

8

Victor is in the kitchen of the clubhouse. He is measuring the gap for the new dishwasher that Mr Mende ordered last week. Lucy and Anna are watching him.

Victor: 60 cm wide, 63 cm deep and 85 cm high. That's the size of the dishwasher Mr Mende ordered last week. Hmm, the gap is a little bit too small! We need a dishwasher that has a width of 50 cm. The depth and height are o.k.

Lucy: Should Mr Mende ask 'Elektro-Garbe' if they have a smaller one?

Anna: Yes, and what about the new fridge? When are they delivering that?

Victor: Well, Mr Mende told me that they want to deliver the fridge next Tuesday. They said somebody has to be here from 7 o'clock in the morning until 2 p.m. I hope they can bring a new dishwasher of the right size together with the fridge.

1. **Find a word in the text above that is similar in meaning.**

a) A machine to wash the dishes.
b) An open space between two things.
c) When something is not large then it is …
d) To bring something.
e) The one immediately following.
f) Early time of the day.
g) To want something and to think that it is possible.
h) With other things.

2. 9

Mr Mende is busy on the phone when Lucy and Viktor come into his office. Listen to what Mr Mende tells Lucy and Viktor after he finishes his phone call. Answer the following questions.

a) Who is on the phone?
b) What is the problem?
c) Does 'Elektro-Garbe' have the dishwasher Mr Mende wants?
d) What does 'Elektro-Garbe' offer Mr Mende?
e) What are the dimensions of the smaller dishwasher?
f) When does 'Elektro-Garbe' want to bring the new dishwasher?

PHRASES		Dimensions
How long is it?	It's 1 cm long. It's one centimetre long. It's 10 cm long. It's ten centimetres long.	The **length** is 10 cm.
How wide is it?	It's 45 cm wide. It's forty five centimetres wide.	The **width** is 45 cm.
How high is it?	It's 80 cm high. It's eighty centimetres high.	The **height** is 80 cm.
How deep is it?	It's 35 cm deep. It's thirty five centimetres deep.	The **depth** is 35 cm.
What is the size of ...? What size is ... ?	It's 45 x 65 x 80. It's forty five centimetres by sixty five centimetres by 80 centimetres.	

3. **Work in pairs:**

a) Measure two things in your classroom and write the measurements down.

b) Practise talking to your partner about the dimensions of the kitchen equipment.

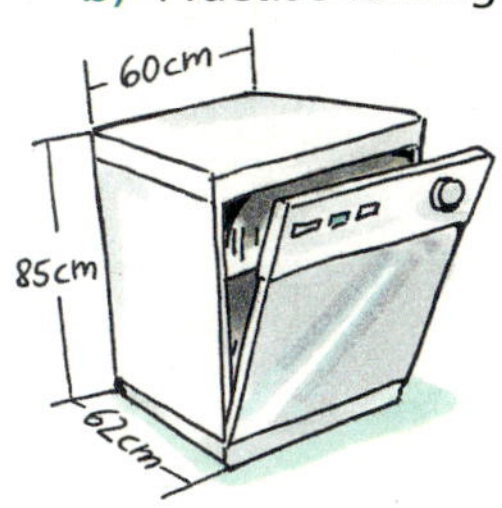

dishwasher

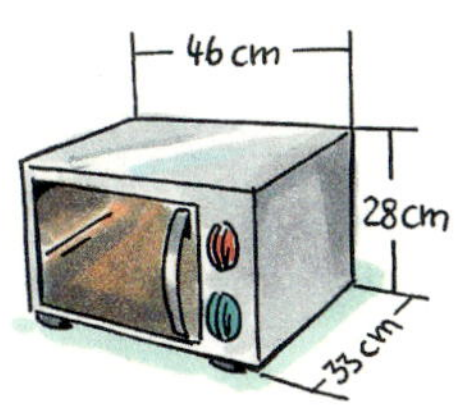

microwave

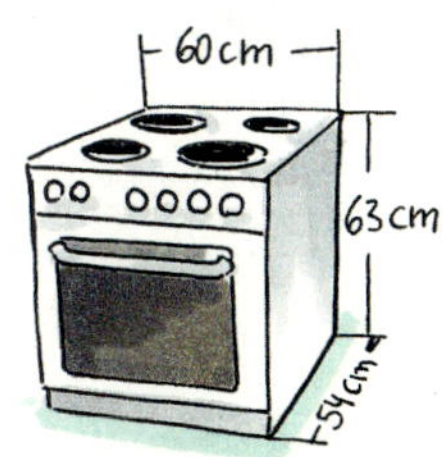

cooker

fridge freezer

4. **Copy the sentences and fill in the gaps with words from the phrase box above.**

a) The dishwasher is 85 cm .... Its ... is 60 cm and its ... is 62 cm.

b) What about the microwave? How ... is It? 28 cm. And how ... and ... is it? 46 cm and 33 cm.

c) What did Victor say? What are the ... of the cooker? The cooker is 63 cm high, 60 cm ... and 54 cm ....

d) The ... of the fridge freezer is 1.80 m ... 60 cm ... 54 cm. 1.80 ... is its ..., 60 cm is its ... and 54 cm is its .... However the refrigerator itself is only 1.20 cm ... but its ... and ... are of course of the same ... as the freezer.

VOCAB

size Größe	**gap** Lücke	**depth** Tiefe
dimension Dimension	**to order** bestellen	**height** Höhe
to measure messen	**wide** breit	**to deliver** liefern
to block verstopfen	**deep** tief	**immediately** sofort
drain Abfluss	**width** Breite	**busy** beschäftigt

2. Kitchen

The blocked drain

As promised 'Elektro-Garbe' brought the replacement dishwasher and the new refrigerator at 1.30 p.m. So the next problem in the kitchen could be tackled. When Victor wanted to clean the sink in the kitchen of the clubhouse he realised that the water didn't run off. He talks to Lucy and Anna about it:

a) Use a **measuring tape** to measure the new pipe to be **inserted**. In order to insert the pipe in the space, the measurement of the **coupling sleeve**, which will **protrude** on either side of the pipe, must be **deducted** when calculating the length of the pipe to be fitted.

b) Finally **wipe** off any **excess grease** on the outside of the pipe with a **cloth** and make sure that the drain pipe is not **leaking** and that the water is running off **properly**.

c) When cutting the **pipe**, a **bucket** or similar container should be placed under the pipe to catch any water which is in the pipe. After removing the piece of pipe, look into both ends to **ensure** that there is no dirt still in the pipe.

d) Oh, I know what the problem is. The drain is blocked and a part has to be **replaced**. We had a similar situation at the building site the other day. Let me show you how it works best.

e) Next **deburr** both ends of the pipe both inside and outside with a **half-round file**. File an **angle** on the outside of the pipe and clean the pipe with a cloth.

f) Apply grease on all ends and push a coupling sleeve onto both ends of the new pipe and fit the pipe between the two ends of the old pipe. If necessary use a hammer to gently ease the coupling sleeve in the direction of the pipe. Make sure that the rubber ring is not **twisted** and that the measured insertion depth is correct when the coupling sleeve is pushed onto the pipe.

g) Firstly, the blocked part of the **drain** has to be cut out. This part should be marked both on the left and right side and then cut out with a saw. The cut must be **straight** so that the **join** is **impervious** when the new piece is joined later. Use this simple trick. Before cutting, attach a **clamp** on either side of the piece of pipe to be replaced. One side of the clamp must **be flush** with the line to be cut. When the clamp is then **tightened**, you have a straight surface along which to cut. If the space for the saw is not big enough, you can also use a single machine **blade**.

h) The new piece of pipe should also be deburred at both ends both inside and outside. File an angle on the outside of the pipe. Measure the length of the insertion and mark it accordingly.

5. **Put Viktor's explanation into the correct order and write it down.**

6. **After putting Victor's explanation into the correct order answer the following questions.**

a) Which tools do you need to repair a blocked drain?
b) What is the first step to repair a blocked drain?
c) What can you do to make sure that the cut at the drain is straight?
d) What is the bucket for?
e) What has to be done after removing the blocked piece of pipe?
f) Which tool do you need to deburr the pieces of pipe?
g) What is important when you calculate the length of the pipe to be fitted?
h) How can you fit the new pipe between the two ends of the old pipe?

7. Find the expressions for the items shown in the pictures in Victor's explanation above. Which item is not mentioned?

a)  Schiebemuffe	b)  Hammer	c) 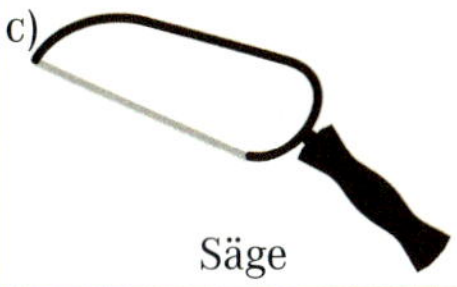 Säge	d)  Bleistift
e)  Gleitmittel	f)  Eimer	g)  Schraubendreher	h) 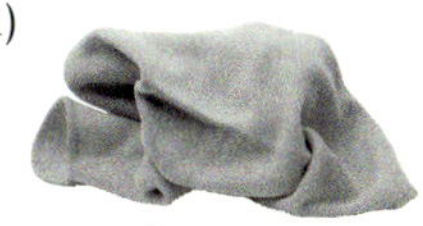 Lappen
i)  Maschinensägeblatt	j)  Rohrschelle	k)  Halbrundfeile	l) 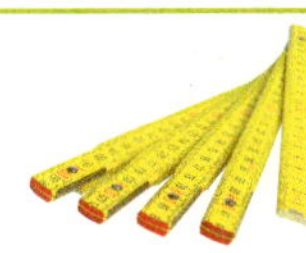 Gliedermaßstab

8. Match the verbs with a corresponding noun.

Verbs		Nouns	
to apply	to measure	an angle	grease
to attach	to place	a bucket	the length
to catch	to remove	a clamp	the pipe
to deburr	to replace	dirt	water
to file		the drain	

9. Mediation: Explain how to fix a blocked drain in German.

VOCAB

replacement Ersatz
to tackle a problem ein Problem angehen
sink Spülbecken
measuring tape Maßband
to insert einfügen
coupling sleeve Schiebemuffe
to protrude überstehen
to deduct abziehen
to wipe off abwischen
excess überschüssig
grease Gleitmittel
cloth Tuch
to leak lecken
properly ordentlich
pipe Rohr
bucket Eimer
to ensure sicherstellen
to replace ersetzen
to deburr entgraten
half-round file Halbrundfeile
angle Winkel
to twist verbiegen
drain Rohr
straight gerade
join hier: Verbindungsstelle
impervious undurchlässig
clamp Schelle
to be flush bündig sein
to tighten festziehen
blade Sägeblatt
expression Ausdruck
item Gegenstand
corresponding zugehörig

2.2

TO DO

- Get to know different kinds of food
- Talk about meals and dishes

A delicious dinner

After Victor repaired the blocked drain, he cleans the sink. Anna and Lucy help him clean the rest of the kitchen. Anna mops the floor and Lucy cleans the cupboard.

Anna: Oh boy, what a **mess**, but this "Spezialwischtuch" actually makes cleaning easy.
Lucy: Haha, "Spezialwischtuch", that sounds funny but it really works.
Anna: Yes, and I'm so happy that we will have such a **well-equipped** kitchen.
Victor: Yes, that's really true. Why don't we celebrate it with a "kitchen-warming" party?
Lucy: Yes, why don't we make a delicious **dinner** for us all? We could make hot-dogs and hamburgers, pizza and spaghetti.
Anna: Oh, that's a great idea, Lucy.
Victor: Hot dogs, pizza?? That's not delicious, that's a lot of **junk food**, Lucy.
Lucy: Yes, well that's right. But you could make a green vegetable salad.
Anna: Yes, and I could prepare a fruit salad ...

dinner
a warm meal, is not connected with a **certain** time, but lunch is always connected with a meal eaten at noon

1.

a) Look at the pictures of many different kinds of food. Match the pictures with the words. What are the German expressions?

pepper can be both in German 'Pfeffer' and 'Paprika'

almonds	curry	peanuts
apples	garlic	**pepper**
bacon	ginger	pineapple
beef	hazelnuts	**plaice**
broccoli	herring	**pollack**
cherries	kiwis	**pumpkin**
chicken	**lettuce**	sausage
chives	onion	tomatoes
cereals	oranges	vinegar
cucumber	**parsley**	walnuts

b) Group the kinds of food **according to** the **headings** given in the table.

Vegetables	Fruits and Nuts	Fish	Meat	Herbs and Spices

c) Anna wants to prepare a mixed salad. Which **ingredients** from the table would she use? Would you **add** anything that is not in the table?

2. **How is food usually processed? Match the food with the correct processing verb.**

Verbs		Food	
to bake	to peel	tomatoes	oranges, apples
to boil	to pickle	a fruit salad	pepper
to chop	to prepare	a potato	cherries
to crack	to remove the core of	broccoli	plaice, bacon
to fry	to skin	walnuts	herbs, almonds
to mill		herring	

VOCAB

to mop wischen
mess Sauerei
well-equipped gut ausgestattet
junk food minderwertige Kost
certain bestimmt
chives Schnittlauch
lettuce Kopfsalat
parsley Petersilie
plaice Scholle
pollack Seelachs
pumpkin Kürbis
according to entsprechend
heading Überschrift
ingredients Zutaten
to add hinzufügen
to process verarbeiten

2. Kitchen

Preparations for a delicious dinner

Hakan comes into the kitchen and is really surprised about the equipment and how clean it is.

Hakan: Hey, you guys. How's it going? Wow, what a nice kitchen! The first room in our clubhouse that is finished and **usable**! How cool...

Lucy: Yeah, great isn't it? And now we want to have a kitchen-warming party with hamburgers, hot-dogs, pizza and spaghetti.

Hakan: Aha, good idea, but that sounds like a lot of **pork** to me. Typically German, can't we have some more **beef**, or chicken?

Anna: Of course, we can, sorry Hakan but why don't you eat pork?

Hakan: Because of my religion. Muslims don't to eat pork.

Anna: Ah, so what would you like to eat then, Döner?

Hakan: Oh, come on Anna, Turkish people eat a lot more than Döner! Let me, for example, bring Lahmacun for you. It's a typical Turkish pizza. My mother can make some for us. And for **dessert** she could make Baklava. It's sweet and very **delicious**. My mother would love to make it for us.

Lucy: Great, so, you don't want to make it here?

Hakan: No, Baklava is really not easy to make, at least for me.

Lucy: All right. And what do we have to drink. What do you think about beer, Coke, juice, lemonade or "Alcopops"?

Hakan: Well no beer for me, but Coke and orange juice would be fine. We Muslims don't drink any alcohol at all ..., not even at **weddings**.

Lucy: Aha, okay, so what do you want, Anna and Victor?

Victor: Well Lucy, no "Alcopops"! You drink them and don't **realize** that you get drunk, no thank you. Let's have some beer, the soft drinks and "Apfelschorle". Lucy what is "Apfelschorle" in English?

Lucy: Oh, there is no word for it in English. You have to **describe** it. It's a mixture of apple juice and **sparkling** mineral water.

Victor: Ok, so we need apple juice and sparkling water, too.

Anna: Yes, and who's going to buy it?

Victor: Anna, we could go and buy the drinks.

Anna: Yes, ok. And the others buy what is needed for their dishes, all right?

Lucy: Oh, that means I have to **carry** everything for the hamburgers, the hot-dogs, the pizza and the spaghetti for everybody. Puh, that's a lot!

Anna: Well, we only need 3 frozen pizzas, 2 packets of spaghetti and a bit of cheese. For the hamburgers, we need some beef and **rolls**. Ketchup and mayonnaise is here. Victor will bring the lettuce. Then for the hot-dogs: 4 jars of sausages, some **roasted** onions, a glass of **gherkins** and also rolls. **Mustard** is here as well. Why don't you ask Patrick or Sebi to help you?

Lucy: Do you think they will help me?

Anna: Well, if they don't, they won't get anything to eat! Come on now let's make a list of what we need ...

3. **Find words in the conversation above that have a similar meaning to the ones in the box.**

boys – in working condition – characteristically – faith – forbidden – persons – tasty – fruit drink – explain – combination

4. **In the conversation German and Turkish nationalities are mentioned. Copy the table and complete it by filling in the nationalities and the German translations.**

German word	Country	Nationality
Kanada	Canada	Canadian
	Germany	
	Turkey	
	France	
	Hungary	

5. **Answer the following questions on the text "Preparations for a delicious dinner".**

a) What does Hakan think of the new kitchen?
b) How will the friends celebrate the new kitchen?
c) Does Hakan eat meat?
d) What does Hakan say about Baklava?
e) What is Apfelschorle?
f) Who is doing the shopping for the dinner?

6. **Read the dialogues on page 26 and page 28 and**

a) write down who wants what,

name	food and drinks the friends want to have
Victor	
Lucy	
Hakan	
Anna	

b) complete Anna's list. What do you think the friends will buy for their dishes?

VOCAB

to be surprised überrascht sein
usable benutzbar
pork Schweinefleisch
beef Rindfleisch
dessert Nachtisch
delicious lecker
wedding Hochzeit
to realize merken
to describe beschreiben
sparkling sprudelnd
to carry tragen
rolls Brötchen
to roast rösten
gherkin Gewürzgurke
mustard Senf
to mention erwähnen

2.3

TO DO

- Talk about daily routines and duties
- How to be polite
- Talk about dishes one likes/dislikes

Hakan's story

On their way home, Lucy and Anna ask Hakan a lot of questions about his cultural background and life.

This is me

I'm Hakan Eskikaya. I was born in Istanbul, but now I live in Hamburg. I'm 18 years old and I am in my second apprenticeship year to become a car mechanic.

A day in my life

I work from Monday to Wednesday and on Friday. On Thursday I go to vocational school. I get up at 6:30 a.m., I have breakfast at 7 o'clock and leave the house at 7:30. I travel to work by bus. I start work at 8 o'clock, I eat my lunch at 12:30 and go home at 5 o'clock. At home, I have supper with my family. My mother usually cooks for all of us, that's my dad, my two sisters, my brother and me.
Twice a week, I go to the gym to keep fit and I sometimes go to the clubhouse to meet my friends.

At work

My duties include doing oil and filter changes, brake and clutch repairs, and some auto electrical work. I repair cars that have broken down or have been involved in accidents. And I make routine checks according to a list, finding faults or problems, then overhauling or replacing worn or faulty parts. I use special equipment and do road tests to make sure the vehicle performs as it should.

1. **Read above what Hakan says about himself and make a vocabulary list with unknown words.**

English	German
vocational school	Berufsschule
...	

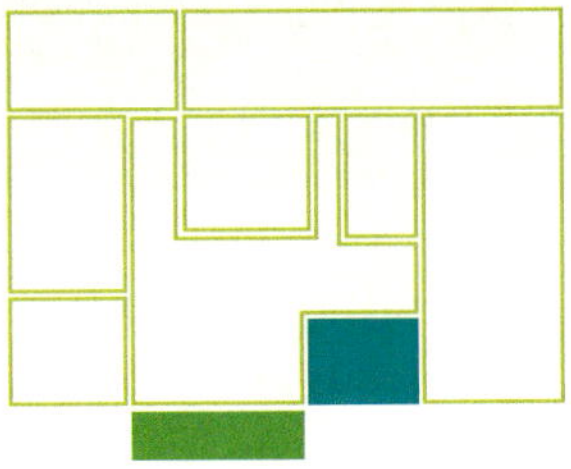

2. **Make sentences about Hakan.**
He was born …
He's a …
At work he …

3. **Write about you.**

- What's your name?
- How old are you?
- Where are you from?
- Which vocational school do you go to?
- What do you usually do during the day?
- What is your daily routine at work?

4. **Now describe Victor's daily routines as a plumber. Use the phrases below to form complete sentences.**

A plumber has to

- read and interpret drawings, plans and **specifications**
- install and repair pipes and other plumbing equipment used for the **supply of water** and **wastewater drainage**
- install sinks, toilets and other plumbing **fixtures**
- **unblock drains** and toilets
- measure, cut, **bend** and **thread** pipes made of **lead**, **copper** and plastic using hand and **power tools** or machines
- test pipes for leaks using air and water pressure **gauges**
- repair and maintain boilers
- **seal** roofs

5. **What are Victor's daily routines in German. Tell your classmates about him.**

VOCAB

duty Pflicht	**supply of water** Wasserversorgung
to be polite höflich sein	**wastewater drainage** Abwasserabfluss
supper Abendbrot	**fixture** Armatur
twice zweimal	**to unblock drains** Abflussrohrverstopfungen beseitigen
clutch Kupplung	**to bend** biegen
to be involved hier: verwickelt sein	**to thread** einziehen
fault Fehler	**lead** Blei
to overhaul überholen	**copper** Kupfer
worn gebraucht	**power tool** elektrisches Werkzeug
vehicle Fahrzeug	**gauge** Messgerät
to perform hier: funktionieren	**to seal** abdichten
specification Beschreibung	

The kitchen-warming party

The friends are sitting in the new kitchen and celebrating that their new kitchen is finished.

Lucy: Olga, come and sit here. It's a good place to **reach** everything. Would you like something to drink?
Olga: Yes, please. A Coke, thank you.
Lucy: You're welcome. The pizza is good, isn't it?
Olga: Yes, very tasty.
Victor: Why don't you try my salad, Lucy?
Lucy: Oh no, green vegetable salad, that's far too **healthy** for me. **Just kidding**, Victor. There are carrots in it and I'm not so **fond of** them.
Victor: Oh, I see. I'm sorry.
Hakan: But, I like your salad, Victor. The dressing is good. It tastes a bit sweet.
Victor: Yes, there is a little bit of honey in it.
Hakan: Oh, good.
Anna: Excuse me, Victor would you pass me the salt, please? I need a little bit for my spaghetti.
Victor: Here you are.
Anna: Thank you.
Victor: You're welcome. But Anna, these **pre-processed** sauces for spaghetti are usually already very salty.
Anna: Yes, well, my mother also says that I shouldn't eat so much salt because it's so unhealthy.
Mr Mende: Yes, too much salt is actually very unhealthy, Anna.
Anna: I know.
Mr Mende: Hakan, your Turkish pizza is delicious. It's very **spicy**!
Hakan: Yes, my mother made it. And she also made the Baklava.
Patrick: That's also very delicious. Lecker! Say thanks to your mother.
Hakan: I will, thank you.

just kidding: **colloquial** expression for making a joke

6. Find the following German expression in the text above.

a) Möchtest Du etwas trinken?
b) Ja, bitte.
c) Danke.
d) Bitte sehr.
e) Entschuldigung, könntest Du mir das Salz reichen/geben?
f) Bitte schön/Hier, bitte schön.

HOW TO ... Be polite

Would you like something to drink/eat?	Yes, please.
Excuse me, would you **pass**/give me the salt, please?	**Sure**. Of course. **Here you are**.
Thank you.	**You're welcome**.

7. **Get together in a group and role-play the kitchen-warming party above. Use polite phrases.**

8. **The friends and Mr Mende like the food they prepared in the new kitchen as well as the dishes brought from home. Only Lucy didn't like Victor's salad.**
What about you? Look at the pictures below and say which of these kinds of food you really like/dislike.
Form 10 sentences; the words and phrases given below should help you.

I don't like baklava, because there is too much sugar in it.

to taste delicious / to be healthy / to be unhealthy / to taste sweet, sour, salty, spicy, **unpleasant**, bitter, sharp, fatty / to be too sweet, sour, … / there is too much sugar, **garlic**, … in it

VOCAB

to celebrate feiern	**pre-processed** vorbehandelt	**here you are** bitte sehr
to reach erreichen	**spicy** gewürzt	**you're welcome** bitte
healthy gesund	**polite** höflich	**to prepare** vorbereiten
colloquial umgangssprachlich	**to pass something** etwas reichen	**unpleasant** unangenehm
to be fond of mögen	**sure** sicher	**garlic** Knoblauch

2.4

TO DO

- Talk about the daily routines of a joiner
- How to ask questions
- Talk about general feelings

Cleaning the kitchen – again

12

After their dinner the friends clean the kitchen again.

Lucy: Come on Justin, here is a **cloth**. Can you **wipe** the table?

Justin: Oh, I worked so hard today. The only thing I want to do now is sit. **Especially** after such a delicious dinner. Can't you do it for me?

Lucy: Oh, you must be joking, you did nothing for our dinner. You didn't prepare anything, you didn't go shopping with me or the others but you ate more than anybody.

Justin: I was really hungry after such a hard day.

Sebi: What's the matter? What did you have to do today?

Justin: I **laid parquet** in a big hall of a school. First, I had to carry the wood blocks from the transporter to the school which lies on a hill. Then I had to cut **irregular** wooden parts to **fit** and **join** them **together**. I was on my knees the whole day putting things together.

Anna: Do you often lay parquet?

Justin: Well, this is only a part of my job. I usually work in the **workshop** and **assemble** furniture. But my boss and my colleague are ill at the moment.

Anna: How long do you have to work on your own?

Justin: **At least** until the end of this week.

Anna: Poor you.

1. **Match the English expressions with the German ones.**

cloth, to lay parquet, hall, to carry, workshop, to assemble, furniture, to be ill, at least, until

tragen, Möbel, krank sein, Tuch, bis, mindestens, Parkett legen, Werkstatt, zusammenbauen, Vorhalle

2. **What do joiners usually have to do? Write down a short report about a few of Justin's daily routine tasks.**

A lot of questions

Use **during** with a noun and **while** with a verb!

During their conversation **while** cleaning the kitchen again the friends asked each other a lot of questions: Can you wipe the table? What did you have to do today? How long do you have to work on your own?
Look at how questions are usually formed.

HOW TO … Form questions

There are two general ways of forming questions.

1. Yes / No questions

These questions begin with an **auxiliary verb** (be, do, have) or modal auxiliary verb (will, shall, would, should, can, could, …).

Are	you	waiting	for Anna?
Does	she	go	to vocational school?
Is	**there**	a clubhouse?	
Have	you	got	the key?

Structure:

auxiliary verb	subject	verb	rest

Is/are there …? is often translated with „Gibt es …?"

2. Wh-questions

These questions begin with a question word (when, where, how long, who, why, …).

Where	is			the key?
When	are	they		in the clubhouse?
Who	are	you	talking	to?
Why	do	you	go	to the gym?

Structure:

question word	auxiliary verb	subject	verb	rest

3. **Change the following sentences into questions.**

a) Lucy can wipe the table.
b) They are cleaning the kitchen.
c) Patrick works on his own.
d) The transport of wood is part of my job.
e) My boss is ill at the moment.
f) I usually work in a workshop.
g) Mr Mende goes to the clubhouse every day.
h) Hakan doesn't eat pork.

VOCAB

cloth Tuch	**irregular** unregelmäßig	**to assemble** zusammenbauen
to wipe abwischen	**to fit together** anpassen	**at least** mindestens
especially besonders	**to join together** zusammensetzen	**during, while** während
to lay parquet Parkett legen	**workshop** Werkstatt	**auxiliary verb** Hilfsverb

2. Kitchen

Bad feelings

Justin is really frustrated with his job. His boss and his colleague are ill and he has to do the work alone. It's not only that he has to carry everything which is exhausting and boring, but the headmaster and the caretaker also asked him about other things which have to be done in the building. He was embarrassed, because he always had to say that he didn't know. It was especially embarrassing when the caretaker asked him about the planned time for finishing the parquet flooring. When he again said that he didn't know, the caretaker was angry about it and said that although he is an apprentice he should know about plans and times. Justin felt so uncomfortable that his cheeks went completely red.

4. How do the people in the text feel?

5. Get together with a partner and find as many words about feelings as possible.

6. Look at the words of feelings below and complete the table with their nouns and the German translation of both, the adjective and the noun.

Adjective	angry	bored	comfortable	painful	relaxed	sad	stressed	strong	tired	weak
German	ängstlich									
Noun	anger									
German	Ärger									

7. How do these people feel? Can you read their emotions from their faces?

An:	Chris@yahoo.ca
Cc:	
Betreff:	worn out

Hi Chris,
I have so much work to do. My boss and my colleague are ill so that I have to work alone. We are laying parquet in a school. And I had to carry all the wood blocks up a hill to get to this school. It was not **possible** to use a **load lifter**, because the path to the building is so narrow that everything has to be carried. What a job!!! And then they asked me so many things I didn't know. It was really embarrassing.
This is only a short mail. I'm completely **worn out**. Hope everything is alright.

CU,
Justin

8. **Justin's email to Chris is very short because Justin is very tired.**

a) What is missing? Copy the email and write another paragraph to Chris so that the email has a little bit more information about Justin's life. Read through Unit 2 again.

b) Reply to Justin's email.

VOCAB

exhausting	anstrengend	**although**	obwohl	**possible**	möglich
headmaster	Schulleiter	**apprentice**	Auszubildender	**load lifter**	Lastenheber
caretaker	Hausmeister	**uncomfortable**	unbehaglich	**to be worn out**	erschöpft sein
embarrassed	verlegen	**cheek**	Wange	**the other day**	neulich

3. Workshop

3.1

TO DO

- Use the present tenses
- Explain jobs on a building site

A phone call

After school Sebastian phones Justin at home. Justin answers the phone.

Justin: 735 8807.
Sebi: Äh, hallo, hier ist ...Hi, this is Sebi. Is that you Justin?
Justin: Yes. How are you? What's up?
Sebi: Äh, fine. Do you always say your phone number when you answer the phone?
Justin: No, but it's quite common. How do you answer the phone in Germany?
Sebi: You say your name.
Justin: I'll remember that. Thanks. So what's up, Sebi?
Sebi: I'm at home, watching TV – but it is boring. What do you do?
Justin: **Come off it**, you know I'm a joiner, too.
Sebi: No, what do you do right now.
Justin: Ah, I see, you mean what **am I doing** right now. You Germans often mix up the simple and the continuous. I'm listening to music.
Sebi: Continuous music?
Justin: No, I wanted to explain that we have two ways to talk about the present:
- First there is the **simple present**. We use this to talk about things in general.
- Then there is the **present continuous**. This is used to talk about things that are happening at the time we are talking.

Do you understand?
Sebi: More or less. I think I need to practise that.
Justin: Okay. What is your father's job?
Sebi: He is a bus driver.
Justin: What does your father do?
Sebi: He sleeps. He is on **night shift**.
Justin: Hahaha, I'd like to be a bus driver, too. No, the two questions "What is your job?" and "What do you do?" mean the same. Your father is a bus driver. What does he do? He drives buses regularly. What is he doing at the moment? He is sleeping because he **is on duty** tonight.

Sebi: Ah yes, so I'm telephoning right now.
Justin: **You got it**. Okay, I'll help you to improve your English and you can give me some German lessons. I need to know all the jobs on a **building site**.
Sebi: There is a **building under construction** in Claudiusstraße. We can go there and talk about the jobs. Let's meet at Wandsbek Markt in half-an-hour.
Justin: Fine. See you then.

1.

page 170

Explain the use of simple present and present continuous.

a) Give rules for the usage of both tenses.
b) How are the tenses formed (positive sentences/negative sentences/questions).
c) Name keywords.
d) Illustrate the usage and write down 10 sentences for each tense.

On a building site

A little later Justin and Sebi arrive at the building site. They are talking about the different jobs and what the people are doing at the moment.

bricklayer
carpenter
carpet layer
electrician
foreman
gardener
joiner
metal worker
painter
plumber
roofer
tiler
scaffolder
site manager

2. **Who is who on a building site?**
Copy the job titles, translate them and match them with the numbers in the picture.

3. **Look at the picture. What are the workers doing at the moment?**
Work with a partner and write down as many sentences as possible.

A painter is varnishing the window.

A ...	build carry erect fix install lay look	mend plant read tile varnish	the	building site burglar bar carpet carport construction drawing door plant	roof scaffolding sink tile wall window wiring

VOCAB

come off it Red keinen Unsinn	**you got it** du hast es (verstanden)
night shift Nachtschicht	**building site** Baustelle
to be on duty Dienst haben	**building under construction** Neubau

3.1

3. Workshop

What does a site manager do?

Soon after they arrive the site manager notices Justin and Sebi and asks them what they are doing there. Sebi explains that they are talking about the jobs and activities of the workers in German and English.
Although the site manager seems to be a little surprised, he smiles and says:

Mein Name ist Andreas Ludanecki und ich bin der Bauleiter auf dieser Baustelle. Ich koordiniere die Arbeiten auf der Baustelle, sorge für eine termingerechte Umsetzung, überprüfe die Qualität der **Bauleistungen** und auch die Rechnungen der einzelnen Firmen. Ich bin sozusagen das Bindeglied zwischen Handwerkern, Architekt und **Bauherrn**. Außerdem bin ich verantwortlich für die Einhaltung von **Vorschriften** und rechtlichen **Bestimmungen.** Dazu gehören auch Umweltschutz und Arbeitsschutz, das heißt die Sicherheit und Gesundheit von den Arbeitnehmern auf der Baustelle. So muss ich zum Beispiel die Sicherheit der Gerüste überwachen.

4. **Summarise the statement of the site manager in English.**

5. **In conversations there are often words, especially technical terms, which are not quite clear or more or less unknown to other people.**
Therefore you should explain these words.

Explain the following words in English:

a) Geselle
b) Handlanger
c) Chef
d) Maschinenführer
e) Bauleiter

On a construction site

Firstly, there is the **client**. This could be the owner, a company or a **contracting** authority. The client has or raises the money for the building and puts an architect in charge of the planning.
The architect designs the building. There is normally a **civil engineer**, a **draughtsperson** and a **quantity surveyor** in his team. The draughtsperson draws the building plans, the civil engineer is in charge of the technical designs and the quantity surveyor calculates the costs of the building.

Then there is the **main contractor** who **requests** offers from various subcontractors. These are the tradespeople responsible for the actual construction work.
Furthermore, there is always a site manager, who is responsible for the quality of the construction work and the completion of the building **on schedule**. A **safety engineer** is in charge of the safety at work on huge building sites.

Tradespeople like bricklayers, plumbers, painters and electricians are skilled workers who completed a three-year apprenticeship. A **foreman** is responsible for their work. Then there are, of course, the apprentices who do a three-year on the job training. There are also unskilled workers who assist the tradespeople by handling materials and cleaning up the site.

6. **Read the text and answer the questions.**

a) Who designs the building?
b) What do unskilled workers do on a building site?
c) Who **hires** an architect?
d) Who trains on the job?
e) What is the task of a safety engineer?
f) Who draws the building plans?
g) How long does an apprenticeship normally last?
h) Who calculates the quantities?
i) Who inspects the quality of the construction work?
j) Who pays the bills?
k) Who keeps an eye on the progress chart?
l) Who bids for the different jobs on a building site?
m) Who **actually** builds the new houses?
n) Who could be a client?

actually ist ein sogenannter false friend (= falscher Freund): Es meint nicht aktuell, sondern tatsächlich/wirklich.

7. **Create an organigram for a building site.**

client

owner ____ ____ ____

⇩

____

VOCAB

site manager Bauleiter	**quantity surveyor** Kostenplaner
construction work Bauleistung	**main contractor** Generalunternehmer
client Bauherr, Auftraggeber	**to request** anfordern
rule/regulation Vorschrift/Bestimmung	**on schedule** termingerecht
conracting authority öffentlicher Auftraggeber	**safety engineer** Sicherheitsingenieur
civil engineer Bauingenieur	**foreman** Vorarbeiter
draughtsperson Bauzeichner	**to hire** einstellen

3.2

→ TO DO

- Label tools
- Look up vocabulary

Tools

Before Sebastian and his friends start working they have a look at the clubhouse's workshop to check if there are enough tools.
This is what they found:

1. Draw a chart like this. Who uses these tools?

Gardener	Painter	Bricklayer	Plumber	Mechanic	Joiner	Metalworker or Locksmith

2. Which other tools do the young people need to do their work?
Make a list of tools you use in your job.
Use a dictionary, a picture dictionary or search the web.
www.leo.org www.google.de http://dict.tu-chemnitz.de

HOW TO … **Look up vocabulary**

Jeder kennt die Möglichkeit, Vokabeln im Wörterbuch oder im Internet nachzuschauen, doch gerade Fachvokabular ist nicht immer einfach zu finden. Oft erhält man mehrere Möglichkeiten als Antwort, weiß damit aber immer noch nicht welche die richtige ist.
Hier gibt es die Möglichkeit Antworten zu „googeln", indem man erst den deutschen Begriff eingibt und sich die Bilder dazu anschaut, danach den englischen Begriff eingibt und die Bilder vergleicht.

3.

a) Look for the English expressions of the following words and pictures.
b) Write down a list in your exercise book and create a similar page with pictures of tools and their names in English and German.

 Kneifzange	 Kombizange	 Seitenschneider	 Telefonzange
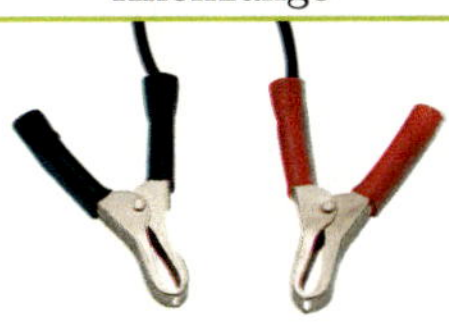 Ladezange, Betterieklemme	 Zeckenzange	 Rohrzange	 Abisolierzange
 Rundzange	 Flachzange	 Fliesen(brech)-zange	 Lochzange
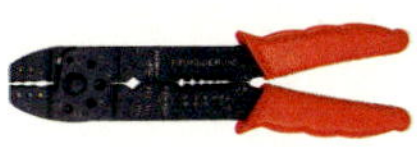 Crimpzange	 Wasserpumpenzange	 Fliesenlochzange	 Sicherungsringzange

4. **Take a photo of your workshop and label all the tools on the picture.**

3. Workshop

A messy workshop

Before Lucy starts painting the billiard room she goes to the workshop to get the tools she needs.

Lucy: I need a brush, a roller and an **extension pole** so that I can start in the billiard room.

Justin: Well, let's have a look. I think the extension pole is here in the corner. Oh no, it's just a **broomstick**.

Hakan: There's a brush on the shelf next to the radio.

Victor: The roller is in the paint bucket between the shelf and the door.

Lucy: Great, ... but the brush and the roller are full of dried paint. That's just rubbish. I thought you Germans are so **neat**. Don't you ever clean your tools?

Sebi: I do! But I'm not the only one who works here and the problem is that not everyone cleans up their own **stuff**.

5. Where are the tools? (See 'Where is it?' on page 13.) Who can find the most tools and say where they are?

6. Write down at least five tools and what you have to do to **maintain** them.

7. **What do you do with these tools? Write down sentences.**

You use a folding rule to measure the height of a door.

folding rule	to move earth
hammer	to measure the height of a door
screwdriver	to pull out nails
spade	to cut firewood
pincers	to **insert** and **remove** screws
plumb bob	to **release** or **tighten** nuts of different size
wheelbarrow	to cut **wire** and to **grip** small parts
water pump pliers	to lift and move sand
spirit level	to find a vertical line
shovel	to **plane** wood
plane	to **drive in** nails
pencil	to clean rust and remove paint
bow saw	to **indicate** whether a surface is **level** or **plumb**
file	to **apply** paint
brush	to dig earth
spanner	to write or draw
combination pliers	to cut paper, plastics and ropes
wire brush	to shape metal or wood
filling knife	to fill small holes and scrape off wallpaper
snap-off knife	to turn **bolts** and **nuts**

8. **Write five sentences about the use of tools of your trade. Your classmates should guess these tools.**

You use it to drill holes into wood. Powerdrill.

9. **Lucy said, "I thought you Germans are so neat."**
What do you think about this statement? Is it true or is it simply pointing out how we tend to stereotype nationalities? Do you know of any stereotypes? Discuss in class.

VOCAB

messy unordentlich	**to remove** herausschrauben	**to indicate** anzeigen
extension pole Teleskopstange	**to release** lösen	**level** eben, horizontal
broomstick Besenstiel	**to tighten** festziehen	**plumb** lotrecht
neat ordentlich	**wire** Draht	**to apply** auftragen
stuff Zeug, Kram	**to grip** greifen, erfassen	**bolt** Schraube
to maintain pflegen	**to plane** hobeln	**nut** Mutter
to insert einschrauben	**to drive in** einschlagen	**stereotype** Klischee

3.3

TO DO

- Understand instructions
- Give instructions

A flat tyre

On Thursday morning Justin arrives twenty minutes late at school.

Justin: Good morning. Sorry, I'm late.
Teacher: Good morning Justin. What happened? Did you oversleep?
Justin: No, I didn't. I got up in time, at 6:45 as usual. Lucy and I left home at 7:30, but unfortunately, Lucy's bike had a flat tyre and I had to pump it up three times.
Sebi: You're a real gentleman.
Justin: Stop kidding. Lucy doesn't have a bike pump and I don't want to give her mine. Lucy loses everything, she's the kind of girl with three left-hand gloves. Every winter she loses one of her gloves.
Sebi: Poor boy. Couldn't you repair the tyre?
Justin: Great idea. Do you always have a bike repair kit with you when you ride to school?
Sebi: Äh,... no, I don't. But I know how to fix a tyre.
Justin: So do I.
Teacher: Alright you smart boys, please tell me how to fix a flat tyre.

How to **fix** a **flat tyre**

Remove the **wheel** with the flat tyre. **Remove** one side of the flat tyre from the **rim**.

Once you have one side of the flat tyre open you can pull the **bicycle tube** out. After the tube is out run your hand around the inside of the flat tyre to feel for sharp points that could **cause** a flat.

First you need to find the hole. Pump air into your tube and **dip** it under water and watch for bubbles.

In most cases you will first clean and **buff** the area around the hole using a piece of sandpaper. Make sure the area you clean and buff is bigger than the size of the **patch** you will be using.

After you clean and buff the hole area, apply **adhesive** to the same area and let it dry. Don't apply the patch until the adhesive has dried.

Place the patch over the hole and press it on the tube. Put the tube back into the tyre.

Depending on the tyre/rim combination you will be able to get most of the tyre **seated** with your hands but the last little bit may be difficult.

Make sure the tyre is **properly** seated all the way around the rim.

Pump your tyre about half way up to its normal pressure and inspect again to make sure the tyre is properly seated on both sides all the way around the rim. If all looks good finish pumping the tyre up to your normal riding pressure.

Put your wheel back onto your bike. Test ride your bike.

1. Find the right sequence of the pictures and write down the instruction.
Begin each sentence with a verb.
You can use the text on the left as a guide.

1 = e) Remove the wheel with the flat tyre.

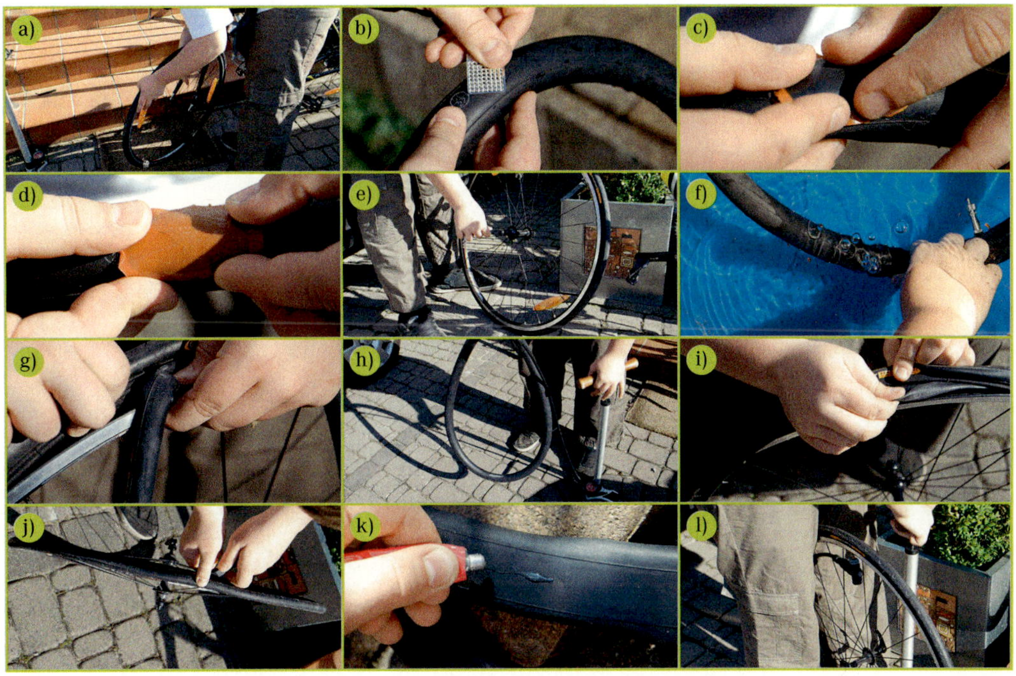

2. Listen to the instruction and say what it is about.
Give it a heading and write down eight main instructions.

15

How to …

1.

2.

VOCAB

to fix reparieren	**to dip** tauchen	**angle** Winkel
flat tyre Platten (Ugs.)	**to buff** aufrauen	**surface** Oberfläche
wheel Rad	**patch** Flicken	**burial chamber** Grabkammer
to remove ablösen	**adhesive** Klebstoff	**tomb** Grab
rim Felge	**to seat** platzieren	**level** Ebene
bicycle tube Fahrradschlauch	**properly** richtig	**calculation** Berechnung
to cause verursachen	**to enslave** versklaven	**evidence** Spur, Hinweis

A water rocket

After school Sebi wants to show Justin how to make a water rocket. He has found pictures on the internet but unfortunately there was no text.

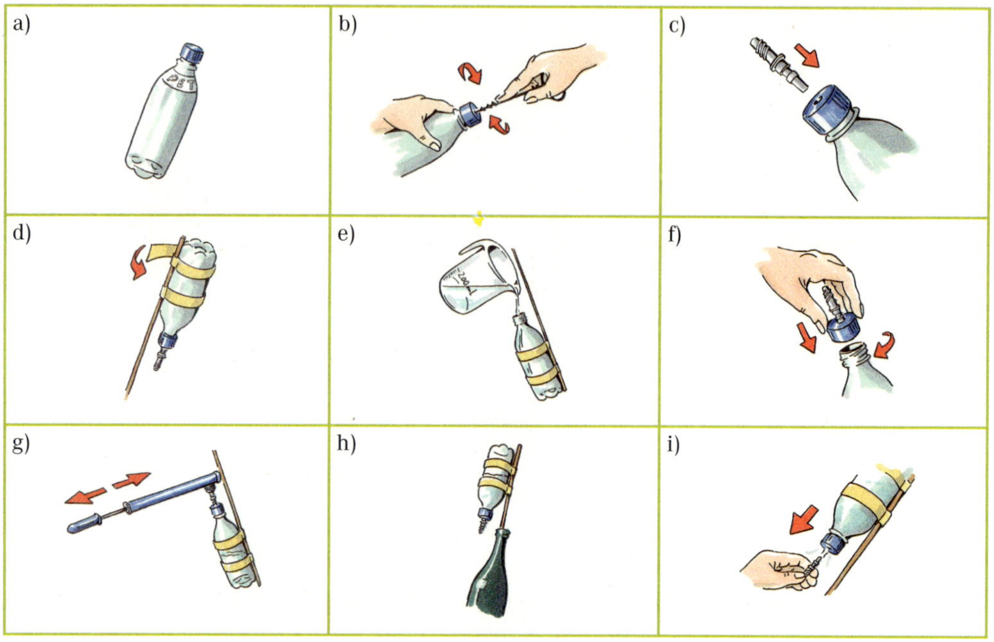

3. **Look at the pictures and write instructions on how to construct a water rocket.**

a) Take a half-litre PET bottle.

4. **Write instructions about one of the following:**

a) make **concrete**.
b) plant a rose.
c) unblock a washbasin.
d) fold a **seam** on **sheet metal**.
e) install a door.
f) set up a wallpaper **paste table**.
g) change an oil filter.
h) make coffee.
i) fix a shelf to a wall.
j) make cocktails (choose one you like).

Power tools

Justin and Sebi used a drill to put a hole into the cap of the bottle. Sebi wants to know the names of other power tools.

drill –
cordless drill –
circular saw –
jigsaw –
angle grinder –
spray gun

a)

b)

c)

d)

e)
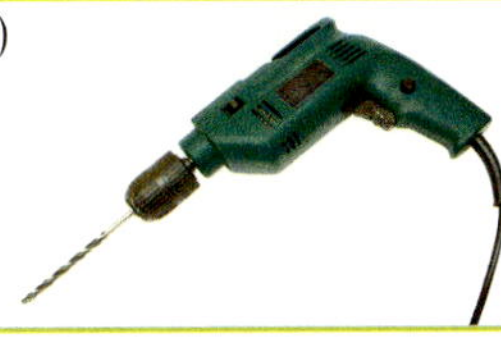

f)

5. Which of the power tools above do you use in your job?

a) Match the words and the pictures.
b) Make a list of all power tools you use at work.

6. Read the safety instructions and find out which tool is meant.

1. Use safety footwear, **snug-fitting** clothing, protective gloves, and eye, hearing, and head protection.
2. When working, hold the tool firmly with both hands, with thumbs and fingers on both handles. Grip the tool with the right hand on the rear handle (**throttle**) and the left hand on the front handle, even if you are left handed. A firm grip will help you maintain control of the tool in the event of a **kickback** or other unexpected reaction.
3. Do not overreach or work above shoulder height. It is very difficult to control the tool in **awkward** positions.
4. Do not operate the tool in a tree or from a ladder unless you have been specifically trained. There is a risk that you can lose your balance because of cutting **forces** on the tool or movement of material being cut.
5. Carry the tool with the engine stopped and the cutting chain to the rear.
6. Do not allow other people to be near the tool when starting it or cutting with it. Keep people and animals out of the work area.
7. Cut while standing slightly to the side, out of the plane of the cutting chain and guide bar to reduce the risk of injury in case you lose control of the tool.
8. Do not start cutting trees until you have a clear work area, secure footing, and a planned retreat path from the falling tree.
9. Keep all parts of your body away from the cutting chain when the engine is running.

VOCAB

concrete Beton	**paste table** Tapeziertisch	**kickback** Rückschlag
seam Falz	**snug-fitting** festsitzend	**awkward** schwierig, ungünstig
sheet metal Blech	**throttle** Gashebel	**force** Kraft

3.4

TO DO

- Express frequency
- Talk about maintenance and repair
- Describe problems at work

Repairs

16

After school Sebi and Justin are riding home. As always Sebi is showing Justin some short cuts. Suddenly Justin stops.

Justin: Hey Sebi, look at this old house. Isn't it **run-down**?
Sebi: Yes, ... definitely ... What does run-down mean?
Justin: Shabby! Let me explain: When a house looks run-down or shabby it's not well kept, nobody cares for it.
Sebi: I see. If no-one looks after the house, more and more parts need to be repaired. I've ridden past here many times. At first it was just the garden but now it's the entire house. Look at the windows and doors.
Justin: And the gutters and the roof. Who lives in such a house?
Sebi: Some years ago I used to see an old couple in the garden, perhaps they have moved to an old people's home.
Justin: Or they've already died. Let's have a closer look.

1. **Match the sentence starters with words from the bubble.**

a) The drain pipe is
b) The lawn is
c) The window is
d) The car is
e) The outside light cable
f) The **bulb** doesn't
g) The door is
h) The plaster is
i) The paint is
j) The flowers are
k) Some roof tiles are
l) The sink is

leaking
squeaking work
dirty **crumbling**
overgrown dry
peeling broken
blocked

2. **What has to be done to get things straight?**
Use these verbs:
clean, fix, mend, mow, oil, paint, plaster, repair, replace, unblock, water
Start like this: a) The drain pipe has to be fixed.

3. **Think of your trade. What regular maintenance or repairs do you do? How often do you have to do this maintenance?**

VOCAB — **Expressing frequency**

once einmal **twice** zweimal **three times** dreimal **X times** Xmal	**every** jede **every second** jede zweite **once a** einmal pro	**day** Tag **week** Woche **month** Monat **year** Jahr

I change the motor oil every 20,000 kilometres.

I clean up the workshop twice a week.

VOCAB

maintenance Pflege- und Wartungsarbeit **short cut** Abkürzung **run-down** heruntergekommen	**bulb** Glühlampe **to squeak** quietschen **to crumble** bröckeln	**to peel** abblättern **to get something straight** etwas in Ordnung bringen

Trouble at work

In the evening the young people meet at the youth club. Justin is in a bad mood. He thinks his boss is being unfair. Hakan and Lucy also talk about their problems at work.

4.

17

a) **Look at these three pictures and listen to the reports. What is happening in the pictures? What are Justin, Hakan and Lucy talking about?**

b) **Now listen and answer these questions:**

1) Why did Justin go to the customer?
2) What did the boss tell him to measure?
3) What did the customer tell him to measure?
4) Why were the boss, the colleague and the customer angry with Justin?
5) Who is responsible for the wrong measurement?
6) What would you do if you were Justin.

borrow – lend
borrow = sich etwas von jmd. leihen (take)
lend = verleihen (give)

7) What did Hakan's brother **borrow**?
8) When did the accident happen?
9) What was damaged?
10) How did Hakan's brother try to hide the damage?
11) How did the boss know about the accident?
12) What happened to Hakan's brother?
13) What would you do if you were Hakan's brother?

to back rückwärts fahren
post Pfosten
dent Beule
to smear schmieren
spot Stelle, Fleck
to turn out sich herausstellen
attempt Versuch

14) How long has Lucy been working with her colleague?
15) How does Lucy describe her relationship to her colleague?
16) What happened at the farewell party?
17) How did Lucy respond to her colleague after the farewell party?
18) What **suggestions** do you have for Lucy?

to have a crush on somone in jemanden verknallt sein
to be disgusted angeekelt sein
suggestion Vorschlag

5. **What kind of problems have you experienced at work? Tell your classmates.**

An:	Chris@yahoo.ca
Cc:	
Betreff:	empty houses

Hi Chris,
You won't believe what has happened this week. On our way home from school Sebi and I passed an old shabby house. We stopped and had a look. The house looked empty and so we decided (I mean it took a while to **convince** Sebi, in the end he didn't want to be a **coward**) to go into. Luckily the back door wasn't locked. First we went into the kitchen. Chris you should have seen it, there were spider webs everywhere. The entire house was **damp** and smelled **mouldy**. Then we entered the living room. Although the flowers were dried and the furniture was covered with dust I had the feeling somebody was living there. Even a TV magazine lay on the table. Sebi was a little **scared** and wanted to leave, but his **curiosity pushed** him to follow me when I went upstairs. The stairs **creaked** at each step. It was **quite** dark upstairs, so I struck a match when suddenly something big rushed towards us. We screamed, flew down the stairs, ran out of the house, jumped on our bikes and rode away as fast as possible. Finally we stopped at an ice-cream parlour and had a huge spaghetti-ice.
There was something in the house, Sebi says it might have been just an owl but I'm not that sure, really **spooky**.
I will never go into an empty house again. That's for sure!

That's it for today.
See ya.
Justin

VOCAB

- **to experience** erfahren, erleben
- **to convince** überzeugen
- **coward** Feigling
- **damp** feucht
- **mouldy** schimmlig
- **to be scared** ängstlich sein
- **curiosity** Neugier
- **to push** drängen
- **to creak** knarren
- **quite** ziemlich
- **spooky** gruselig

4. Billiard Room

4.1

TO DO

- Record vocabulary
- Calculate quantities
- Measure objects

What do we need?

Justin and Sebi are on a class trip to Ireland and are coming home next Friday. Lucy, Olga and Hakan want to surprise them with a newly decorated billiard room. They are cleaning up the cellar of the clubhouse to see what they already have and what they need to buy. Lucy knows exactly what they need.

to want to in English means "wollen" in German. I will means "Ich werde".

1.

18

Look at the picture above and listen to the three friends talking in the cellar. Can you identify the tools and painting equipment they found? Work with a partner and list the tools and material.

Tools and material
1. a pasting brush 2. two step ladders

2. **The three friends are taking stock of what they found in the cellar. Hakan is packing their box of treasures, Olga is making a list of everything and Lucy is telling them what the tools are used for.**
What does Lucy say?

a) Follow the lines and find out the uses of the different tools.
They need a pasting brush to put the glue onto the wallpaper.

Tool/equipment	Use
a pasting brush	to create a vertical (reference) line
a paint roller	to flatten the joins in the wallpaper
sandpaper	to protect window frames from paint
a roller tray and grid	to mix and carry paint
a measuring tape	to put the glue onto the wallpaper
a paint bucket	to roughen painted surfaces
a seam roller	to paint the walls
a plumb bob	to measure things
masking tape	to load rollers with paint

b) Work with a partner and ask each other questions.
Why do they need a pasting brush?

3. **Can you think of any other tools, material or equipment the friends need to redecorate the billiard room?**

a) Make a list. Use your dictionary to look up any words you do not know.
b) Why do they need them? Discuss with a partner.

VOCAB

to clean up aufräumen	**masking tape** Abdeckklebeband
to need to do something etwas tun müssen	**plank** Brett
pasting brush Kleisterbürste	**to take stock** Bestand aufnehmen
step ladder Trittleiter	**treasure** Schatz
seam roller Nahtroller	**sandpaper** Schleifpapier
measuring tape Maßband	**plumb bob** Senklot
paint roller Farbenroller	**join** Naht
roller tray and grid Farbwanne und Gitterrost	**to roughen a surface** eine Fläche aufrauen
putty knife Kittspachtel	

4. Billiard Room

HOW TO ... **Record vocabulary**

Draw a **word map**. The main topic is written in a cloud in the middle of the page. Link other words to this topic. Words can always be added at any time. In this way all the vocabulary about a **special topic** is on one page. This makes it easy to find the word you need and it helps you to remember it.

4. **Complete this word map with all the vocabulary you need to redecorate a room. Group the words under the following headings:**

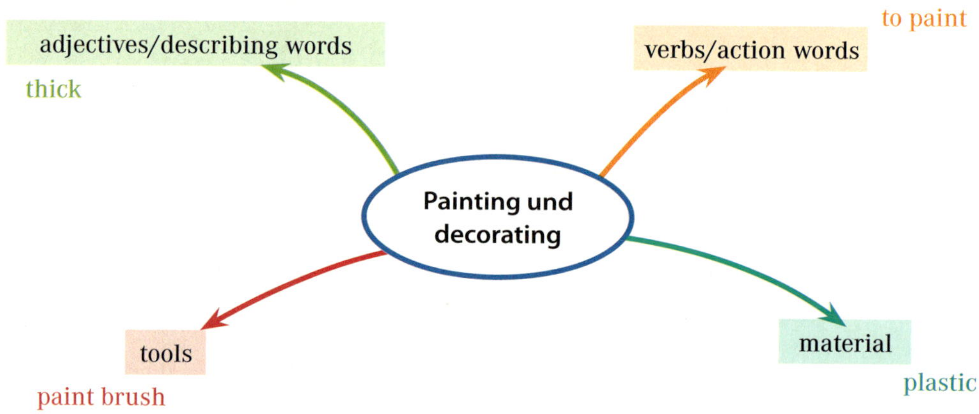

5. **Work with a partner. Each choose either picture A or picture B.**
Find out the differences between the two pictures.
In picture A/B …….. is ……..ing ………. but in picture A/B ………is/are ….ing ……

In picture A Anna is cutting off dead leaves but in picture B she is watering the plants.

A

B

How much wallpaper and paint do we need?

Back in the billiard room the three friends measure the walls and calculate how much paint and wallpaper they need.

6. (CD 19)

Listen to the dialogue.
Copy the plan and fill in the measurements of the billiard room.
When you are finished, check with your partner to see if you both have the same answers.

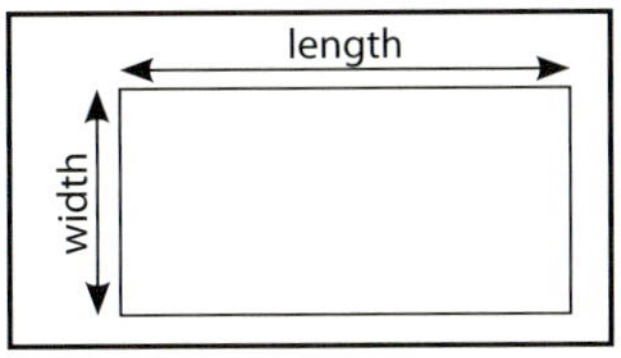

7.

Sometimes we don't have a measuring tape at hand when we need to measure something, so we use different things instead.
Today you and your partner need to measure your desk and your classroom.
You don't have a measuring tape so you should use some part of your body as a unit of measurement.

My desk is three and a half Toby-hands long.

8. (CD 20)

Listen to Lucy telling Olga how to calculate how much paint and wallpaper they need for the billiard room.

a) Write down the formula.
b) Now calculate how much paint and wallpaper the friends need. Use the measurements from exercise 6. Check your answer with your partner.

false friends:
formular = Formel
form = Formular

VOCAB

word map Wortkarte	**heading** Überschrift
special topic besonderes Thema	**to calculate** berechnen

4.2

TO DO

- Say where things are
- Describe packaging
- Use much and many

Off to the DIY shop

Back in the billiard room Lucy, Olga and Hakan are finishing their shopping list so that they can go to the the DIY shop to buy their supplies.

DIY = Do it yourself

Shopping list
8 litres of paint - water-based
4 rolls of wallpaper
1 roll of masking tape
1 large plastic protection sheet
2 packets of wallpaper glue
1 tub of multi-purpose Polyfilla
1 large roller sleeve

1. **Look at the layout of the DIY shop and together with a partner discuss:**

a) Which departments Olga, Lucy and Hakan will go to for their supplies.

b) What you can buy in the different departments.

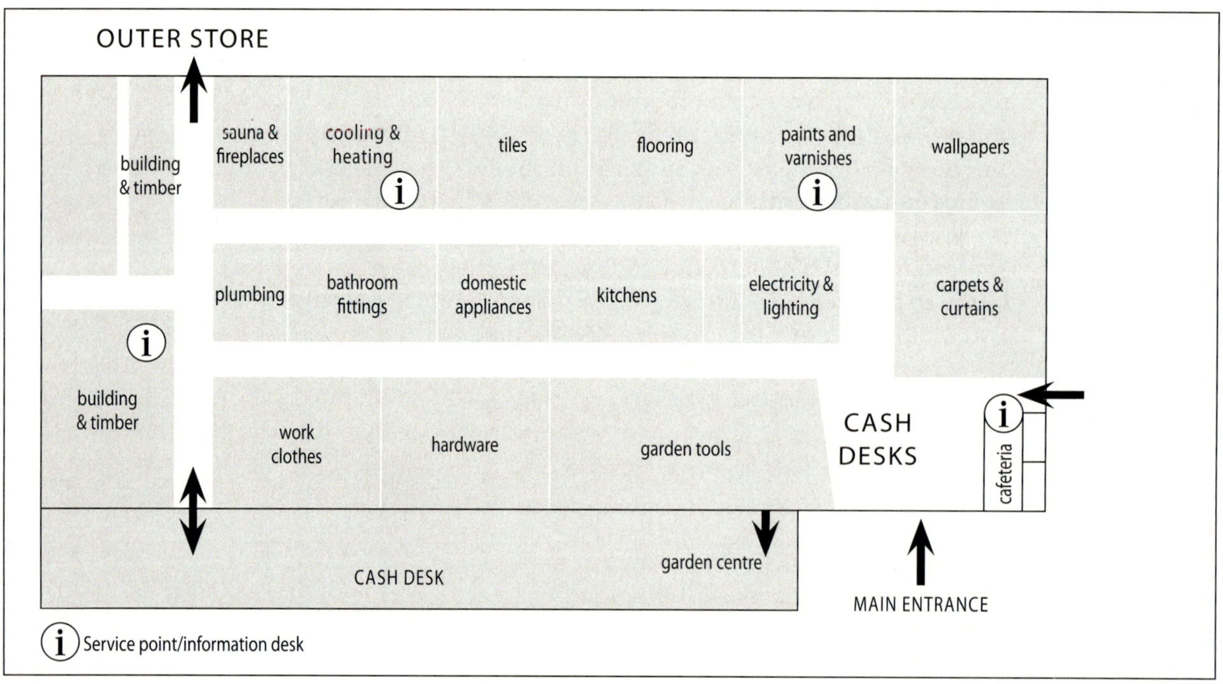

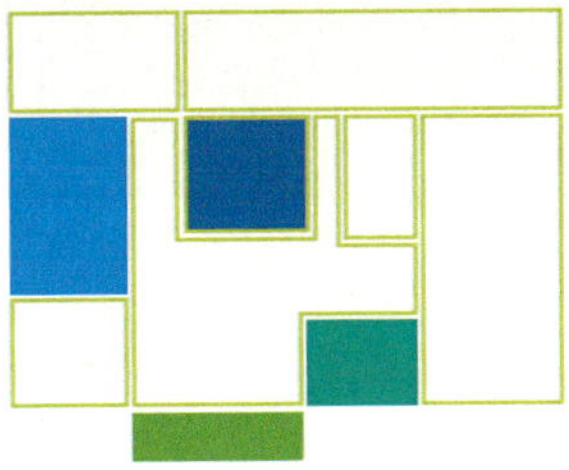

2. **Together with your partner practise asking and telling each other where the different departments are in the store:**

Student A: Where is the **work clothes** department?
Student B: It's opposite the **plumbing** department and next to the **hardware** department.

PHRASES — **Asking for assistance**

Can you help me, please?	Certainly, sir/madam.
Where is ..., please? Excuse me, where are ..., please? Where can I find ..., please?	It's in the second **aisle** on the right/on the left. They're against the back wall. Go **straight on/ahead**. It's over there, next to the ...
Thank you very much. Thanks a lot.	You're welcome.

3. **It is not always easy to find what you need in a store and sometimes you have to ask a shop assistant. Practise a dialogue with your partner.**
Take it in turns to be a customer and a sales assistant:

	hardware
Customer:	Excuse me, where is the **hardware** department, please?
Shop assistant:	It's in the first aisle next to the garden tools.
Customer:	Thank you very much.

4. 21

While they're in the store Lucy's mobile rings. Can you guess what Mr Mende wants Lucy to buy?

VOCAB

supplies hier: Arbeitsmittel **water-based paint** wasserlösliche Farbe **multi-purpose** Mehrzweck ... **department** Abteilung	**aisle** Gang **straight on/ahead** geradeaus **to take turns** abwechseln

More supplies needed

That was not the only thing Mr Mende wants Lucy to buy.

Lucy: Mr Mende needs coffee, milk, ice-cream, toothpaste, playing cards, nails and light bulbs.
Hakan: I'll get the nails. How many does he want, Lucy?
Lucy: He wants a box of 100 nails.
Olga: And how many light bulbs does he need?
Lucy: He needs two 40 watt light bulbs.
Hakan: What about the playing cards?
Lucy: I'll get those over there. He wants three packs. I think he wants to play poker.
Hakan: What about the other things, Lucy?
Lucy: We'll buy those at the supermarket on our way back to the clubhouse. Mr Mende wants a **jar** of instant coffee, two **cartons** of milk and a **tub** of chocolate ice-cream. I think he wants **to give us a treat** as we're working so hard.
Hakan: Should we also buy some **tins** of Coke?
Lucy: Oh Hakan, you mean some **cans** of Coke. Yes, that's a good idea.
Hakan: But why can't I say tins of Coke?
Lucy: Because when it's something to drink, we normally use the word can, for example, a can of beer.
Hakan: And when do I use the word tin?
Lucy: We normally say a tin of fish or a tin of tomatoes.
Hakan: So that means we use tin when there is something to eat inside, is that correct?
Lucy: That's right.
Olga: Come on you two! That's enough, let's go.

5.

Read the dialogue and identify all the countable and uncountable nouns.
Make a list and check with your neighbour to see if you identified the same words.

many	much
nails	ice-cream

6.

We can also use words which make it easier to say how much we want or need.
These units or containers are countable.

Mr Mende wants a tub of ice-cream.
Ice-cream is sold in tubs, otherwise it would be difficult to carry the ice-cream.
I drink a lot of milk and I buy it in cartons.

Read the dialogue once more and explain the use of tin and can to your partner.

PHRASES — Using much/many/a lot of

We use **much** and **many** when we ask questions and when we use not:

I didn't drink **much** beer last night. I didn't eat **many** cheeseburgers.

We use **much** for things we cannot count (uncountable):

How **much** coffee did you drink? I had two cups of coffee.

We use **many** for things we can count (countable):

How **many** people were at your party? Eight people.

We use **a lot of** in positive statements:

I drank **a lot of** water.
I ate **a lot of** hamburgers.

7.

Look at the pictures above and find out what they are packed into. Use the words below and write the sentences down

a **bag** of …, a **mug** of …, a **carton** of…, a **glass** of …, a **bottle** of …, a **tub** of …, a **jar** of …, a **crate** of …, a **pack** of …, a **box** of …, a **bucket** of …, a **barrel** of …, a **basket** of …, a **packet** of …

8.

What other items can we buy in these containers?
Brainstorm with a partner and find out which partners in the class can think of the most items.

VOCAB

jar Glas	**tin** Konservendose
carton Karton	**can** Dose
tub Kübel	**countable** zählbar
to give someone a treat jmd. eine Belohnung geben	**uncountable** nicht zählbar

4.3

TO DO

- Talk about colours
- Safety signs and colours

Brightening up the billiard room

The friends cannot decide what colour to paint the billiard room, but Lucy as an idea.

At school we learnt that colours affect our **moods**. For example blue makes a room look smaller but also seems very cold. Yellow, on the other hand, makes a room very **bright** and sunny. I think that would be a good colour for the billiard room. We want to be in a good mood when we are in there, don't we? Even if we lose it doesn't matter, we are playing because it's fun.

1. **Is Lucy right? Does colour affect our moods? Discuss in class.**

2. **Do you believe that colours affect our emotions?**
Research and experiments have been carried out on the effect of colour on our emotions and have been scientifically proven. However, not all scientists believe the results.
Write down a list like this and discuss with a partner.

Colour	Moods	Feelings and emotion
red		love, warmth, danger
orange		happiness

3. a) **Interview a partner:**
What is your favourite colour?
How many shirts, pullovers, jackets and trousers do you have in this colour?
What colour is your bedroom?
What colour is your furniture?
What colours are you wearing today?

b) **Carry out a survey with your classmates to find out which colours are most popular.**

4. **Colour partnerships:**
Which of the words in the box belong to which colour?
a) Each of the above colours have three partners.
Find their correct partners.

yellow + pages

back, ~bell, **belt**, ~berry, blood, box, card, **carpet**, Christmas, -collar worker, -collar worker, Cross, fingers, ~horn, House

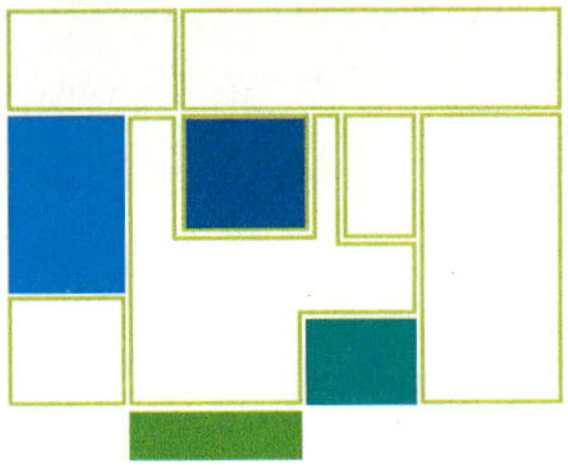

b) Match the meanings to the colour partnerships.

1 a factory worker
2. snow at Christmas
3. an aircraft flight recorder
4. an international organization
5. a carpet for celebrities
6. **of noble birth**
7. US dollar bill
8. office worker
9. the US president lives here
10. a martial arts expert
11. to send a player off the pitch
12. a plant with blue flowers
13. a soft fruit
14. someone with no **experience**
15. a good gardener

HOW TO … Make it easier to remember

Mnemonics

This is a tool to help you remember important things. Once you learn them, you never forget them.

The phrase **"Spring forward – Fall back"**
helps you remember how to adjust your clock for standard and daylight saving time.
In spring the clocks are turned one hour forward and in autumn they are turned back one hour.

Do you sometimes forget how to spell a word?
It is easy to remember the word **because** if you remember this sentence:
"**B**ig **e**lephants **c**an **a**lways **u**nderstand **s**mall **e**lephants."

Here is another example for the handyman who wants to remember which way to tighten or loosen a screw:
"righty tighty, lefty loosy"

Do you know the colours of the rainbow?
"**R**ichard **o**f **Y**ork **g**ave **b**attle **i**n **v**ain"
The first letter of each word is the first letter of the colours of the rainbow.
Red **o**range **y**ellow **g**reen **b**lue **i**ndigo **v**iolet

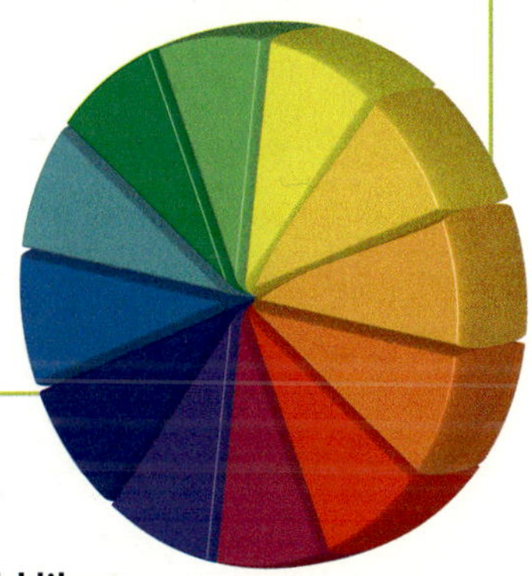

5. **Now it's your turn.**
Make up a mnemonic for at least three new words you would like to remember from this unit.
Join up with some other classmates and exchange your mnemonics.

VOCAB

mood Stimmung	**to prove** beweisen	**belt** Gürtel
bright heiter, leuchtend	**scientist** Wissenschaftler	**of noble birth** von edler Herkunft
research Forschung	**survey** Befragung	**experience** Erfahrung
scientifically wissenschaftlich	**carpet** Teppich	**mnemonic** Eselsbrücke

4. Billiard Room

Lucy noticed this sign in the DIY store and asked Olga and Hakan what it meant.

6. Can you explain what it means?
Is it a symbol sign or a text-message sign?
What is the English sign for this?

Safety Colours and Safety Signs

There are four types of safety signs: warning signs, **prohibition** signs, **mandatory action signs**, and safety information signs. They **differ** in **shape**, colour and symbol.
Well-designed symbols communicate information quickly and do so across language barriers. Text-message-only safety **labels** are practically meaningless to product users who are **illiterate** or do not speak the language of the label text.

The **ability** of symbols to communicate across language barriers is an important **benefit** in Europe, where many languages are spoken and products often cross borders. The blue mandatory-action and yellow-and-black triangular warning sign formats are unfamiliar to many people in the United States.

Prohibition signs: red, black and white, round			
1 	2 	3 	4 
Warning signs: yellow and black, triangular			
5 	6 	7 	8 
Mandatory signs: blue and white, round			
9 	10 	11 	12 
Safety information signs: green and white, square			
12 	14 	15 	16 

7. **Read the text and find the answers to these questions:**

a) How many different types of safety signs are there?
b) What are the different types of safety signs called?
c) How do the safety signs differ?
d) Why are symbols better than text-message-only safety labels?
e) What do you think of text-message-only safety labels?

8. **Look at the safety symbols on page 64 and match them with the explanations below. Watch out! Not all the explanations are correct.**

1 No Smoking

Ear Protection Area	Hard Hat Area	Wear Safety Glasses	Wear Respirator
First Aid Kit	Conserve Water	Wear Your Goggles	Keep Out
Crane Overhead	Restricted Area	Slippery When Wet	Buckle up
Poison	Wear Hard Hat	Watch for Forklifts	Meeting Point
Not Drinking Water	Falling Material	Emergency Exit	Wear Your Respirator
Asbestos	Wear Your Gloves	Radioactive	Do Not Touch
Electical Hazard	Out of Order	No Pacemakers	No Smoking
Water Fountain Signs	Emergency Door	Fire Hose	Watch Your Head
Caustic	Eye Wash	Fire Extinguisher	Hair Net Required
Don't Be A Litterbug	Hazardous Chemicals	Emergency Phone	Do Not Block Door

9. **In English we often use colours to express something. Do you know what these expressions mean?**

Look them up in your dictionary or do some research on the internet. See if you can find another two examples to present to the class.

Colourful English	
to paint the town red	out of the blue
to see red	to have a yellow streak
to be green with envy	a white elephant
to be a greenhorn	a white knight
to feel blue	to black out

VOCAB

prohibition Verbot	**ability** Fähigkeit
mandatory vorgeschrieben, zwingend erforderlich	**benefit** Vorteil, Nutzen
mandatory-(action-)sign Gebotsschild	**hazard** Gefährdung
to differ in sich unterscheiden	**caustic** ätzend
shape Form	**hose** Schlauch
label Hinweisschild	**to buckle up** anschnallen
to be illiterate Analphabet sein	**to watch out** aufpassen

4.4

TO DO

- Talk about the environment

An environmental scandal!

Lucy, Olga and Hakan meet to clear up and finish the billiard room. Olga is very angry when she arrives and the other two are surprised and ask her what has happened. Olga shows them a newspaper article.

Stinkender Schlick erbost Urlauber

Unter den Urlaubern herrscht Empörung: Am Strand von Wackerballig sollte neuer Seestrand angefahren werden. Dazu sollte das Material genutzt werden, dass bei Baggerarbeiten des Sportboothafens gewonnen wurde. Nun musste am Strand eine Sperrzone errichtet werden, schwarzer stinkender Schlick bedeckt den gesamten Strand.

23

Lucy does not unterstand, so Olga explains:

Something happened in Wackerballig at the Baltic Sea. My grandmother has a caravan on the camping site and I have spent many holidays there. There is a beautiful natural beach where you can swim and normally there are also a lot of surfers as well. There is a marina about one kilometre from the camping site.
It was necessary to dredge the harbour so that bigger yachts could moor there. All the alluvial mud was then dumped on the beach. Now it is impossible to swim there as the mud is so thick that you can no longer walk in the shallow water. You sink right up to your knees in the thick mud and it is difficult to get out of it. This is very dangerous as small children could drown there. If they fell over they wouldn't be able to stand up again by themselves.
Swimming is now prohibited on this beach and it is not clear whether the water is contaminated or not. The campers have all signed a petition which was taken to the mayor, who now has to do something about this. The summer holidays are coming and the beach is closed!

1. **Imagine you are**

a) a seagull
b) a camper
c) a small child
d) a parent
e) a local surfer

in Wackerballig
How do you feel about this issue and how will it affect you and your daily life?

2. **Do you know of any other environmental problems either past or current? Discuss with your group.**

PHRASES		Modals
must	Vorschrift, Aufforderung	You **must** close the paint tin tightly when you finish painting.
must not	Verbot	You **must not** pour old paint down the drain.
have to	Notwendigkeit	We **have to** buy paint because we don't have any.
should	Ratschlag, etwas zu tun	We **should** wear a mask when painting so that we don't breathe in the fumes.
need to	Bedarf	We **need to** cover the floors with plastic before we start painting.
needn't	keine Notwendigkeit	We **needn't** wear goggles because we are not using a spraypainter.
can	Fähigkeit/Möglichkeit	We **can** clean the brushes in water.

3. **Look at these photos and discuss what happened and how or why it happened.**

4. **Choose one of these disasters and research what happened and present your results to your class.**

- Killer bees
- 9/11
- Chernobyl
- Plastic shopping bags
- Global warming in Germany

VOCAB

environment Umwelt **to clear up** aufräumen	**to dredge** ausbaggern **alluvial mud** Schlickwatt **prohibited** verboten	**seagull** Möwe **current** aktuell

4. Billiard Room

The friends have completed the billiard room and are busy cleaning up.

Never throw paint away in open tins with the normal household garbage. Paint is liquid and can **seep into** the soil and cause contamination.

What schould we do with the old paint we found in the cellar, Lucy?

Lucy immediately tells Olga and Hakan about the **strict rules** regarding the **disposal** of paints etc.

1. Latex paint can be disposed of together with the household waste if it is dry. Leave leftover paint in the paint tins without a lid so that it can dry.
2. Oil based paint must not be disposed of in normal household garbage. This must be taken to a collection point for **hazardous waste**.
3. Empty spraypainter guns can be put in normal household garbage.

5.

How can, should, need or must you dispose of the following items?

6.

What do you or your family do with your rubbish?

a) How do you separate it in your home?

b) How do other countries separate their rubbish?

7.

Think of the different types of jobs: painter, teacher, dentist etc.
What kinds of rubbish do these jobs produce and how do these people dispose of their rubbish/ waste?

a) Categorize according to: household rubbish, hazardous waste, potential recyclable waste, organic waste

b) Name 5 different examples for each category.

An: Chris@yahoo.ca
Cc:
Betreff: Dublin was great!

Hi Chris,
Wow has this been an exciting week! We were in Dublin, Ireland with our class for a few days. That was absolutely phenominal! I could hardly understand the Irish people as they speak with such a strange accent. We went to a Dublin vocational school and had some lessons there and the guys also showed us around Dublin. There's a lot of partying going on in the Temple Bar area.
We got back yesterday evening to find that Lucy and two other friends, Olga and Hakan, had been very busy renovating our billiard room in the clubhouse and they had also organized a billiard tournament. Guess who won? Yeah, you're right, not me!
That's okay I enjoyed it very much and we had a really good laugh.
You'll like the gang at the clubhouse. They're really great.
That's me signing off for now.
Take it easy mate and cu.

8. **Tell your partner about it.**

a) Do you play billiards or pool?
b) Are you a good player?
c) Have you ever won a billiard or pool **competition**?
d) Have you ever won a competition? If yes, which competition did you win and what did you win.

VOCAB

to seep into rein sickern	**hazardous waste** Giftmüll
strict rules strenge Regeln/Vorschriften	**competition** Wettbewerb
disposal Beseitigung	

5. Office

5.1

TO DO

- Talk about office equipment
- Use the internet
- Read an email address correctly

The search for new office equipment

Someone has broken into the office at the clubhouse.

24

Justin: Oh, Mr Mende, what happened?

Mr Mende: When I came in this morning I found everything in chaos. Look, the computer and printer have been stolen. They broke the cupboard open to get the camera. The swivel chair is damaged because they tried to use it as a footstep.

Justin: Did they get in through the window?

Mr Mende: Yes, as you can see they cut a hole into the glass and levered the window open.

Justin: And now? What are we going to do now? I mean, you need your office here. What about the equipment? It'll be very expensive to buy it all new.

Mr Mende: Yes, indeed. We only wanted to clean up the office a bit and redecorate it with new plants, lamps etc. But now ...

Justin: Yes, now we need a lot more.

1. **What is needed in the office of the clubhouse? Read the dialogue between Mr Mende and Justin above again and make a list.**

2. **What kind of equipment do we usually find in an office? Match the words with the letters in the picture and write the words down.**

a = tower

adapter – adhesive tape
bookshelf – cable –
cupboard – desk –
filing cabinet –
filing trays in and out –
keyboard –
mouse – photocopier –
printer –
ream of paper –
ring binders –
swivel chair –
telephone – tower

3. **What does the office in your company look like? Describe it.**

Internet search for office equipment

Later that day Lucy and Olga come to the clubhouse. They are also very shocked about the chaos the burglars left behind. When they hear that new equipment is needed, they enthusiastically search the internet for the cheapest equipment.

HOW TO … Use the internet

The internet offers a lot of information. Here is advice to make searching internet websites easy.

- If you only have a **vague** idea about what you are looking for, use a search directory. The search directory is a special directory page you have to go to. Yahoo is probably the most well known.
- If you know exactly what you are looking for (so if what you are looking for are facts) use a normal search engine like Google or Yahoo.
- Be as specific as possible. Search engines can search for many keywords **at once**. The keywords don't have to be written in a special order. The more keywords the better the results.
- Use **quotation marks** "…" to find the exact phrase you want to have. If you want to read the lyrics of a song, type the song title and the word *lyrics* into the search engine: "slicker than your average" lyrics
- Limit your search with a **hyphen**: pizza salami -olives
- If you want more than one alternative use **OR**: croque ham **OR** bacon
- After the search service has listed the websites click on **Cached** to find the keywords you have typed into the search engine highlighted in many colours.

4. **Write keywords in German about the information given above and explain them to your partner. Use a dictionary to help you.**

5. **Find out what these abbreviations mean. What do they mean in German? If possible search the internet for answers.**

www http faq url html

.net .org .edu .gov .com

frequently asked questions	for non-profit organizations
hypertext mark up language	for educational institutions
world wide web	for companies
uniform resource locator	for network infrastructure
hypertext transfer protocol	for government agencies (mainly USA)

VOCAB

office equipment	Büroausstattung
search	Suche
swivel chair	Bürostuhl
to lever something open	etwas aushebeln
burglar	Einbrecher
vague	undeutlich/wage
at once	auf einmal
hyphen	Bindestrich
abbreviation	Abkürzung
frequently	häufig
non-profit	nicht kommerziell
educational	bildend
government agency	Regierungsbehörde

New office equipment via the internet

Lucy and Olga are very angry about the burglary and really want to help Mr Mende with his office. They are sitting at the computer looking for new office equipment and furniture.

6.

a) **Listen to their conversation and complete the following table. Find out**
- what they want to buy,
- how much it costs.

b) **Calculate the total costs.**

Office equipment	cost
cupboard	180.00 €
Total	

HOW TO … Read internet sites and email addresses correctly

www.leo.org (w-w-w dot l-e-o dot o-r-g)
www.tradukka.com (w-w-w dot t-r-a-d-u-k-k-a dot c-o-m)
www.lyrics.com (w-w-w dot l-y-r-i-c s dot c-o-m)

B_Jarvey-Ryan@flexbond.com

capital B underscore capital J-a-r-v-e-y hyphen capital R-y-a-n at f-l-e-x-b-o-n-d dot com

J.Mende@gtl.de

capital J dot capital M-e-n-d-e at g-t-l dot d-e

com, org, net, co
These abbreviations are pronounced like words. They are not **spelt** letter by letter as in 'de'.

7. **Read these emails to a partner.**

a) L.Briggs@yahoo.co.uk
b) blackhead_33@magic.com
c) Frank.Messer-Waldner@service.center.de
d) info@village.real.estate.org
e) M_Oezpal@turk-travel.com
f) helpdesk@grammerton.edu

8. **Spell your most favourite internet addresses to a partner.**

Home-made office equipment

Justin and Sebi are talking about the burglary.

26

Sebi: We **certainly** have to buy a new computer and printer and all the other electronic equipment, the camera and so on. But we don't have to buy a desk and a bookshelf. We can make them ourselves, can't we?
Justin: Yes, of course. I mean the desk won't be a **luxurious** one with **the latest mod cons**, but functional.
Sebi: Yes, right. And we also need a cupboard and filing cabinet. That's a bit more **difficult** to make.
Justin: You're right. We should buy these things. But for the other things, I can make a list of the materials we need.
Sebi: Good idea. And as we also need a new window, we should ask about that, too.
Justin: Yes, should we build in a window with special **burglar-proofing**?
Sebi: Well, windows like those are very expensive. But I thought about **welding** burglar bars over all windows.
Justin: That's a good idea! Then, the window won't be so expensive, that's true. We should ask Olga about it. I'm sure she can weld burglar bars.
Sebi: Yes, so let me talk to Olga about the window. Now you make a list of the materials and things we need for the desk and bookshelf.
Justin: Alright ...

9. **Here is Justin's material list. Sebi wants to understand the list completely. Help him to translate the list into German.**

desk	bookshelf
1 piece of wood 2 by 1 m	1 wooden **board**
4 table legs made of metal	4 screws
4 x 4 screws	4 **rawl plugs**
4 flooring **felt pads**	2 “L“ **brackets**

10. **The two friends want to make the desk and the bookshelf with the materials listed above. Which tools do they need? Make a list.**

VOCAB

to spell buchstabieren
certainly sicherlich
luxurious luxuriös
the latest mod cons mit modernstem Komfort
difficult schwierig
burglar-proofing Einbruchsicherung
to weld schweißen
felt pads Filzscheiben
board Brett
rawl plugs Dübel
bracket Befestigungsarm

5.2

TO DO

- How to speak on the telephone

A telephone call from England

Justin and Sebi were able to build the office furniture with the help of Justin's boss. They also talked to Olga, and she promised to ask her boss about the window and the burglar bars. Anna and Lucy decorated the room with some plants so that Mr Mende's office looked really neat and organized again. The friends are really happy that the office is shipshape again. Only the telephone isn't working yet. While Olga is trying to fix it, she tells a story about what happened in her company's office the other day.

Olga: Das war witzig, ich kam rein und die Kollegin war völlig aufgeregt. Der Chef war nicht da und sie musste nun den Anruf aus England selbst entgegen nehmen. Die Arme...

Mr Mende: Kannst Du eigentlich genug Englisch um mit Engländern zu telefonieren, z. B. um einen Kunden hinsichtlich der Einbruchsicherung seines Hauses zu beraten?

Olga: Ach, das geht schon ganz gut, wir haben es gerade in der Berufsschule gehabt. Aber bei der Kollegin im Büro ging es um eine spezielle Werbekampagne, die mit einer Niederlassung in England verhandelt werden musste.

Lucy: And was she able to manage the phone call?

Olga: **Unfortunately**, I had to go to one of our building sites again so that I didn't hear the end of the story. But, I can tell you, she was really nervous.

Mr Mende: Well, I can imagine that your **colleague** in the office is afraid of a phone call from England. I remember that when I phoned to change my **return flight** when I was in England last year I had quite a few problems. It was really hard for me to understand the other person. And, you know, when you don't feel self-confident, understanding people in another language becomes even worse.

Lucy: Yes, it's because you can't see the other person's body language when your're on the phone.

1. **Look at Olga's colleague in the picture above.**

a) How does she look?
b) How does she feel?
c) How would you feel in such a situation?
d) What can be done to make the situation better?

2. **Listen to the telephone conversation about an advertising campaign with a marketing company in England that Olga's colleague had the other day. List all problems that can occur before, during and at the end of a telephone conversation.**

27

HOW TO … Handle a telephone conversation successfully

1. **Be prepared**
   You should know who you want to talk to and exactly what you want. Have something to write with near you.
2. **Learn key phrases**
   Learn the key phrases listed below and use them. Copy the phrases and put them next to your phone.
3. **Be clear and precise**
   Speak clearly and use simple language.
4. **Be polite**
   Smile when you are on the phone, **avoid** direct language. Say "Could I ..." and not "Can I ...". And don't forget the little word "please": Could I speak to Mr Cartwright, please?
5. **Control the call**
   Ask the caller to speak more slowly, politely **interrupt** the caller when you don't understand. Repeat the details at the end of the call again.
6. **Be able to spell**
   B as in butter, C as in Caesar

3. **Which of the above points do you find easy to follow? Give reasons.**

4. **Listen again to the telephone conversation about the advertising campaign between Viktoria Altmann and Paul Evans. Make notes about how the conversation can be improved.**

VOCAB

to promise versprechen	**during** während
neat ordentlich	**to prepare** vorbereiten
shipshape tiptop	**key phrases** Schlüsselsätze
the other day neulich	**precise** genau
unfortunately unglücklicherweise	**polite/ly** höflich
colleague Kollege/Kollegin	**to avoid** vermeiden
return flight Rückflug	**to interrupt** unterbrechen
advertising campaign Werbekampagne	**to spell** buchstabieren
to occur auftreten	**to improve** verbessern

PHRASES **Telephoning**

At the beginning
Good morning/afternoon. This is Manning, **Peter Manning** from Germany speaking.
I would like to talk to Mary Skinner in marketing, please.
Could you tell me ...?
I'm calling about ...

Say your full name

Offer help
How may I help you?
May I ask what it is about?
Can I give her a message?

Connect the caller
One moment please, I'll see if Ms Skinner is **available**.
Just a moment, please, I'll **put** you **through**/I'll connect you.

The person is not available
I'm sorry; the line's **busy/engaged**.
I'm afraid Ms Skinner is not in.
I'm afraid she's away on business. Can she call you back when she gets in?
Can I take a message?
Would you like to **leave a message**?
I'll give her the message as soon as possible.

Handle problems
Who is speaking please?
Sorry, **I didn't quite catch that**/your name.
Could you spell that/your name, please?
Sorry, could you speak more slowly, please?
I'm sorry; could you repeat that, please?
Sorry, what did you say?

At the end
Thank you for calling. Goodbye. → Thank you. Goodbye.
Have a nice day. Goodbye. → You too. Goodbye.
Thank you for your help. → **You're welcome.** Goodbye. → Goodbye.

5. **Copy the phrases in the box above and find similar German phrases.**

6. **Create a telephone conversation with the help of the phrases above. Start like this:**

Partner A
Brendon Enterprises. Hawthorne speaking. How can I help you?

Partner B
Hello Ms/Mr Hawthorne. This is ...

...

7. **Have a look at the conversation below. Brenda and Frank are very impolite. Rewrite the sentences making them more polite. The phrase box on page 76 should help you.**

Brenda	Frank
Jerry White's office. Brenda speaking. What do you want?	
	Hi Brenda. This is Frank Tramp speaking. Give me Mr Baker.
Wait! … The line is engaged. Do you want to wait?	
	No. Give me Mr Baker's extension.
It's -354. Mr Baker will be in the office until 5 o'clock.	
	What? Repeat that.
The extension is -354. Mr Baker will be in the office until 5 o'clock. Got that?	
	Yes, ok. Goodbye.
Goodbye.	

8. **Get together with a partner. Choose one of the situations below and create a telephone conversation using as many phrases from the phrase box as possible. Practise the conversation with your partner and be prepared to present your role play to the class.**

Situation 1: Hedley Hunters in London have a problem with the transport of wood to Fischer Holzverarbeitung in Germany. Hedley Hunters want to call and tell Fischer Holzverarbeitung that the wood will arrive 3 days later.

Situation 2: Anna Paulsen from Metallverarbeitung Paulsen has **received** a fax from Wilkerson Tools Ltd. Her problem is that the quality of the fax is very bad and she cannot read what Wilkerson Tools Ltd. want. She wants to call Mr Champ and ask if Wilkerson Tools Ltd. can send the fax again. **Unfortunately**, Mr Champ from Wilkerson Tools Ltd. is out of office. Anna Paulsen wants to leave a message.

Situation 3: Selma Taylor from Mitch Security Systems wants to tell Hahnen GmbH that the **spare parts** have arrived in England. She wants to call Hahnen GmbH to say that the spare parts can be sent to Germany next week. Unfortunately, Mr Hahnen is at lunch at the moment. She asks if Mr Hahnen can call her back.

VOCAB

to be available	zur Verfügung stehen	**You're welcome.**	Bitte sehr.
to put somebody through	jemanden verbinden	**impolite**	unhöflich
busy/engaged	besetzt	**extension**	Durchwahl
I'm afraid	Es tut mir leid	**to receive**	erhalten
to leave a message	eine Nachricht hinterlassen	**unfortunately**	unglücklicherweise
I didn't quite catch that	Ich habe das nicht ganz verstanden	**spare parts**	Ersatzteile

5.3

TO DO

- Write a simple enquiry
- Write an offer

Enquiries

It was unusual for Viktoria Altmann, Olga's colleague in the office, to have something to do with the advertising campaign. She is normally responsible for the customers of their company. They often enquire about the products and services Bergent Metalltechnik GmbH can offer. Sometimes they ask for certain products from abroad. Here is an enquiry from an English customer.

1 **DYD Metal Services**
15 Wincome Lane, Shaftesbury, Dorset, SP7 9QJ
Telephone 01747 818009 / **Fax** 01747 819482 / **Email** sales@dydmetalservices.co.uk

2 Bergent Metalltechnik GmbH
Industriestraße 16
22309 Hamburg
GERMANY

3 Your ref.:
Our ref.: TW/ab

4 15 September 20XX

5 Dear Sir or Madam

6 **Steps – custum designed**

7 We are a medium-sized company which offers metal services in England and learnt from your website that you offer special steps.

Please send us an offer for the steps as described in the enclosed technical drawing. As we can't get these steps for a spiral staircase on the British market at the moment, we need the information urgently, please let us have your offer by the end of this week.

Please tell us your terms of payment and terms of delivery as well as the delivery date.

We look forward to hearing from you soon.

8 Yours faithfully

9 *Thomas Winter*
Thomas Winter
(Purchasing Department)

10 cc: David Compton, Managing Director

11 Enc.

The subject line usually comes under the salutation

cc stands for 'carbon copy' and means that another person gets a copy of the letter

1. **Olga's boss, Mr Schmüser, asks his secretary, Victoria Altmann, to explain to him what the enquiry is about.**
Help Ms Altmann: Write an explanation of the letter in German.

2. **Match the numbers in the letter with the following terms:**

body of the letter – cc – **complimentary close** – date – **enclosures** – letter head – references – **salutation** – sender's address – **signature block** – **subject line**

PHRASES — Writing an enquiry

Opening

We are a small/**medium-sized**/large company.
We have seen your advertisement in the German magazine "Der Handwerker".
We refer to our telephone conversation of (date).

Details

We are looking for a **supplier** of ...
We urgently need ...
As we want to **extend** our range of products, we are interested in (name of product).
Please tell us your / Please let us have your } terms of payment and terms of delivery.

Beachte: look forward to + ...**ing**

Close

We look **forward to hearing** from you soon.
We hope to hear from you soon.

Salutation and complimentary close

kein Ansprechpartner:	Dear Sir or Madam	Yours faithfully
Ansprechpartner vorhanden:	Dear Mr Brown	Yours sincerely

3. **Write an enquiry for materials you often need in your company.**

- Begin by telling your business partner that you are a large company in your work field.
- Ask for prices, terms of delivery and terms of payment.
- Say that you need your materials immediately.
- Close by saying that you are looking forward to receiving an offer soon.

VOCAB

enquiry Anfrage
abroad im Ausland
offer Angebot
enclosed anliegend
spiral staircase Wendeltreppe
urgent/ly dringend
terms of payment Zahlungsbedingungen
terms of delivery Lieferbedingungen
to look forward to (doing something) sich freuen auf
Yours faithfully Mit freundlichen Grüßen
complimentary close Grußformel
enclosure Anlage
salutation Begrüßung
signature Unterschrift
subject line Betreffzeile
medium-sized mittlere Größe
supplier Anbieter
to extend ausbauen

Offers

Anton Schmüser, Ms Altmann's boss gave her a note with the business terms for the steps DYD Metal Services, the customer in England, wants to order. Ms Altmann translated the terms into English. Here is what she wrote.

Dear Mr Winters

Your enquiry about steps for a spiral staircase – spezcial fabrication

Thank you for your enquiry of last week. We are **pleased** to offer you the following steps for a spiral staircase:

40 Steps – custom designed	58.00 € each		2,320.00
Delivery			800.00
		Total costs	**3,712.80**

Prices **stated** are fob Hamburg. If you **order** by the end of this week we can give you a **discount** of 10 %.

We can deliver by the end of this month.

This offer is **valid** for 4 weeks after date of offer.

We would be pleased to **receive** an order from you soon.

Yours sincerely
A. Schmüser

A. Schmüser
(Managing Director)

4. **Ms Altmann wants to know if she understood the information the boss gave her correctly. She explains the offer to her boss again. Help her and note down in keywords what the offer is about in German.**

5. **Look at the phrases box on the next page for writing an offer and find the English words for the following German expressions.**

Angebot – Anfrage – Rabatt – genannt – Versicherung – sofort – Lieferung – gültig – innerhalb – sich beziehen auf – zufriedenstellend – Bestellung

PHRASES — Writing an offer

Opening
Thank you for your enquiry of ...
We **refer** to your email/letter of ...

Details
We are pleased to offer you the following ...
We are pleased to give you a discount of 10 %.

Prices **stated** are	... cif London (cost, insurance, freight)	Kosten, Versicherung und Fracht bezahlt bis London.
	... fob Hamburg (free on board)	frei an Bord Hamburg
	... EXW (ex works)	ab Lager

Shipment can be made **immediately/within** two weeks.
The offer is **valid** until ...

Close
We hope that our prices and terms **meet with your approval** and that you will **place an order** with us.
We hope that our offer will be **satisfactory** and that you will decide to place an order with us soon.

6. **Look at Anton Schmüser's memo to his secretary about the offer he wants to make to Macro Ltd., 77 Dale Street, Manchester, M1 2HG, UK. Help Mr Schmüser's secretary. Write a letter to Marco Ltd. using the notes made by the managing director. Use the proper layout and today's date.**

- *Firma Macro Ltd. hat Interesse an unseren Brandschutztüren (fireproof doors)*
- *beziehen Sie sich auf ihre Anfrage vom ..., telefonisch habe ich ihnen letzte Woche angeboten:*
- *889 €/Stück, Preis: fob Hamburg, 15 % Rabatt, Lieferung sofort, Angebot bis Ende des Jahres gültig*
- *Freundlichen Schlusssatz nicht vergessen*

VOCAB

to be pleased erfreut sein
to state angeben
to order bestellen
discount Nachlass/Rabatt
valid gültig
to receive erhalten
to refer to sich beziehen auf
shipment Transport
immediately sofort
within innerhalb
meet with your approval ihre Zustimmung finden
to place an order eine Bestellung aufgeben
satisfactory befriedigend
proper passend

5.4

TO DO

- Talk about things in the past

28

Burglar bars for the clubhouse

Olga's boss was very thankful for the help of his secretary with the English customer. He was able to offer very good terms so that finally the English customer ordered the special steps.

Olga: My boss said that she did a "good job" when she helped him with the English expressions. That's nearly all he can say in English.

Lucy: Mmmh, but she really did a good job. There are a lot of words and phrases that you need to understand to be able to write enquiries and offers.

Olga: Yes, that's true.

Lucy: Olga, were you able to ask about the window and the burglar bars for the clubhouse?

Olga: Oh, when I told my boss about our clubhouse and the burglary that happened, he praised me for my commitment there. He said that it is important for young people to take responsibility for something. That's why he gave us the material for free. Yesterday, he gave me the iron bars and I welded the burglar bars together – with his help, of course. And now we can install them together with the window.

Lucy: Great! So, no more burglaries in the future anymore!

Olga: Yes, exactly. And these burglar bars have a special element. They have a quick-release mechanism. In an emergency you can use it to quickly unlock the bars from inside the clubhouse and so escape immediately.

Lucy: How thoughtful!

1. **Say whether these statements are true or not.**

a) Olga's boss did not want to give any material to the clubhouse.
b) Olga's boss did a good job.
c) People have to know a lot of English words and phrases to write an enquiry.
d) Lucy praised Olga for her commitment to the clubhouse.
e) Olga welded the burglar bars.
f) People cannot get out of the clubhouse through the windows because of the burglar bars.
g) The burglar bars have a special mechanism to unlock them.
h) There is an emergency at the clubhouse.

2. page 168, 184

Identify all simple past forms in the dialogue. Which of these words are regular verbs and which are irregular verbs?

HOW TO …

page 168

Use the simple past

We use the simple past to talk about things and periods of time in the past.

1. Regular form:
   add -ed at the end of the **infinitive** (to walk/walk**ed**, to cook/cook**ed**, ...)
   sometimes the infinitive ends with an "e" then only add -d at the end
   (to move/move**d**, to hope/hope**d**)
2. **Irregular** form
   change the infinitive **according to** the list in the grammar section (to take/took, to bring/brought, to put/put, ...)
3. **Specialities**
   y → i + ed (to study/stud**ied**, to **tidy**/tid**ied**)

3. **Mr Mende told the friends about his past. Here is his report. Copy it and fill in the gaps with the correct form of the simple past.**

I … (leave) school when I … (be) 19 and … (do) an **apprenticeship** as an **office management assistant**. I … (work) in a small company which … (specialise) in security systems. After my apprenticeship I … (work) there for two more years. Then I … (study) **social science** at university. After that I … (work) for a **health care organisation**. I … (be) in charge of organising the transport of sick people to and from the hospital. A year ago I … (start) to work in the clubhouse here. I really like working with young people.

4. **Now give a report about Olga's boss Mr Schmüser in English. Use a dictionary if necessary.**

Anton Schmüser

- verließ die Schule mit 16 und machte eine Ausbildung zum Tischler,
- arbeitete 3 Jahre lang in einer kleinen Tischlerei (joinery).
- Danach gründete er sein eigenes Unternehmen (to set up a business).
- Vor 10 Jahren ist sein Geschäftspartner, Herr Hohmann, in sein Unternehmen gekommen.
- Heute ist er zusammen mit Herrn Hohmann für 30 Mitarbeiter verantwortlich.

VOCAB

burglar bars Fenstergitter
customer Kunde
finally schließlich
expression Ausdruck
nearly fast
burglary Einbruch
to praise loben
commitment Engagement
to take responsibilty Verantwortung übernehmen
iron bars Eisenstangen
quick-release mechanism Schnelllösemechanismus
to unlock aufschließen
infinitive Grundform
irregular unregelmäßig
according to entsprechend
specialities Besonderheiten
to tidy aufräumen
apprenticeship Ausbildung
Office Management Assistant Bürokaufmann
social science Sozialwissenschaften
health care organisation Gesundheitsorganisation

Emergency exit

Lucy wanted to know more about the burglar bars and the mechanism that allows people to get out of a house through a window quickly. She searched the internet for more information. Read the text and then do the following exercises.

burglar bars

Tragedies happen when children and adults become trapped inside their homes, unable to escape a fire because of burglar bars!

Requirements for the installation of burglar bars:

- Ideally they should be able to be opened from the inside without the use of a key, easy to open and without much **effort** (a child should be able to open the bars and get out easily).
- If the burglar bars need a key to be opened, keep the key near the bars at all times, for an easy way out in case of fire. **Practise** opening and closing the burglar bars with your family and make sure the key is always kept in the same place, so the burglar bars can be unlocked quickly.
- DO NOT install burglar bars that cannot be opened from the inside on windows or doors used for **escape routes**, because in the event of a fire your life will be at risk. However, installation on guest toilet windows is **advised** as this is often the **preferred point** of entry for burglars.
- If burglar bars are installed, you should have **smoke detectors** to protect the place where you sleep or the **hallway**. The signal from a smoke alarm must be able to be heard from every bedroom.

5. **Find words in the text that have a similar meaning as the following words and phrases:**

a) grown up people
b) to be caught
c) when people run away quickly
d) a special **device** to open a door
e) to open a door with a key
f) mother, father and children
g) very simple
h) period of time that a person or animal exists
i) white, grey or black gas produced by something that is burning
j) place where people sleep

6. **Lucy wants to tell Olga about the information in the article. Help her to note down in German what is important about burglar bars.**

An: Chris@yahoo.ca
Cc:
Betreff: burglary

Hi Chris,
We had burglars in our clubhouse. Everything was in chaos. ...
...
...

Yours
Justin

7. **Imagine you are Justin. Complete the email to Chris and tell him what happened at the clubhouse. Read through Unit 5 again. Tell him about the burglary, what Justin and Sebi did, what the girls did and how they helped to make the office comfortable again.**

VOCAB

adult Erwachsener	**to practise** üben	**hallway** Flur
to be trapped in der Falle sein	**escape route** Fluchtweg	**similar** ähnlich
to escape flüchten	**to be advised** hier: geboten sein	**device** Vorrichtung
requirement Erfordernis	**preferred point** bevorzugter Punkt	**comfortable** bequem
effort Aufwand	**smoke detectors** Rauchmelder	

6. Extension

6.1

TO DO

- Arrange a delivery
- Arrange a meeting
- Describing the way

Equipment

In the evening they discuss how the garage should be equipped.

Hakan: We need a car lift, an engine analyser, a tyre changer, a brake test rig, a tool box with casters and all the tools.
Victor: Hakan, are you planning to start a business?
Hakan: Errm, why?
Mr Mende: What Victor is trying to say is that it sounds like you want equipment for a professional car repair shop.
Viktor: First of all we should think about what we would like to do in the garage. Not everybody is a professional car mechanic and we might need the space for other work as well.
Hakan: But I ...
Olga: A tyre changer would be great but how often do you really need it? When you buy new tyres, tyre changing is often included or doesn't cost that much extra. Most of us are apprentices and don't have that much money, especially for cars. So, our old cars might need welding; we should rather buy welding equipment rather than state of the art stuff.
Patrick: That's true. Look at my car! It's full of dents.
Hakan: That's because you can't drive.
Patrick: It was my grandfather's car; it already had the dents when I got it.
Hakan: Maybe you could fix or weld bumpers all around your car?
Lucy: Welding won't help. Patrick, if you want a great looking car then the dents have to be removed and the whole car needs to be sprayed. So it would be good to have a spray gun and a compressor in our workshop.
Justin: Could we use it for airbrushing, too?
Lucy: No, unfortunately not. We need smaller spray guns for airbrushing. Maybe there are air compressors that can be used for spraying and airbrushing as well. We'll have to found out.

Anna: What about solvents? They can be dangerous, as well as unhealthy and could cause an explosion.
Lucy: We can use water-based paint and wear respirators.
Sebi: I think it's really important to have a well-equipped tool box. I can only do small repairs, but I often don't have the right tools. I would like to use the garage to do oil changes and to replace air filters or spark plugs. I don't know how an engine analyser works. We have an inspection pit, so we don't need a car lift as well, a hydraulic car jack will do.
Mr Mende: Thanks for all the ideas. However, we should remember that we only have 3,000 euros left for the equipment and we can't buy everything.

1. **Which pieces equipment would you buy? What do you think is necessary? Discuss in class.**

Delivery

29

After Hakan and his friends agreed on what to buy, they found out that new equipment was too expensive. Finally they ordered second hand equipment from Ireland.
Mr Mende is talking on the phone with Mr Daniels from *Used Garage Equipment Direct Online Shop*.

Mr Mende: Jugendclub Escape, Mende.
Mr Daniels: Good morning. My name is Jack Daniels from Used Garage Equipment. Do you speak English?
Mr Mende: Yes, a little. How can I help you?
Mr Daniels: We've just put your order together and we are ready to deliver. I'd like to sort out the details of the delivery. We can send it by Parcelforce Worldwide or by DPD UK, but it's very expensive because your equipment is so heavy. However, I can recommend using a **freight forwarder**. This firm delivers directly to Hamburg **every fortnight**. This only costs half as much.
Mr Mende: Our garage isn't finished yet, so that sounds perfect. When would the equipment arrive?
Mr Daniels: **Next** Tuesday or two weeks later on 7 June. If that's too early then four weeks later on Tuesday, the twenty-first.
Mr Mende: Well, then I would prefer the 21 June. What time will the **lorry** arrive?
Mr Daniels: The carrier leaves in the evening, takes the overnight ferry and should arrive in Hamburg at midday.
Mr Mende: Oh, we're only open from 5 o'clock in the afternoon.
Mr Daniels: That's not a problem. There are other customers in Hamburg. I'll ask the forwarder to deliver to you last. Can I give him your phone number just in case there are any problems?
Mr Mende: Yes, of course.
Mr Daniels: Alright, your equipment will be delivered on 21 June at 5 p.m. Thank you for your order. Goodbye Mr Mende.
Mr Mende: Bye Mr Daniels. Thank you for organizing such a quick delivery.
Mr Daniels: You're welcome.

You don't use a **preposition of time** with **last, next, this, every.**

2. page 177

Read the dialogue above. When do you use at, on, in (= prepositions of time)?
... on 21 June ... = When you talk about dates.

VOCAB

delivery Lieferung	**casters** Laufrollen	**pit** Grube
car lift Hebebühne	**dent** Beule	**car jack** Wagenheber
engine analyser Motortester	**bumper** Stoßstange	**freight forwarder** Spediteur
brake test rig Bremsenprüfstand	**solvent** Lösemittel	**fortnight** zwei Wochen
	spark plug Zündkerze	**lorry** Lastwagen, Lkw

6. Extension

Describing the way

It's 4.15 on Tuesday afternoon and Mr Mende is sitting at his desk working when Hakan walks in and asks:
"Has the lorry arrived with our equipment yet, Mr Mende?"
Before Mr Mende can answer Hakan the phone rings. A problem has cropped up!

3. 30

page 180

Listen to the dialogue and find the route to the youth club on the map.

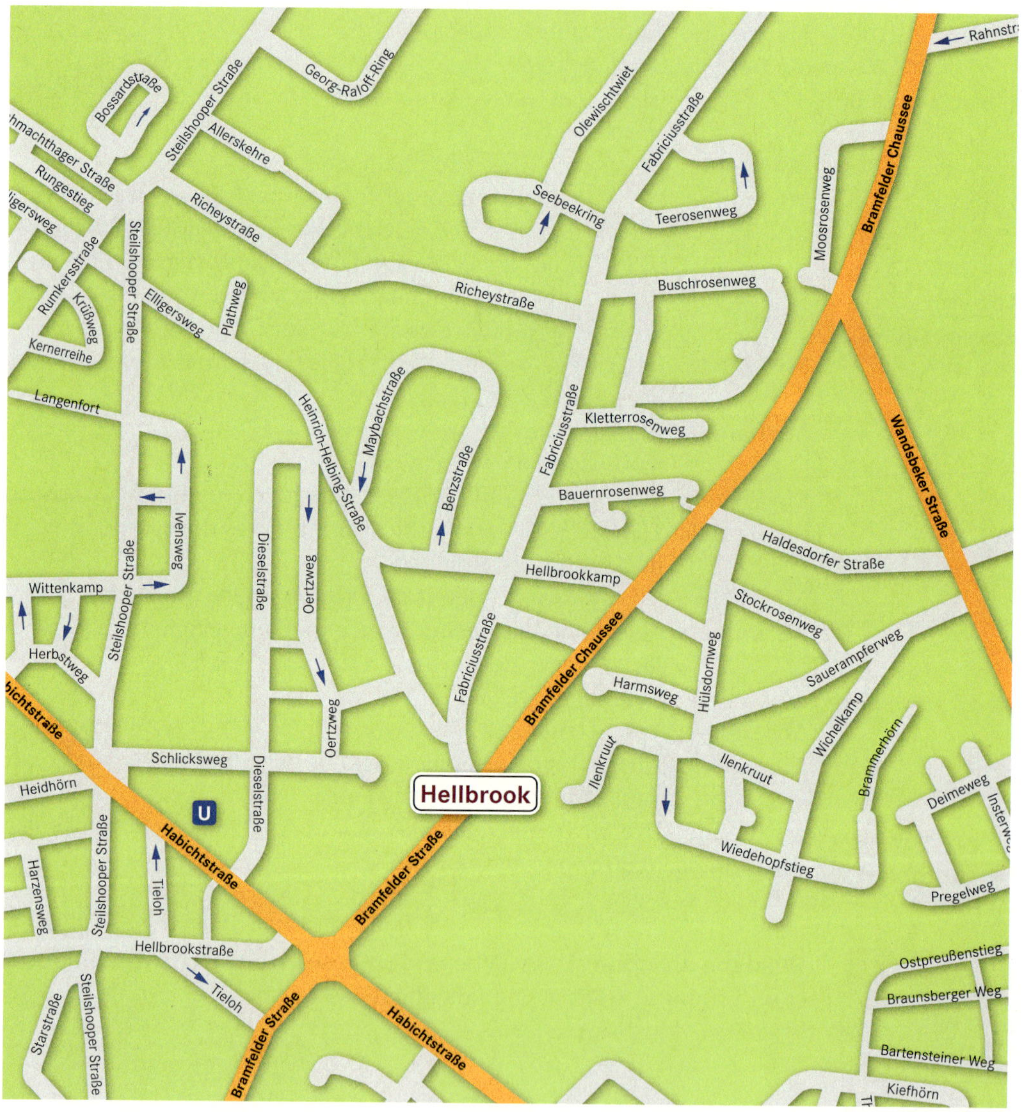

4. Work with a partner. Explain how to get from "Kletterrosenweg" to "Wiedehopfstieg".

5. Work with a partner. Take turns explaining the different points of your choice.

Arrange a meeting

On Thursday evening Olga and Lucy are planning what to do at the weekend.

Lucy: I don't want to spend the whole weekend here at the clubhouse.
Olga: What about going to the cinema?
Lucy: I've heard that the Zeise-Kino is a beautiful place. What's on there?
Olga: Yes, it's amazing. They've set up a cinema in an old factory for **marine propellers**. Let's have a look at their program.
Lucy: Are they showing a comedy?
Olga: Yes, but only on Sunday morning.
Lucy: What's being shown on Saturday evening?
Olga: There's "Soul Kitchen" with Moritz Bleibtreu. It's a film by Fatih Akin which won a special prize at the Venice Film Festival in 2009. They are also showing "A Serious Man", a **black comedy** film by the Coen brothers.
Lucy: I've always wanted to see that film. When does the performance start?
Olga: There's is one at 19:45 and then the late show is at 22:30.
Lucy: Let's go to the late show and go for a drink afterwards.
Olga: Great idea! We can also have a pizza before the film at the restaurant next to the cinema.
Lucy: Terrific! Let's meet at 8:30 in front of the restaurant.

6. What's on at the cinema?

Work in pairs and make a dialogue. Decide on a film, date and time.

Programm vom 18.3. bis zum 24.3.

	Do, 18.3.	Fr, 19.3.	Sa, 20.3.	So, 21.3.	Mo, 22.3.	Di, 23.3.	Mi, 24.3.
Kino 1 [369 P.]				11:30 Das weiße Band			
	14:30, 17:00, 19:45 Soul Kitchen						
	22:30 Soul Kitchen	22:30 Kampf der Künste - Shortfilm Slam	22:30 Soul Kitchen		22:30 Soul Kitchen	22:30 Sneak Preview	22:30 Soul Kitchen
Kino 2 [95 P.]				11:00 Willkommen bei den Sch'tis			
			13:15 Willi und die Wunder dieser Welt				
	15:00 Willi und die Wunder dieser Welt						
	17:00, 19:45 A Serious Man						
	22:30 A Serious Man	22:30 Soul Kitchen	22:30 A Serious Man		22:30 A Serious Man	22:30 Soul Kitchen	22:30 Soul Kitchen
Kino 3 [67 P.]				11:00 Vicky Cristina Barcelona			
			13:15 Neues von Pettersson und Findus				
	15:00 Bolt						
	17:00, 19:45 Neuseeland auf eigene Faust						
	22:30 Neuseeland auf eigene Faust				22:30 Neuseeland auf eigene Faust		

VOCAB

marine propeller Schiffsschraube	**black comedy** schwarzer Humor

6.2

TO DO

- Explain mandatory signs
- Give safety instructions

Safety clothes

When Justin and Sebi arrive at the clubhouse the old birch tree has been felled and is lying in the garden. Mr Mende tells them gardeners from the garden & parks department chopped it down, sawed off the branches and removed them. The trunk of the tree should be used for firewood. Therefore it has to be sawed up and split. Anna also arrives.

Anna: Hi, have you seen the birch tree in the garden? What a shame that it had to be cut down; it was such a beautiful tree.

Mr Mende: It was old, decayed and dangerous.

Justin: It was also too close to the garage; its roots could have damaged the foundations and the walls.

Anna: So, I've brought a chain saw from my firm to saw it up.

Sebi: Great, Justin and I will do that. We are joiners, we were born to work with wood.

Anna: Have you ever worked with a chain saw? Are you trained to use a chain saw? Do you know the safety precautions? Have you got any safety clothes?

Justin: We have to wear ear protection in our workshop as long as planing machines or saws are running.

Sebi: I have to wear safety shoes on building sites. But I don't have to wear a hard hat all the time. And I was instructed on how to operate the chain saws. In the beginning I wasn't allowed to work alone with those machines.

Mr Mende: Anna is right. Last year I was in a forest getting some firewood for my fire place at home but I wasn't allowed to use a chain saw. Even fire fighters have to go on a training course before operating chain saws. I think we'll get into a lot of trouble if somebody gets hurt with a chain saw here at the youth club.

1. **What are your answers to Anna's questions?**

a) Have you ever worked with a chain saw?
b) Are you trained to use a chain saw?
c) Do you know the safety precautions?
d) Have you got any safety clothes?
e) Which safety clothes do you have to wear when you work with a chain saw?
f) Which safety precautions do you know for operating a chain saw?

2. **Think of your job.**

a) Which safety clothes do you wear in your job?
b) Which safety precautions do you have to follow? Think of machines, tools and places where you work (ladder, roof ...).

Dangerous places of work

In the evening Justin and Sebi search the internet to find out more about safety at work. Suddenly they start laughing. They have just found a page with some 'funny' pictures of unsafe places of work.

3. **Look at the photos. Work in pairs and present the results to your class.**

a) Explain why these places of work are very dangerous and why the workers are careless.

b) What precautions should to be taken to make these places of work safe?

VOCAB

birch Birke	**branch** Zweig	**precaution** Vorsichtsmaßnahme
to fell fällen	**trunk** Stamm	**decayed** morsch, verfault
to chop down fällen	**to saw up** zersägen	**fire fighter** Feuerwehrmann
to saw off absägen	**to split** spalten	

6. Extension

Mandatory signs

4. **Do you remember these mandatory signs? What do they mean? Use modal verbs to explain them to your partner.**

5. **Match the safety symbols and the explanations. Then make sentences and explain.**

page 183

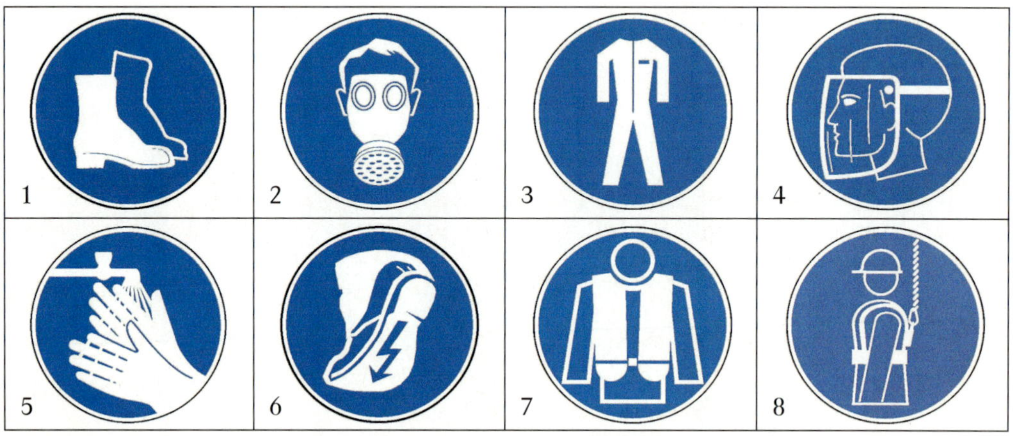

a) respirator
b) face mask
c) safety boots
d) chained cylinders
e) safety belt
f) **lifejacket**
g) wash hands
h) protective clothing
i) **conductive** shoes
j) face shield
k) **safety harness**
l) **apron**
m) wear **heavy duty**
n) wear **easy duty**

1 c) safety boots:
Safety boots must be worn in this area. You must wear foot protection.

6. **What else should you do to protect yourself? Look at the three pictures and write three sentences. Together with a partner brainstorm any other things you should do to protect yourselves at work, on the road, on holiday or when doing sport.**

Personal protective clothing

When working with a chainsaw it is important to make the work as safe as possible. Chainsaw injuries are dangerous and very common.
Protective **pants** are a must for anyone using a chainsaw. The saw-stopping power in these pants comes from layers of Kevlar, a lightweight fibre but five times stronger than steel.

Chainsaw protective clothing can be worn all day and is machine washable.
Clothing must be **tight** but shouldn't reduce freedom of movement. Do not wear loose clothing or a scarf which can get caught on a branch of a tree or even worse, in a chainsaw. If you have long hair cover it with a hair net or a cap.

pants = American English
trousers = British English

7. **Match the headings and the paragraphs with the picture.**

- leg protection
- hearing protection
- hand protection
- helmet
- facial protection
- safety boots

a) **sturdy** gloves, preferably leather, some have **cut retardant** material sewn in
b) closely fitting trousers with cut-resistant inlay; **threads** like Kevlar can **halt** chains immediately on contact
c) helps to reduce the sound pressure and frequency of power-driven machines in noisy conditions
d) protects head from falling branches
e) a face shield protects against **woodchips** and **rebounding** branches; it's a good idea to wear additional goggles or sunglasses
f) with **cut-resistant** inlay, non slip soles and **steel toe caps**

VOCAB

lifejacket Rettungsweste	**protective clothing** Sicherheitskleidung	**to halt** blockieren
conductive leitend	**tight** enganliegend	**woodchips** Sägespäne
apron Schürze	**sturdy** robust, strapazierfähig	**to rebound** zurückschnellen
safety harness (Auffang)Gurt	**cut retardant** schnitthemmend	**cut resistant** schnittfest
heavy duty schwerer Atemschutz	**thread** Faden	**steel toe cap** Stahlkappe
easy duty leichter Atemschutz		

6.3

TO DO

- Describe processes
- Use sequence words

Describing processes

Lucy hasn't been to the clubhouse for a fortnight. When she arrives, she is surprised to see a huge stack of firewood close to the entrance. She sees Sebastian and asks him about it.

32

Lucy: Where did all this wood come from? Did Mr Mende order it?
Sebi: No way! Your brother, Anna and I made it. Didn't Justin tell you?
Lucy: No, he didn't. What does "we made it" mean? Where did you get the wood?
Sebi: Take a look in the garden behind the house. There was an old birch tree, remember? The gardeners chopped it down. Then they sawed off the branches. Then Anna chopped up the trunk and Justin and I split the logs. Then we put the pieces into a wheelbarrow and took them to the front of the building. Then we stacked the pieces of wood there.
Lucy: I see. By the way, can you help me with my "Berichtsheft"? I have to explain how to hang wallpaper.

HOW TO … Use sequence words

When Sebi explained where the firewood came from he linked the events with "then". This type of sequence word does not present the various events in any sort of relationship to each other. It is important to know the order or sequence that events take place in a story or explanation. It helps you understand what you hear or read.

Sequence Words
first second next before after that then later afterwards finally last

You can also use:
to begin with following once that was done during while earlier meanwhile

1. Look at Sebi's explanation in the dialouge above and replace each "then" with one of the sequence words in the box.

2. Tell your partner what you do in the morning before coming to school. Link the different actions using the sequence words.

3. Rewrite the story of Olga making a raspberry jam roll. Link the different steps using sequence words.

Olga took a knife. She cut the roll into two halves. She spread butter on both halves of the roll. She spread raspberry jam on one half of the roll. She put the two halves of the roll together. She ate it. It was delicious!

How to hang wallpaper

Later in evening Lucy is working on her "Berichtsheft". First she makes some notes. Before she writes her report she compares her headings with an article she found in a DIY-magazine.

4.

a) Read the article below from an English DIY-magazine and match the headings to the paragraphs.

1. Hang the Wallpaper
2. Smooth the Wallpaper
3. Fold the Wallpaper
4. Measure and Cut the First Strip
5. Create a Plumb Line
6. **Trim** the Wallpaper
7. Pasting Wallpaper

a) Start at a corner and measure out the width of the paper minus 2 cm. Use your carpenter's level or a plumb bob and draw a vertical line. This line will be your guide when you hang the first strip of wallpaper.

b) Now you'll need to measure and cut the first **strip** of wallpaper. Leave about ten extra centimetres so that you have something to trim at the bottom and top.

c) Put the strip of wallpaper down on the table so that the wrong side is facing you. Apply a light, gentle coat of **paste** with your brush.

d) Fold the top two-thirds down so that the paste is facing the paste. Fold the bottom third up again with the paste facing the paste. Now fold or roll up the wet strip gently so that you don't **crease** it. Let the wallpaper soak for about 10 minutes.

e) Unfold the top of the wallpaper strip. Put the wallpaper into position so that it's in **alignment** with the plumb line you've drawn. Press the wallpaper gently with your brush against the wall. Unfold the bottom of the strip and brush it into place. Because you don't want the wallpaper to stretch while you position it brush it gently in a vertical direction.

f) Use your hands to press the strip of wallpaper into the corner. Cut a diagonal line into the corner at the **baseboard** and at the ceiling. Use your brush to smooth that extra 2 cm onto the adjoining wall and use a wet sponge to wipe off the extra paste.

g) Trim the bottom and the top of the wallpaper. Press the strip into the corner with your hands and mark the edge with a pencil or the back of your scissors. Pull off the wallpaper a little so that you can cut along easily. Use a sharp pair of scissors. Brush the wallpaper against the ceiling and the skirting board. Don't forget to wipe off the excess paste.

b) Read the text to your partner but this time put in sequence words.

VOCAB

stack Stapel	**relationship** Beziehung	**paste** Kleister
to stack stapeln	**trim** Zierleiste	**to crease** verknittern
to link verbinden	**strip** (Tapeten-)Bahn	**in alignment** in Flucht
event Ereignis	**to trim** abschneiden, kürzen	**skirting board** Fußleiste

6. Extension

How to change a wheel

33

Late in the afternoon everybody is waiting for Anna to turn up. She should have arrived at 5:30 pm. It's already past 6 o'clock, but no Anna. She wanted to bring her boss' pick-up so that they could get a long ladder from the DIY-store. Suddenly the door opens, Anna rushes into the room and falls exhaustedly into an armchair.

Lucy: Anna, are you alright? What's happened?

Anna: Everything is okay but I nearly had an accident. I was driving along the main road when all of a sudden the car in front of me stopped. I **slammed on the brakes** and turned the steering wheel to the right. Although I managed to avoid a crash I had a new problem. When I drove onto the **sidewalk** the right front wheel crashed against the curb and I damaged the tyre. Unfortunately, it's flat now.

Hakan: Why didn't you change a wheel?

Anna: First, I was still shaking because I almost had an accident. Secondly, I have never changed a wheel before, nor do I know where to find the spare wheel. Hakan, can you change a wheel on a pick-up?

Hakan: Of course! There's no difference between changing a wheel on a car or a wheel on a pick-up. I've already done it several times. Where's the pick-up now? Is it still on the sidewalk?

Anna: No, it isn't. It happened on the sidewalk in front of the supermarket. So I drove slowly to the parking site.

Hakan: I'll change the wheel for you. Does anybody here need some practice in changing wheels?

Justin: Nice try, I'll help you anyway.

Anna: Thank you boys. Here are the car keys.

Sidewalk = American English
pavement = British English

5. **Describe how to change a wheel. Use as many sequence words as possible.**

How to make Swedish meat balls

Two hours later Hakan and Justin return to the clubhouse.

Hakan: Here we are. We've changed the wheel and parked the car opposite the entrance.
Anna: Thanks a lot. It took a long time, it's too late to go to the DIY-store now. It has already closed.
Hakan: A long time! All the nuts were rusty. It was difficult to loosen them. If I hadn't had penetrating oil I wouldn't have been able to change the wheel. And you're talking about a long time.
Anna: Sorry Hakan. You're right. What about sex on the beach as a reward.
Hakan: Äh, you mean we should ...
Anna: No, Hakan. I'm talking about inviting you and Justin for a cocktail.
Hakan: I see. But I don't drink and drive. I won't risk my driving licence for a cocktail with you.
Anna: Well, then I could offer to make you my homemade Swedish köttbullar.
Hakan: Köttbullar? What's that?
Anna: They're Swedish meat balls.
Hakan: Oh, I love meat.
Anna: Then let's go. Lucy are you coming as well?
Lucy: I wouldn't miss that. Let's go.

Köttbullar (Swedish meat balls)

Ingredients
250 g ground beef
250 g ground pork
30 ml **grated** onion
1 large egg
200 ml single cream
50 g bread **crumbs**
soaked in the cream above
salt and pepper
about 20 ml oil to fry

Mixing Instructions
First mix all the ingredients together and leave aside for at least half an hour.
Next make balls about 2 cm diameter.
After that fry the meatballs in an iron **griddle pan** for about 5 minutes until they become brown on all sides.
Turn them as necessary, but do so gently.
Lastly serve with boiled potatoes and cranberry sauce.

6. **Describe how to make your favourite meal. Remember to use linking words.**

VOCAB

to slam on the brakes eine Vollbremsung machen	**crumb** Brösel, Krümel **to soak** aufquellen	**grated** gerieben **griddle pan** Grillpfanne

6. Extension

6.4

TO DO

- Describe goods
- Compare things and people

Materials and Shapes

After the Swedish dinner Anna and Lucy start talking about fashion and Anna tells Lucy about her latest bargain.

This ring is made of silver. → It's a silver ring.
but
a <u>woollen</u> pullover
a <u>wooden</u> ladder

Anna: Look at this **hoody**. Isn't it cool?
Lucy: Yes, it looks hot. What's it made of? Cotton?
Anna: No, it's made of wool. It's a **woollen** hoody.
Lucy: It's really soft and I like the **pattern**.
Hakan: Justin these girls are on about fashion again. Did you see that Porsche parked outside the supermarket earlier? It had black leather seats, aluminium wheel **rims** and the **dashboard** was made of **burl wood veneer**. Those parts must have been really expensive.
Justin: Yeah, it's really interesting to know what different materials cost. In the workshop we also work with different types of material like wood and **plywood** for example.

1. **Look around your classroom. What are things made of?**

2. **Draw a chart and answer these questions.**

a) What are textiles made of?
b) What kinds of metal do you know?
c) What is paint made of?
d) What types of wood do you know?

3. **Fill in the adjectives. Look up unknown words in your dictionary.**

Surface	Textiles	Common adjectives
polished	soft	old

dark red, big, small, large, bright, light blue, striped, curved, thick, thin, polished, glossy, matt, old, new, rough, cheap, expensive, wavy, lined, soft, smooth, floral, hot, cold, warm, flat

shapes	descriptions
	A circle is round or circular.
	A square is square.
	A rectangle is rectangular.
	A triangle is triangular.
	An octagon is octagonal.
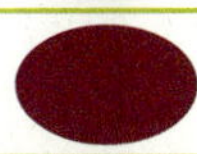	An oval is oval.
	A semi-circle is semi-circular.
	A quadrant is a shape that is a quarter of a circle.
	A sphere is spherical.
	A cube is cubic.
	A cuboid is cuboidal.
	A cylinder is cylindrical.
	A cone is conic or conical.
	A pyramid is pyramid(al).

This chair is made of wood and steel. Its four legs are cuboidal and made of stainless steel. The seat and the back are made of teak wood. The seat has five bars, the back has three. The surface looks smooth and is probably oiled.

VOCAB

bargain Schnäpchen
hoody Kapuzenpullover
pattern Muster
dashboard Armaturenbrett
rim Felge
burl wood veneer Wurzelholzfurnier
plywood Sperrholz

6. Extension

4. **Describe these pictures.**

5. **Describe a tool or a product of your trade. Classmates should guess what it is.**

HOW TO … Compare things

Comparatives are used to compare two things or people.
A Ferrari is faster **than** a lorry.
Superlatives are used to compare more than two things or people.
London is the biggest city in Europe.

as big **as**
= so groß **wie**
bigger **than**
= größer **als**

6. **Look at the table below and compare Justin, Lucy and Patrick.**
Patrick is older than Lucy. Justin is the oldest.

page 182

	Justin	**Lucy**	**Patrick**
age (old)	18	16	17
body height (tall)	1,80 m	1,72 m	1,88 m
weight (heavy)	78 kg	62 kg	90 kg
grades in English (good)	1-	1	2
grades in **social studies** (bad)	6	5	4-
room (big)	14 m²	16 m²	14 m²
clothes (fashionable)	casual	latest fashion	old fashioned
costs of holidays (expensive)	€ 750.00	€ 900.00	€ 1,500.00

An: Chris@yahoo.ca
Cc:
Betreff: Gliedermaßstab

Hi Chris,
You won't believe what happened to me yesterday. I broke my folding rule at work, so I went to a DIY-store to buy a new one. Before that I looked up the German word in my dictionary, it is called a Gliedermaßstab. At the DIY-store I asked for this Gliedermaßstab, but nobody seemed to know what it was. First they sent me to the household articles, next to the electronics section and then to the metal goods, but I couldn't find a Gliedermaßstab. Nevertheless, I didn't give up. Finally I found one in the tools department. On the way to the cashier I passed the information desk and told those idiots where to find a Gliedermaßstab. And what did they reply? "Ah, you mean a Zollstock. Why didn't you say so?" I couldn't believe it.
At home I looked up the meaning in my dictionary. These guys were right; a folding rule is a Zollstock. It's just an old expression. "Zoll" means inch and "Stock" is a stick. Although the Germans normally use meters, they also use inches or "Zoll" as well for screens, for bicycle rims, **screen definition** (96 **dpi**), vinyl discs (7", 10" and 12"), pipes, **waists** and the lengths of jeans (W32"/L34").
I still can't believe that you are coming to Hamburg next month. Please let me know what time you are arriving at the airport so that I can pick you up.

So long,
Justin

7. Which other old measurements are still in use?

VOCAB

social studies Gemeinschaftskunde	**dpi = dots per inch** Punkte pro Zoll
screen definition Bildschirmauflösung	**waist** Bundweite

7. Lounge

7.1

TO DO

- Apply for a job
- Write a CV

A year abroad

Patrick has nearly finished his apprenticeship as a bricklayer and wants to leave home after he finishes school. He is not happy there.

http://www.hunt4jobs.co.uk/had/jobs/advert?adid=220911376

hunt4jobs

You are here: Home » hunt4jobs » Search results » Job details

« *Back to search results* | Email me jobs like this | Send to a friend | Save this job | Print

BRICKLAYER: Manchester, Greater Manchester.

Job type: Permanent

Insustry sector: Construction, Property Maintenance & Surveying

Construction4U is a market leader in social housing refurbishment with a future order book of over £1. 1bn

Staff are required for our housing contract due to start soon. The contract includes repairs, and property improvements with the work taking place throughout the North West.
MULTI SKILLED BRICKLAYERS
Good competitive rates of pay.
Excellent terms and conditions.

We also have vacancies for site managers and building surveyors at our other partnerships within the area.

Construction4U is an equal opportunities employer and recognizes diversity in the communities it serves.

Adfinder code: Ref 22091137

Recruiter information

1. Together with a partner discuss and answer these questions.

a) What is Patrick looking at?
b) What is the URL address of the page on the screen? Spell it to your partner.
c) What does **hunt4jobs** mean?
d) What can you find on this website?

GB: football and soccer
USA: soccer

2. **A year abroad: In groups discuss your ideas, feelings and suggestions about:**

- working abroad for a year
- living abroad for a short time
- where you would like to go
- why you would like to go there
- why you don't want to go abroad

3. **What are the pros and cons of spending a year abroad?**
Together with a partner brainstorm the advantages and disadvantages of going abroad for a year.

Working and living abroad for a year

pros	cons
make new friends	miss my friends

VOCAB

CV/curriculum vitae Lebenslauf
Manu Machester United football team
Old Tafford Manu's stadium
ad/advertisement Anzeige
hassle Auseinandersetzung
to need a change eine Veränderung benötigen
football, soccer Fußball
job application Bewerbung
interview Vorstellungsgespräch
abroad im Ausland
pros and cons Vor- und Nachteile
advantage Vorteil
disadvantage Vorsilbe ‚dis' ändert das Wort in die umgekehrte Bedeutung

4. 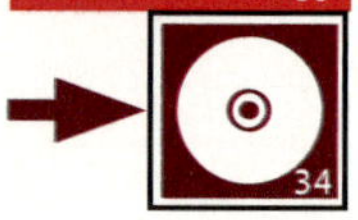

Patrick and Justin are reading the advertisement and brainstorming all the things that Patrick has to do to get the job in Manchester.
Listen to Patrick and Justin talking and put these sentences in the correct order.

a) "I have to speak to Mr Harrison on the telephone."
b) "You need to write a CV."
c) "What's a **covering letter**?"
d) "Let's read the advertisement and find out what you need to do."
e) "What are my interests and hobbies?"
f) "What's the difference between **form** and **formula**?"

5. **Patrick wrote his CV but forgot to put in the headings. Where do these headings go? Match the words below with the numbers in the CV.**

interests and hobbies – **additional information** – **references** – **work experience** – **education and training**

Curriculum Vitae

Name:	Patrick Johanssen	Tel. No.:	0049 40 275 89 630
Address:	12 Böhmestrasse	Email:	patrick1988@gmx.de
	22041 Hamburg	Date of birth:	30.03.1990

1.

08.2005 – 08.2008	Vocational school for construction as a certified bricklayer
08.1999 – 07.2005	Realschulabschluss (school-leaving qualification)

2.

08.2005 – 08.2008	Apprentice bricklayer in the company, *Stein auf Stein GmbH*, Hamburg. Duties: Learning about and working on all aspects of construction

3.
All types of sport, but especially football: member of a club team since the age of five.
Member of a youth clubhouse (Escape) in Hamburg; helping to renovate the clubhouse.

4.
Full, **clean driving licence**

5.

Mr Michael Mende	Mrs Josephine Lynch
(Clubhouse social worker)	(English teacher)
Escape Clubhouse	Josephstr. 11
Wandsbekerstieg 19	22041 Hamburg
22041 Hambrug	Tel.: 0049 40 663 890
Tel.: 0049 40 686 932	

6. **Now it's your turn. Write your own CV.**

HOW TO … Write a CV (Curriculum Vitae)

When writing a CV make sure that it is:

Clear: The layout is very important; use headings for the different sections and space your information well.

Short: Only give the important facts about yourself. One to two sides of an A4 page is enough.

Honest: Always tell the truth. No **white lies**!

Positive: This is about your life. **Remain** positve and **sell yourself** well.

Remember:

- If the company likes your CV then they will invite you to an interview.
- You have a good chance of getting the job if you are well prepared and present yourself well.
- When you apply for a job at a company you either have to write a CV or you have to fill in a job application form. These are important documents for your future employer as they **contain** all the information and details about who you are, where you live and what you know.

7. **Now that you have completed your CV, look at the application form below. How would you fill in this application form using your own details?**

Remember to:

- read the form carefully
- use a black pen
- write neatly and clearly
- check whether you have to write in capital letters

Application Form

Please use **BLOCK CAPITALS**

Job Title: .... Job No.: ....

Your details

Name: .... Date of Birth: ....

Address: .... City: ....

Postcode: .... Tel No.: ....

VOCAB

covering letter Bewerbungsschreiben
form Formular
formula Formel
additional information hier: Zusatzqualifikationen
references Empfehlungen
work experience Berufserfahrung
education and training Schul- und Ausbildung
clean driving licence punktefreier Führerschein
clear übersichtlich
short knapp
honest ehrlich
white lie Notlüge
to remain bleiben
to sell yourself sich verkaufen
to contain enthalten
block capitals große Druckbuchstaben

7.2

TO DO

- Write a covering letter

Writing a job application

The next afternoon the two boys meet at the clubhouse to finish Patrick's job application. Patrick is already busy at the computer when Justin arrives.

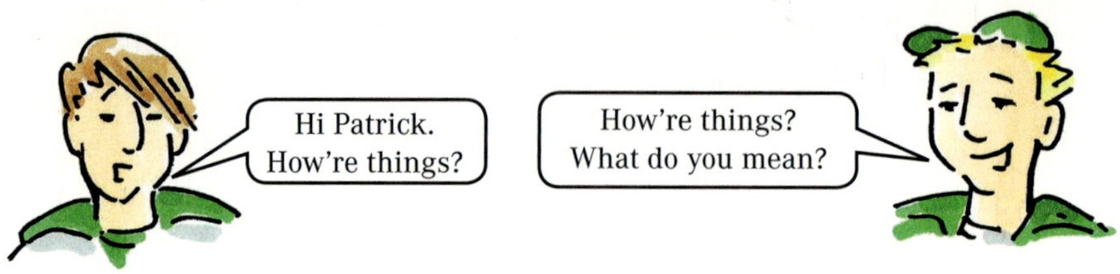

1. 

Listen to the dialogue and answer the following questions.

a) What does 'How're things?' mean?
b) How was Patrick's day?
c) Is Justin good at maths?
d) How does Patrick **encourage** Justin?
e) What did Justin's father give him?

2. **Look at the following "Dos" and "Don'ts" statements for job applications and decide in which column they should go:**

a) Write clearly.
b) Write on A4 size paper.
c) Keep your letter short and simple.
d) Use contractions **e.g.** I'm, don't etc.
e) Use any colour ink (blue, black, red). Colour is not important.
f) In your letter **mention** why you want to work for that company.
g) Save postage and fold your letter to fit in the smallest envelope.

Do	Don't
Write clearly.	

3. **Sometimes abbreviations are used in job advertisements.**
Do you know what these abbreviations mean?
Use a dictionary to find the answers.

circa – co – CV – exp – f – m – pa – prev – p/t – ref – tel – yr

4. **Look at this covering letter and answer the questions below.**

The **recipient's** address can be written either on the left or the right side.

Joe Soap
32 Hill House Road
Streatham
SW16 2AL
England
joe.soap@gmail.com
Tel. +44 2087 486033

Mr John Green
Recruitment Manager
Employ Me Agency
10410 51 Avenue
Edmonton, Alberta T6H OK3

15 April 20..

Dear Mr Green

Joiner (Ref. JO18/00)

I would like to apply for the job of a joiner as advertised in the Employment Pages on 9 April 20...

I completed my apprenticeship **recently** and would now like to get a **permanent job** in Canada. I am a Canadian **national**.

I am enclosing my **resume** containing details of my **qualifications**, **skills** and experience. I am able to work in a team and reach the **targets** as **required** in your job description.

I would like to work for your company and I look forward to hearing from you soon.

Yours sincerely

Joe Soap

The difference between qualifications and skills:
qualification = a certificate or degree you get when you have finished a course or study period
skill = something you are able to do well

a) Who is applying for the job? What nationality is he?
b) Where does he live?
c) What kind of a job is he looking for?
d) Where did he find the job advertisement?
e) What other information does he give his **prospective employer**?

VOCAB

to encourage ermutigen	**national** Staatsangehörige(r)
e.g. = for example zum Beispiel	**resume (US)** Lebenslauf
to mention erwähnen	**target** Ziel
recipient Empfänger	**to require** benötigen
recently kürzlich	**prospective** voraussichtlich, zukünftig
permanent job unbefristeter Arbeitsplatz	**employer** Arbeitgeber

HOW TO … Write a covering letter

- The covering letter is important because it explains why you want the job.
- Always send a covering letter with your CV when you apply for a job.
- All the important information about you **is included in** your CV.
- Therefore, your letter should follow the **KISS** rule: **K**eep **I**t **S**hort and **S**imple. Your letter should be **brief** and clear.
- Make sure that you put in the date, your full address and telephone number, quote the job title, reference number and the **source** of the advertisement.
- Also say exactly what you are **enclosing** with your letter.

Remember:
Always end with 'Yours sincerely' if you started with 'Dear Mr/Mrs/Ms' and end with 'Yours faithfully' if you started with 'Dear Sir or Madam'.

5. **Justin and Patrick have written the covering letter in paragraphs but they are jumbled up. Put them in the correct order.**

a) I am enclosing my CV containing details of my qualifications, skills and experience.
b) I would really like to work for your company and I look forward to hearing from you soon.
c) I would like to apply for the job of bricklayer as advertised on the website hunt4jobs on 12 May 20.. .
d) I have worked on many different building sites with many different nationalities during my apprenticeship and I am a good team player.
e) I will complete my bricklayer apprenticeship in June 20.. and would like to get a job in England **to gain experience** in a foreign country and to also **improve** my English.
f) Bricklayer (Ref. FI4175)

6. **Read these covering letters and together with a partner discuss what you think is wrong with them.**

Hello,
I want the job of bricklayer. I can do everything.
Here is my CV.
I wait for your answer.
Faithfully, Burt Brickford

Dear Sir or Madam,
I saw your advert for a plumber.
I want the job. I'm good and can everything.
When can I start?
How much money will I get?
Best wishes, Peter Plumming

7. **Choose one of the advertisements on the next page and apply for the job.
Write a covering letter to the company and tell them why you would like to work for them. Include all the information required.
Use the phrases in the box on the next page.**

PHRASES — Writing a covering letter

I would like to	apply for the ... **enquire** whether ...
I am writing to apply for ...	
I saw your advertisement I found your advertisement	on your website in the ... (newspaper)
I enclose Please find enclosed	a copy of my CV. the application form. a copy of my ...
I am responsible/hard-working/intelligent/**cheerful** ...	
I look forward to	receiving your reply. hearing from you.

The Evening News London Classified Ads 19 June 20..

Job Offers

Job Title	Grave Digger	Electrician	Plumber
Job number	172391427	172302528	936314381
Description	must be a qualified gardener, must have experience of working in a cemetery, must have a driver's licence, use a mechanical digger	carry out maintenance service, emergency and weekend shifts, no previous experience required	installation and maintenance of pipework, driving licence, no shifts at least one-year's experience
Working hours	9 a.m. – 5 p.m.	Shift work	8 a.m. – 5 p.m.
Salary/Wages	£ 15.00 per hour	£ 24,000 per year	£ 15.50 per hour
Contact name	Tom Pickford	Mark Pointer	Mary Plunger
Telephone no.	0044(0)20 8592 1804	0044(0)20 7505 2929	0044(0)20 8668 5689
Reference no.	GD007 LON	TE008LON	PM009LON

Please apply in writing. Enclose your CV and and explain why you want to have this job.
Send all applications to:
Seahorse House, 29 Canning Road, London, E15 3ND, UK

VOCAB

to be included in enthalten sein
brief knapp
source Quelle
to enclose beifügen
to jumble up durcheinanderbringen
to gain experience Erfahrung sammeln
to improve verbessern
to enquire anfragen, erkundigen
cheerful fröhlich

7.3

TO DO

- Prepare for a job interview
- Talk about likes and dislikes

Preparation is important

It is Saturday morning and Patrick arrives at Justin and Lucy's house. He has an appointment with Mr Time, who is going to help him prepare for the job interview. He is very nervous and not sure what to expect. Mr Time offered to help him and Patrick is very pleased about that. Mr Time is the head of the Human Resources Department in the company where he works. He has a lot of experience in interviewing job applicants. Patrick has only had one interview before when he applied for his apprenticeship. He has never had an interview in English and he feels unsure about his English, although his marks at school are good. Justin and Lucy have spoken a lot of English to him and he always understands what they say. However, this is not the same as speaking to a stranger from England.

Patrick lifts his hand and rings the doorbell.

The door opens and a dog jumps up at Patrick, who gets a fright.

1. (CD 36)

Listen to the greetings, introductions and conversation at the door. Which of these phrases did you not hear?

- Good morning, my name is Patrick.
- He simply loves visitors.
- Hello. You must be Patrick?
- Come inside.
- Coffee! Down!
- Nice to meet you.
- Nice to see you again.
- Hi Patrick, how're you doing?
- Hello Mr Time.
- Justin!
- Don't worry, he doesn't bite.
- Is Justin here?
- Thank you for helping me.
- Have you ever been to England before?
- I'm only too happy to help.
- So, where do you want to work?
- Yes. That's right.
- I want to go to Manchester.
- Let's go into my study.

2.

Greetings and small talk are important parts of any interview.
Now together with a partner, practise meeting and greeting someone at the door.
Look back at Unit 1 for typical phrases we use when meeting someone for the first time.
Setting the scene: Decide

- who you are (for example Mr Time, your father, Barack Obama, etc.),
- who is at the door,
- wether you know each other

HOW TO … Prepare for a job interview

Before the interview
Find out about the company:
- Look at their website.
- Where is the company?
- Find the address on a map.
- Do they have any other **branches**?
- How many people work for the company?

Think of questions they might ask you.
Think about your answers to these questions.
Practise these questions with someone.
Dress well for the interview.
Arrive in time for the interview.

At the interview
Be polite and friendly.
Speak clearly.
Look at your interview partner.
Sit upright.
Tell the truth.
If you don't understand something then say so.
Be **confident**, but not **overconfident**.
Show enthusiasm.
Have a question ready to ask.
Thank your interviewer at the end.

3.

Look at the job interview advice above.

a) Which points do you think are the most important?
b) Which points do you not **agree** with?
c) Can you add any points to the list?
d) Now discuss your opinion with your partner/s. Do you have the same opinion?

4.

37

Mr Time tells Patrick that companies want to know about prospective employees. These are some of the questions they ask:

- Why do you want the job?
- What do you do in your free time?
- How do you **deal with** difficult colleagues?
- What are your **strengths**?
- What are your **weaknesses**?
- Where do you see yourself in five years?

Listen to Mr Time and Patrick talking and write down Patrick's answers to these questions.

VOCAB

job interview Vorstellungsgespräch	**applicant** Bewerber	**overconfident** hier: überheblich
appointment Verabredung, Termin	**unsure** unsicher	**to agree** zustimmen
to prepare vorbereiten	**fright** Schreck	**to deal with** umgehen mit
head Leiter, Chef	**study** Arbeitszimmer	**strength** Stärke
Human Resources Department Personalabteilung	**branch** Geschäftszweig	**weakness** Schwäche
experience Erfahrung	**confident** selbstsicher	

Breakfast

Justin enters the study to say 'Hi' to Patrick. He has just woken up and wants to have some breakfast. He asks Patrick if he would like something to eat, too.
Patrick is very happy. He did not have breakfast before he came as he was too nervous. Mr Time has some work to do, so the two boys go into the kitchen for something to eat. Lucy joins them. She has a magazine with her and wants Justin to do the test: How well do you know your friend?

5. **Why don't you test how well you know your partner?**

a) Read the **questionnaire** and think about your own answers.
b) Now find a partner and guess what you think their answers are.
c) Compare and see how many you got right.
d) Discuss your **choices** with your partner and find out more about him/her

All about me

1. **What is my favourite magazine?**
   - Bravo
   - Maxim
   - TeenVogue
2. **What is my favourite TV program?**
   - GZSZ
   - DSDS
   - Germany's next top model
3. **What's my favourite season?**
   - winter
   - spring
   - summer
   - autumn
4. **Do I enjoy blogging?**
   - I don't blog
   - I only blog about important things
   - I spend most of my time blogging
5. **Am I popular?**
   - yes
   - no
   - I don't know
6. **What do I like best about myself?**
   - legs
   - eyes
   - nose
7. **Which dessert would I never reject?**
   - chocolate pudding
   - ice-cream
   - strawberries and cream
8. **Who do I most want to hug?**
   - Santa Claus
   - Dracula
   - Heidi Klum
9. **Which trait do I most value in a friend?**
   - kindness
   - loyalty
   - sense of humour
10. **Which song is the soundtrack of my life?**
    - Mercy
    - Viva La Vida
    - (I can't get no) Satisfaction

Now work out your score. You get one point for each correct answer.

Score

0-5
Basically you do not know your partner very well. You should spend more time together to get to know each other.

6-7
That's not bad. However, there is still a lot to learn about your partner. Go out for a coke together.

8-10
You know a lot about your partner. How much time do you spend together?

6.

page 172

Mr Time and Patrick spoke about Patrick's plans, intentions and dreams.

a) Do you know why Mr Time and Patrick use different ways of speaking about the future?
Look at the questions and answers below.

plans = Zukunftspläne
"We're laying the carpet tomorrow."
intentions = Absichten
"I intend to stay in Manchester for a year."

When are you going to Manchester?
I'm going at the end of July.

How are you getting to Manchester?
I'm flying with one of the cheap airlines.

Where will you stay in Manchester?
I don't know yet. Maybe I'll rent a flat, or I'll look for a room somewhere.

How long will you stay in Manchester?
I think the job will last for one year.

What are you going to do at the weekends in Manchester?
I'm not sure. I'm definitely going to go to a Manu game.
Perhaps I'll go to Liverpool and see where the Beatles lived.
I think I'll go to London for a long weekend.

b) What about you? Do you have any fixed plans, wishes or intentions for the future?
Where do you see yourself in 5 years?
Discuss these questions and use the different ways of speaking about the future.

VOCAB

questionnaire Fragebogen	**to hug** umarmen	**kindness** Freundlichkeit, Güte
choice Wahl	**trait** Charaktereigenschaft	**loyalty** Treue
popular beliebt	**to value** schätzen	**sense of humour** Humor
to reject ablehnen		

7.4

TO DO

- Talk about famous football clubs
- Present yourself

Happy Hour

Lucy, Patrick and Justin arrive at the clubhouse where Sebi, Olga and Hakan are trying out cocktail recipes – non-alcoholic, of course. They want to serve these at the party and now want Lucy, Patrick and Justin to taste them.

Sebi sits down at the computer and the next thing he shouts:

1. **Football is an popular sport in Germany and also in England. Can you answer these questions? Discuss with some of your class mates.**

a) What do you know about Old Trafford?
b) Are you a Manu fan?
c) Which English football team do you **support**?
d) Which stadium in Germany is as spectacular as Old Trafford?
e) Which German team do you support?
f) Who's going to win the league this year?

38

What are Manchester United's beginnings?

It all began when **wrokres** from the Lancashire and Yorkshire Railway at Newton Heath in Manchester started playing **otoflalb** on the **itpch** near the engine sheds in their free time. Their changing rooms were in a public house on Oldham Road.
In 1893 they moved to a pitch in Bank Street, Clayton, Manchester. They stayed and played there until 1910 when they moved to **dol fratford** which became their permanent **ohme**.
However, before that the club experienced cash **smelprob** and had to be reformed with a new constitution. From then on the **bluc** was called Manchester United.
In March 1906 Manchester United played against Woolwich Arsenal in an English Cup **emag** at the Clayton ground. 26,500 **nafs** paid a total £ 950 to watch them play and lose. The **roces** was 2:3.
The silverware went to Clayton twice and Old Trafford once before WW1 (World War One). In 1908 they won the League Championship. In 1909 it was the Football Association Cup and again in 1911 the League Championship.
Manchester United won their first major title in the 1907-8 season and they won the First Division with a record number of points. At one stage they had a string of ten successive wins but they still came a cropper against Fulham, a Second Division team, who knocked them out of the F.A. Cup.

2. **Read the story and test your knowledge about football.**

a) What are the words written in bold? Look at these clues and rearrange the letters to find the correct words.

• people belong to a ...	• another word for difficulties
• another word for field	• people employed by a company
• another word for match	• another word for soccer
• the place you go to after work	• the people who support Manu
• how many goals	• the name of the Manu stadium

b) Who played football at Newton Heath?
c) What do you think a 'public house' is?
d) When did they move to Old Trafford?
e) Who beat Manchester United by one goal in 1906?
f) How many spectators watched the game?
g) What do you think silverware is?
h) How many times did Manu win the League Championship before WW1?
i) Which team stopped Manu from winning the F.A. Cup in 1908?
j) What is a penalty?
k) How many players are in a football team?
l) Which German footballer won the FWA Footballer of the Year in 1994–95?
m) Which English club did he play for?

VOCAB

impressive beeinduckend	successive aufeinanderfolgend
to support unterstützen	to come a cropper Schiffbruch erleiden
engine-shed Lokschuppen	bold fett
constitution Verfassung, Satzung	clue Hinweis
string of Folge	

All about me

Mr Time told Patrick that some companies ask their prospective employees to give an introductory presentation about themselves at an interview.

HOW TO … **Give a presentation**

It is important to structure a presentation well. A presentation is divided into an **introduction**, a **body** and a **conclusion**.
The introduction should interest your **audience** so that they listen to you. The body contains the "meat" of the presentation. That means here you talk about all the important facts. Finally, in the conclusion you can summarize the information.

3. **You are going to give a three-minute introductory presentation about yourself. Brainstorm all the important information you think needs to be included in a presentation.**
Look at the graphic organizer below and complete the ideas.

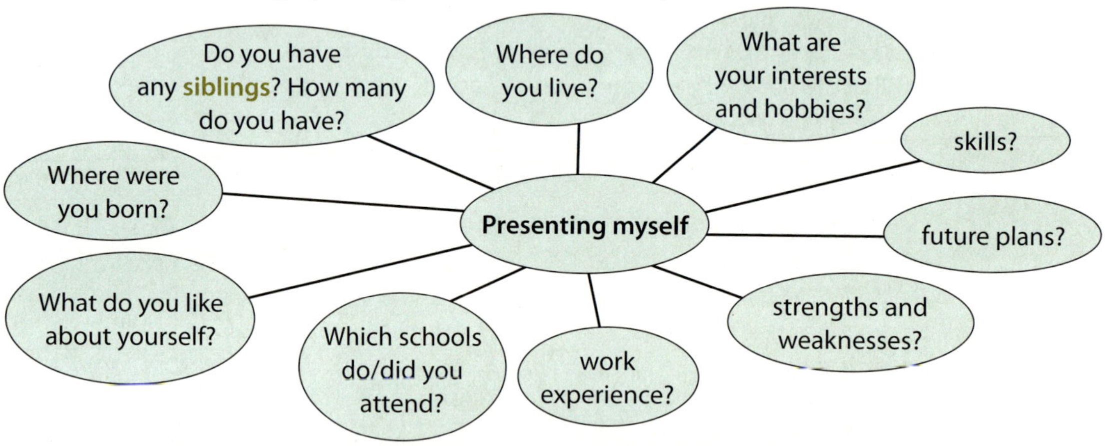

PHRASES **Presenting myself**

Introduction	*My name is …*	*I am …*	*I live in …*
Body	*In 19 … I …*	*I was born in …*	*I went to …*
Conclusion	*I am sure ….*	*I am looking forward to …*	*Thank you for ….*

4. Practise your presentation using these sticker notes. Talk out loud so that you **get used to** hearing your own voice. This makes you more confident. When you are ready, give your presentation to your group.

An: Chris@yahoo.ca
Cc:
Betreff: Your visit

Hi Chris,
Well here I am again. What a week it's been. We sat so many tests at school that **my head is spinning** from all the learning. It really is difficult for me to study in German. It would be so much easier if it were English.
How're your plans coming along? Have you decided when you can come over and visit? It would be great to see you again. My dad says there is no chance for us to visit Canada this summer. He has too much to do at work.
I suppose we could cycle to lakes around the city and enjoy the sunshine. We could even perhaps go up to Denmark by bike. And of course, it would be even better if you were here as well. Let me know when to meet you at the airport.
One of our friends wants to go and work in Manchester and my dad and I have been helping him with his job application. If he gets the job we could even visit him.
Hope your news is positive.

CU soon.

VOCAB

introduction Einführung **body** hier: Hauptteil **conclusion** Abschluss	**audience** Publikum **siblings** Geschwister	**to get used to** sich gewöhnen an **my head is spinning** ich bin ganz verwirrt

8. First Aid Room

8.1

TO DO

■ Make emergency calls

39

Accidents

The friends are in the clubhouse and are discussing an incident that Victor reported about. One of his colleagues was taken to hospital, because he got some tile splinters in his eye. These had to be removed. The friends were all discussing what should be done in the event of an emergency.

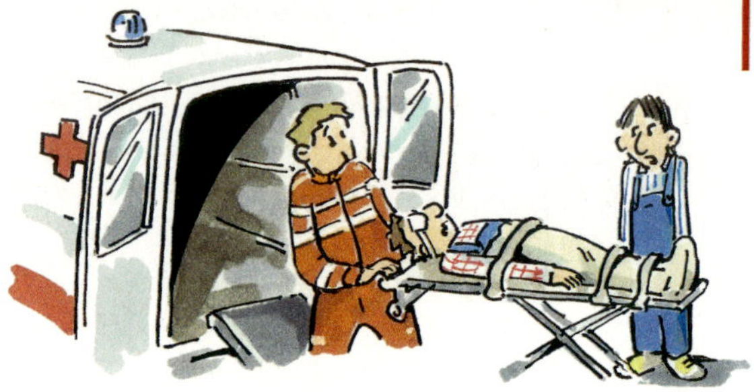

Lucy: How did your colleague get the tile splinters in his eye?

Victor: Two weeks ago we had to repair a bathroom. A pipe was leaking and we also had to replace the sink. My colleague plastered over the slit for the pipe in the wall. We're a small firm, you know, so we do additional jobs as well.
Yesterday we finished our work at another customer early. My colleague **assumed** the wall in the bathroom would be dry enough to **attach** the tiles. Unfortunately, we **got stuck** in a traffic jam, so we arrived late. I suggested that we go home and do the tiling the next day. My colleague didn't want to do this. He said it was only half an hour's work, but an hour of driving. So we started working.
While I was covering the floor my colleague was **stirring** the **tile adhesive**. Working hand in hand we were really fast. I put the adhesive on the tiles and my colleague attached them to the wall. The last tile under the sink had to be cut. It was already after **knocking-off time**, the goggles were in the car and we wanted to go home, so my colleague cut the tile without wearing his goggles.
And then it happened! I don't know if my colleague was tired or careless. Suddenly he was screaming and his eye was bleeding. The tile was cracked and he had some tile splinters in his eye. I didn't know what to do, but my colleague told me to call the ambulance. But I didn't know the number of the emergency hospital.

Lucy: Why didn't you call 911?

Olga: 911 is the emergency number in Canada and the States, isn't it?

Lucy: Yes, that's right. Do you have a different emergency number in Germany?

Olga: Yes, it's 112.

Victor: That's the number I finally called. About ten minutes later the ambulance arrived and took my colleague to hospital. They removed the splinters. My colleague is still in hospital and the last tile still has to be fixed.

Lucy: Is he okay now?

Victor: Yes, but now I'm wondering which number I should call in case of an emergency when I'm abroad.

1. **Answer these questions.**

a) Who called the ambulance?
b) Where did the accident happen?
c) How did the accident happen?
d) When did the accident happen?
e) How many people were injured?
f) What kind of injuries occurred?

112 – The European emergency number

All over the world many countries have a single emergency telephone number to ask for national emergency services (police, fire brigade and ambulance) for help.
Not all countries have the same emergency telephone number, but it is usually a **three-digit** number so that it can be remembered easily. Although there are some countries that have a different emergency number for each of the different emergency services, there is a number that works in all EU countries.
If you need emergency services in the European Union just dial 112.
Millions of Europeans are travelling more and more for holidays or business. If they **witness** or, even worse, are involved in an accident in an EU country which number would they dial to get help? They don't have to remember the emergency number for each single European country any longer, they must only remember 112.
112 is also the emergency number for GSM (= Global System for Mobile Communications) worldwide.
112 is used in Austria, Belgium, Bulgaria, Croatia, Cyprus, the Czech Republic, Denmark, Estonia, Finland, France, Germany, Greece, Hungary, Iceland, Ireland, Italy, Latvia, Liechtenstein, Lithuania, Luxembourg, the Republic of Macedonia, Malta, the Netherlands, Norway, Poland, Portugal, Romania, Serbia, Slovakia, Slovenia, Spain, Sweden, Switzerland, Ukraine and the United Kingdom. 112 is free of charge.
In some countries 112 is the common emergency number, but in most countries, it is used **alongside** the other national numbers.
In Germany 110 is still in use to call the police; in the UK you can still use 999.

2. **Answer these questions:**
a) What are the three emergency services?
b) How much does an emergency call cost?
c) Why is it important to have a common emergency number in Europe?

3. **What's happening in the picture story? What action should be taken? Discuss your answers with a partner.**

VOCAB

incident Ereignis	**to attach** befestigen, ankleben	**knocking-off time** Feierabend
splinter Splitter	**to get stuck** steckenbleiben	**three-digit** dreistellig
emergency Notfall	**to stir** (an)rühren	**to witness** miterleben
to assume vermuten, annehmen	**tile adhesive** Fliesenkleber	**alongside** neben

8. First Aid Room

HOW TO … Act in an emergency

Dial 112 for Emergency Services

When you call 112, please specify:

- **WHO** is calling.
- **WHAT** has happened.
- **WHERE** it happened.
- **WHEN** it happened.
- The number of **CASUALTIES**.
- The nature of any **INJURIES**.
- The **SITUATION** at the scene of the accident.
- What kind of **HELP** you need.

Remember:
Time is of **vital** importance in the case of most accidents.
Act at once and to the best of your ability.

General information
When you call 112 a specially trained **operator** answers your call. The operator either deals with your request directly or puts you through to the most suitable emergency service.
Many operators are able to answer 112 calls in more than one language, which is important for people calling 112 while abroad.
Give your name, address and telephone number. It is necessary to identify callers to **prevent** chaos – the same incident might already have been reported by other people.
Do not hang up if you call 112 by mistake! Tell the operator that everything is OK. Otherwise, emergency assistance may have to be sent out to check there is no problem.
Do not call 112 to **obtain** general information and **inquiries**, traffic or weather reports.

An emergency call

Operator: Hello. This is the emergency 112 operator. Which service do you need – ambulance, police or fire?
Caller: Ambulance, please.
Operator: Please hold the line. I'll put you through right away.
Voice: Ambulance service. Please explain exactly what has happened.
Caller: There's been an accident on the road. A car has **rolled over** a couple of times.
Voice: How many people are involved?
Caller: There's one man lying next to the car. I can't see whether there are still people inside the car or not.
Voice: What's your name, sir?
Caller: Kevin Müller.
Voice: Where's the accident?
Caller: On the M4.
Voice: Where on the M4 exactly? What's the nearest landmark to your location?
Caller: I've just passed junction 11 to Reading and there are roadworks in the opposite direction.
Voice: Okay. Please stay there. I've just **dispatched** an ambulance, it should be there any minute.

4. page 174

Read about the following accidents. Choose one incident and practice making an emergency call in English. Work with a partner.

Scaffolding Collapse in Oxford Street: One dead, one man up to his neck in concrete

A crane lost its **load** of **concrete beams** at a building site on the corner of Oxford Street and Great Portland Street. The beams hit the building and sidewalk scaffolding, part of the 5th floor collapsed onto the 4th floor. One **fatality** has been reported, others are still trapped under the **debris**.

The accident happened at 212 Oxford Street.

Worker P. Smith commented, „When the collapse occurred a whole load of debris and wet cement fell partly on the building and partly on the ground below. One worker was swept off the roof into the safety net attached to the building."

Another worker, Mitchell Miller, told the News, „In the rush of concrete another man missed the net and **literally** fell to his death." The other worker who fell into the safety net was „saved by other labourers who lowered him." He was **tangled** in the net and Miller said, „He was covered up to his neck in concrete. I could only see his head moving."

Accident on Moss Side

Early in the morning of May 22, an electrician was working alone on the roof of a building in Tudor Road. His task was to **disconnect** the electrical services to two air conditioning units to be replaced. The worker was using a **fixed** ladder **attached** to the wall of the building. On the roof he noticed that he needed another screwdriver to disconnect the air conditioning. So he climbed down to get the screwdriver from his van. He put the screwdriver into his back pocket and began to climb up the ladder again. Suddenly the worker missed a step, lost his balance, and fell about five or six feet to the ground. An inhabitant of the building heard a **thud** and went outside to check what was going on. He found the electrician lying on the ground. The resident **administered first aid** and called an ambulance. The worker was transported to a local hospital for treatment.

Schwerer Arbeitsunfall auf der Tunnelbaustelle

Hamburg - Auf der Baustelle des Elbtunnels ereignete sich am Dienstag gegen 15 Uhr 30 ein schwerer Arbeitsunfall.

Der 29-jährige Arbeiter aus Polen war auf der Baustelle zur vierten Tunnelröhre des Elbtunnels damit beschäftigt, ein Bohrgestänge zu wechseln. Dabei geriet der Arbeiter mit der linken Hand zwischen das Bohrgestänge und die Klemmbacken und verletzte sich schwer.

Nach der Erstversorgung durch das Rote Kreuz wurde der Verletzte vorerst zum Arzt nach Altona gebracht, von wo er mit dem Krankenwagen in das Unfallkrankenhaus Boberg eingeliefert wurde.

Laut Polizei kann Fremdverschulden ausgeschlossen werden.

Schwerer Arbeitsunfall in Linden

Hannover – Der Zusammenstoß der Querstrebe eines Krans mit einer Teleskopbühne, in der zwei Arbeiter tätig waren, führte zu schweren Verletzungen.

Am 26. November ereignete sich in Hannover Linden, ein schwerer Arbeitsunfall. Zwei Arbeiter befanden sich auf einer Teleskopbühne mit Lastenkorb in ca. acht Metern Höhe und waren damit beschäftigt, einen Flammschutzanstrich an einer Fabrikhalle anzubringen. Nach ersten Ermittlungen dürfte ein Kranfahrer mit der Querstrebe des Krans die Teleskopbühne samt Arbeitern umgestoßen haben. Einer der Arbeiter erlitt ein Schädelhirntrauma sowie einen Unterarmbruch und wurde mit dem Rettungshubschrauber abgeholt. Der zweite Arbeiter erlitt einen Oberarm- sowie Unterschenkelbruch und wurde ebenfalls vom Rettungsdienst in ein Krankenhaus gebracht.

VOCAB

to specify genau angeben	**to dispatch** abschicken	**tangled** verheddert
vital entscheidend, lebenswichtig	**load** Ladung, Last	**to disconnect** abtrennen
operator Telefonist	**concrete** Beton	**fixed** fest angebracht
to prevent verhindern	**beam** Träger	**attached** angebaut
to obtain erhalten, beschaffen	**fatality** Todesopfer	**thud** dumpfer Schlag
inquiry Auskunft	**debris** Bauschutt	**to administer first aid** Erste Hilfe leisten
to roll over überschlagen	**literally** buchstäblich	

8.2

→ TO DO

- Parts of the body
- Describe health problems

Parts of the body

While Lucy, Victor and Olga are still talking, Patrick enters the room and says he wouldn't be able to make an emergency call because he doesn't know how to describe injuries. He also doesn't know the parts of the body, neither can he talk about health problems, illnesses or injuries.

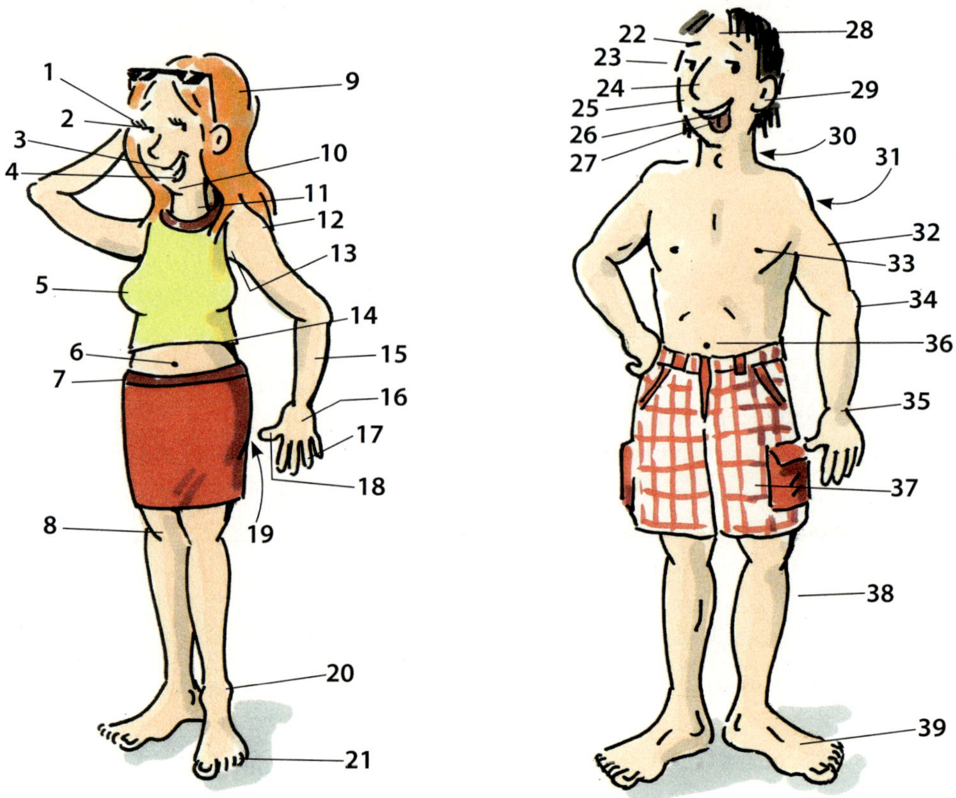

ankle, armpit, back, bottom, cheek, chest, chin, ear, elbow, eye, eyebrow, eyelash, face, finger, foot (pl. feet), forearm, forehead, hair, hand, hip, knee, leg, lips, mouth, navel, neck, nipple, nose, shoulder, stomach, thigh, thumb, toe, tooth (pl. teeth), tongue, throat, upper arm, waist, wrist

1. Can you help Patrick?
Use the words above to label the parts of the body, and fill in the corresponding numbers and the words in the chart.

head	body	limbs
		8. knee

2. Which part of the body is used with the following verbs?

1) **nod**	2) **grab**	3) smell	4) listen
5) shout	6) watch	7) **frown**	8) taste
9) kick	10) walk	11) whistle	12) wear a watch
13) point	14) **comb**	15) **shrug**	16) snap
17) **cough**	18) **sneeze**	19) shake	20) sit

1) You nod your head.

3. Here are some German and English sayings about body parts. Find the equivalent in the other language.

1	Eine Hand wäscht die andere.	a	The way to a man's heart is through his stomach.
2	Eine Krähe hackt der anderen kein Auge aus.	b	You foot the bill.
3	Kopf hoch!	c	**Honour** among thieves.
4	Einem geschenkten Gaul schaut man nicht ins Maul.	d	You scratch my back and I'll scratch yours.
5	Auge um Auge, Zahn um Zahn.	e	An eye for an eye, a tooth for a tooth.
6	Was ich nicht weiß, das macht mich nicht heiß.	f	Give him an inch, he'll take a mile.
7	Aus den Augen, aus dem Sinn.	g	What the eye doesn't see, the heart doesn't **grieve**.
8	Gib ihm den kleinen Finger, und er nimmt die ganze Hand.	h	He's a real pain in the neck.
9	Den Nagel auf den Kopf treffen.	i	Good luck.
10	Du hast es völlig versaut.	j	It's on its last legs.
11	Es pfeift aus dem letzten Loch.	k	Don't look a gift horse in the mouth.
12	Liebe geht durch den Magen.	l	Cheer up.
13	Du zahlst.	m	Down the **hatch**.
14	Er nervt total.	n	Out of sight, out of mind.
15	Man beißt nicht die Hand, die einen füttert.	o	To hit the nail on the head
16	Nicht lang schnacken, Kopf in' Nacken.	p	You made a real pig's ear out of it.
17	Passt wie die Faust aufs Auge.	q	To be a perfect match. Fits like a glove.
18	Hals- und Beinbruch.	r	Don't bite the hand that feeds you.

4. Lucy and Justin have problems to understand these German sayings. Explain the meaning of these sayings.

a) Auf einem Bein kann man nicht stehen.
b) Er gönnt ihm nicht das Schwarze unter den Fingernägeln.

VOCAB

limbs Gliedmaßen	**to frown** runzeln	**to cough** husten	**honour** Ehre
to nod nicken	**to comb** kämmen	**to sneeze** niesen	**to grieve** trauern
to grab greifen	**to shrug** zucken	**to scratch** kratzen	**hatch** Luke

8. First Aid Room

Health problems

5. Look at these pictures. What are the health problems? Match the people and their **ailments**.

No.	Who?		They say:
1	A painter	a	I feel sick./I don't feel well.
2	A man	b	My nose is bleeding.
3	A woman	c	I've broken my leg.
4	A metal worker	d	I've got **flu**.
5	Two teenagers	e	I've got a temperature.
6	A joiner	f	My elbow's **swollen**.
7	An electrician	g	I've got a **rash**.
8	A plumber	h	My finger's **painful**/hurting.

6.

Talk about an accident/injury at work that happened to you, your friend, a colleague or a relative.

What happened?
When did it happen?
How did it happen?
Did anybody help?
Which injuries did you or the person have?
How long did it last till you/they were well again?

7.

40

Listen to nine people talking about their health. Fill in the chart and take notes about the injuries/the problems and write the remedy next to the problem.

Speaker	Problem	Remedy
a)		cough mixture
b)	sore thoat	
c)		tissue
d)		
e)		

8.

Read the two conversations at the chemist's. The patients ask for remedies. The chemist advises the patients. Work with a partner. Make conversations like this. Use the chart you created.

A: What's wrong?	A: Can I help you?
B: I've got toothache.	B: I fell off the ladder and have sprained my ankle.
A: Oh dear. I'll get you some **painkillers**.	A: Wait a minute. I'll get you a bandage.
B: Thanks.	B: Thanks a lot.

At the chemist's
you can ask for a remedy **for**
(*not against*) an illness.
Can I have something **for** toothache?
They haven't found a cure **for** AIDS yet.
But:
Today young people are
inoculated against hepatitis.

VOCAB

ailment Leiden	**painful** schmerzhaft	**tissue** Papiertaschentuch
flu Grippe	**remedy** Abhilfe, Arzneimittel	**to inoculate** impfen
swollen geschwollen	**cough mixture** Hustensaft	**painkiller** Schmerzmittel
rash Ausschlag	**sore throat** Halsschmerzen	

8.3

TO DO

- Learn about a first aid kit
- Deal with minor injuries

First Aid Kit

41

Back in the clubhouse Mr Mende has called all the young people together to discuss something with them.

Mr Mende: The reason for this meeting is that we need to discuss first aid in the clubhouse. How many of you have been on a first aid course?

Olga: I'm a first aider already. I had to do it for the **girl guides**.

Justin: Lucy and I are also first aiders. We did a course at school in Canada.

Mr Mende: Right. Can you three then please organize a first aid kit for the clubhouse? We need to have one on the wall between the two **toilets**. Here is a list of what you need.

Justin: Okay. But what about the others? Do they also have to do a first aid course? We aren't always at the clubhouse, so we might not be there if there's an accident.

Mr Mende: I'm organizing a first aid course for the others as well.

Don't use the word **toilet** in America. Rather use **bathroom** in the USA.

1.

Malteser
...weil Nähe zählt.

Erste Hilfe rettet Leben. Aber leider unterbleiben oft die Maßnahmen der Ersten Hilfe, weil sich die Helfer unsicher sind.
Diese Unsicherheit wird Ihnen der Kurs „Erste Hilfe" nehmen. Er zeigt Ihnen auf, welche Maßnahmen Sie treffen müssen, wenn das Leben eines Menschen durch einen Notfall bedroht ist.

a) Look at the information from the Maltheser on the left and discuss how important first aid is in our daily lives.

b) Have you done or will you do **community service**?

c) How do you feel about
- doing a first-aid course?
- helping when someone is injured?
- joining the **voluntary fire-brigade**?
- working in a hospital?
- caring for the elderly?
- working in a kindergarten?

Lucy, Justin and Olga decide to test what the others know about first aid. They have drawn up a questionnaire and are going to interview the others.

2.

page 183

These are the questions.
Work with a partner and together decide which is the correct action in each situation.
However, always remember to call a doctor if you are unsure.

1. If you burnt your hand would you a) hold it under cold running water? b) put your hand in a basin of hot water?	6. If you have a sore throat would you a) drink some tea? b) **gargle** with honey?
2. If someone sprained their ankle would you a) **encourage** them to keep walking? b) cool the ankle and tell them to rest it?	7. If you have a high fever should you a) stay in bed and sweat it out? b) go to work?
3. If you cut your finger while working in the kitchen do you a) disinfect it first? b) put a plaster on it?	8. If a **wasp stings** you should you put a) vinegar on it? b) cold water on it?
4. If your nose bleeds should you a) put your head forward? b) stuff your nose with tissues and cool your nose?	9. If someone **swallows** something poisonous should you a) give them some water to drink? b) find out what they swallowed?
5. If some chemical **squirts** into your eye would you a) **rub** your eye? b) **rinse** your eye with water?	10. If your friend **faints** should you a) put him in the recovery position? b) lay him on his back?

3.

Have you ever helped someone?
Describe a situation where you helped someone.
Write a description of the situation in 100–150 words.

VOCAB

first aid kit/box Erste-Hilfe-Kasten **minor injury** leichte Verletzung **girl guide** Pfadfinderin **community service** Zivildienst **voluntary fire-brigade** Freiwillige Feuerwehr	**to encourage** ermutigen **to squirt** spritzen **to rub** reiben **to rinse** ausspülen	**to gargle** gurgeln **wasp** Wespe **to sting** stechen **to swallow** schlucken **to faint** ohnmächtig werden

4. **Look at these pictures and write instructions on how to treat these minor injuries.**

5. **Unfortunately, Hakan has had an accident.**

42

a) Look at the pictures and decide which is the correct sequence.
Discuss what has happened with a partner.

b) Now listen to the conversation and check your answer.

6. **The accident happened at the clubhouse and so Mr Mende has to report this to the medical insurance.**

a) Listen to the conversation once more and make keyword notes for each picture.

b) Now write a report explaining

- what happened
- where the accident happened
- what first aid measures were taken

Back in the clubhouse office, Justin, Olga and Lucy are looking at the list Mr Mende gave them.

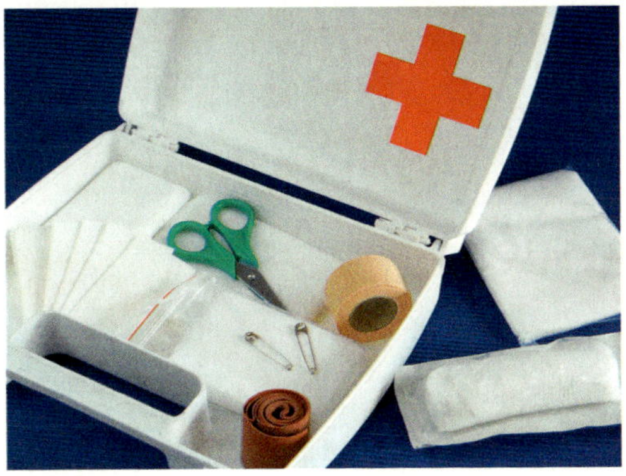

These items should be in the first aid box:

waterproof plasters,
a resuscitation face shield,
sterilised pads, adhesive microtape,
safety pins, disposable gloves,
a thermometer, cold pack,
crepe bandages, gauze bandages,
warm pack

7. (43)

Listen to Olga, Lucy and Justin talking about the contents of the first aid kit and their uses.
Write down the first aid items you hear, their uses and the German word.

First Aid Kit Contents

English	German	Use
painkiller	Schmerztablette	relieve pain/headache

8.

Ask your partner what the German or English words are for the articles in the first aid box.
Use the table you have written to help you.
What is **a pair** of scissors in German? It's 'Schere'.

We use **a pair of** in English for things like scissors, jeans, glasses, as each has two equal parts.

9. (44)

Listen to Justin telling his father what happened at the clubhouse today.
Write down key words as you listen and then write an email to Chris telling him what happened.

VOCAB

medical insurance Krankenversicherung	contents Inhalt

8.4

→ TO DO

- Deal with stress
- Find out how you learn best

Dealing with pressure

Olga, Lucy and Justin are back in the lounge talking to the others about the first aid course when Patrick arrives looking very worried. He is studying for his final exams and tells the others how nervous he is about the exams. Soon everyone is talking about learning to learn, stress and exams.

1. Read this article about stress.
Do you agree with the information and advice given?

Studying and Stress

What is stress?
Tension, anxiety and strain build up inside of us when for example we take exams. We all experience stress and in general stress is important to us because it motivates or challenges us.

How do I know when I'm stressed?
Physical symptoms: You either eat more or less than usual. You sleep too much or too little. Perhaps you feel nauseous, have headaches, cry a lot etc.
Changes in mood: You are angry and irritable. Procrastination is a key word. You may feel guilty, lonely and even isolated.

How can I deal with stress?
- Use positive self-talk: A positive attitude is important.
  - Tell yourself: **I can... and I want to ...**
  - Remember: **"Yes, we can!"** (Barack Obama, the American President)
- Your brain needs oxygen. Do regular breathing exercises: Breathe in deeply through your nose. Hold your breath a few seconds. Relax your shoulders and arms. Breathe out through your mouth. Repeat a few times.
- Plan your time: Use a time planner and don't leave everything to the last minute.
- Take ***small steps***: Set goals you can reach. Do one thing at a time.
- Watch what you eat: a balanced diet is important.
- Drink at least two to three litres of water a day. Your brain needs water.
- Have enough sleep. Go to bed on time.

2. **Discuss the following questions with your class mates:**

a) What stresses you?
b) How do you **calm down** when you feel stressed?
c) Has your mind ever gone blank in an exam?
d) What advice can you give someone who panics in an exam?

3.

a) Work in groups and together discuss what advice you would give someone who suffers from school and/or exam anxiety.
b) Design a poster including all your ideas, and advice.
c) Present your ideas to the class.

Back in the clubhouse the friends are still talking to Patrick about his exam nerves and learning to learn. Mr Mende joins the group and asks them to do the following experiment.

4. **Do you know how you learn best?**

a) Do the three tasks Mr Mende gave the friends and then discuss your **preferences** with the others in your class.

1) Work in pairs. Decide who is partner A and partner B.
Partner A talks for two minutes about their daily routine and partner B only listens and doesn't interrupt. B then paraphrases what A said.
Now it's partner B's turn. Partner A listens and after two minutes paraphrases what B said.

2) Look back at all the new and important vocabulary in this unit. Now create a word map of all these words. Remember to use different colours, drawings, symbols etc. Use the paper horizontally.

3) Work in pairs and look back through this unit. Everyone should take a turn to mime some action or **incident** in the unit and the other has to guess what it is. Partner A begins.

b) Discuss with your partner which activity you liked best and which activity you didn't like at all. Match the activities with the learning styles: visual, auditory, kinaesthetic.

VOCAB

pressure Druck	**nauseous** übel	**goal** Ziel
tension (An-)Spannung	**irritable** reizbar	**diet** Ernährung
anxiety Angst, Sorge	**procrastination** Aufschiebung	**to calm down** sich beruhigen
strain Belastung	**guilty** schuldig	**preference** Vorliebe
to challenge (heraus-)fordern	**attitude** Einstellung	**incident** Ereignis, Geschehnis

8. First Aid Room

HOW TO … Find out what kind of learner you are

We take in information through our senses. Our main senses are visual, auditory and kinesthetic. The information is passed on to the brain for **processing** and understanding through one or more of these channels.

Visual Learners: These learners learn best by using their eyes. They need to see things: images, pictures, diagrams, maps etc.

Auditory learners: These learners learn best by using their ears (hearing). They learn best by listening to people telling them about things: in a conversation, on a CD etc.

Kinesthetic learners: These learners learn best by doing everything themselves. They learn best by using their hands and feet.

Once you know your preferred learning style you can improve your **marks** by **adapting** the way you study to the way you learn best.
But remember: We learn through all our senses.

5. **Read these three statements.**

- I prefer to listen in class. I remember best by hearing everything, listening to dialogues and my class mates.
- I need to move around and feel and touch things. It is important for me to do things myself and not just listen and watch.
- I prefer the teacher to write everything on the board. I see **images** in my mind. I need diagrams, pictures etc. to learn best.

a) Tell your partner which statement best describes you.
b) Together decide which statement fits with which learning style (kinesthetic, visual, auditory).

6. **To find out more about what kind of a learner you are and how you learn best go to the following website and do the test on line:**
http://www.vark-learn.com/english/page.asp?p=younger
or complete the questionnaire your teacher gives you.
Discuss the results with your class mates.

2. **Memory is also very important when preparing for exams. How good is your memory? Discuss these questions with a partner. Now talk about strategies that would help you to do better.**

a) How many of the words you learnt for the last vocabulary test can you still remember?
b) How long does it take you to learn for a vocabulary test?
c) Can you remember telephone numbers easily?
d) Do you remember faces easily?
e) Do you remember names easily?

An: Chris@yahoo.ca
Cc:
Betreff: stress reduction

Hiya Chris!
Wow, this week has been really interesting. Mr Mende is organizing a first aid course for us here at the clubhouse. It'll be good for Lucy and I to have a refresher course. Especially as it'll be in German it can really help to improve our German, although I think we're doing alright now. I understand more and more every day. Remember I told you about Laura. Well her English isn't that brilliant and so I suppose I'll have to talk German to her. I'm still **polishing** my German **chatting-up** skills. I didn't think it'd be so difficult. It really stresses me out a bit. I'll have to follow the stress reducer advice we've been given, like breathing!
Have to go now.
Chat to you soon.
Justin

VOCAB

processing Bearbeitung	**to adapt** angleichen	**to polish** den letzten Schliff geben
mark Zensur	**image** Bild	**to chat-up** „anmachen"

9. Garden

9.1

→ TO DO

- **Talk about technical parts of a lawn mower**
- **Fill a petrol can**
- **Deal with problems with a lawn mower**

Mowing the lawn

Anna and Justin are in the garden.

45

Anna: The first thing that I wanted to do was to **mow** the lawn. It's unacceptable to have such a **neglected** garden. So I **fetched** the lawn mower and tried to start it, but it didn't work. I guess it hasn't been used for quite some time.

Justin: Oh, let's see what it could be ...
Well Anna there's no **fuel** in the tank. We'll have to fill it up again.

Anna: Ok, and what kind of fuel do we need?

Justin: I don't know. Don't you know? You're the gardener.

Anna: Let's ask Hakan.

...

Justin: Hello Hakan, we have to fill the lawn mower, but we don't know what fuel it takes.

Hakan: What kind of lawn mower is it?

Justin: What do you mean? It has a **combustion engine**.

Hakan: Yes, but we need to know if it's a 2-stroke or a **4-stroke engine**. The 2-stroke engine burns a mixture of petrol and oil; the 4-stroke engine needs either petrol or diesel.

Anna: Hakan, I think you have to take a look at the lawn mower. We don't know which type it is, do we Justin?

Justin: No, no idea.

1. **A lawn mower has many technical parts.**

a) Copy the English words of the technical parts of a lawn mower and match each word with the German translation.

a) safety handle
b) **throttle**
c) **petrol** cap
d) recoil starter
e) air filter
f) **carburettor**
g) **spark plug**
h) **exhaust**
i) oil fill tube
j) individual cutting height adjustment
k) pull rope

Auspuff
Gashebel
Luftfilter
Öleinfüllstutzen
Reversierstarter
Schnitthöhenverstellung
Sicherheitsbügel
Tankverschluss
Vergaser
Zugseil
Zündkerze

BE: petrol, AE: gas

b) Make a list of which of these parts are also found in
a car   a **chain saw**   a motorcycle

How to fill a petrol can

After Hakan found out which lawn mower the clubhouse has, he was sure that it needed a mixture of petrol and oil.

Hakan: Do you have a canister for the petrol?
Justin: Yes, there is one in the **shed** but there is some funny stuff in it.
Hakan: Oh, that's too old. We need a new one.
Justin: Ok, I think we can buy it at the service station, too, can't we?
Hakan: Yes, you can. Buy a five-litre canister. But wait a minute. Do you know how to fill the can?
Justin: Sure. I open the **filler spout** and place the **nozzle** of the petrol **hose** into it.
Hakan: Haha, very funny, Justin. Listen, when you fill your petrol can, place it on the ground a few steps from your car – never fill it inside the **boot**. When you transport the petrol in your car, make sure the canister stands safely in an **upright** position and the filler spout, as well as the **vent openings** are **tightly capped**. Make sure there is no possibility of **fume** building up in the boot or **passenger compartment** so that everything doesn't explode on the way.

USA: trunk

2. Find a word in the text that is similar in meaning.

container – small wooden house – filling hole – fuel – **device** to fill petrol into the tank – a kind of pipe made of rubber – **luggage compartment** – gas – space for people to sit

3. Answer the following questions.

a) Who is talking to whom about what?
b) Do the friends have a petrol can?
c) How does Justin want to fill the petrol can?
d) What **advice** does Hakan give about filling the petrol can?

VOCAB

lawn mower Rasenmäher
petrol can Benzinkanister
to mow mähen
neglected vernachlässigt
to fetch holen
fuel Treibstoff
combustion engine Verbrennungsmotor
4-stroke engine Vier-Takt-Motor
throttle Gashebel
carburettor Vergaser
spark plug Zündkerze
exhaust Auspuff
chain saw Kettensäge
shed Schuppen
filler spout Einfüllöffnung
nozzle Zapfventil
hose Schlauch
boot Kofferraum
upright aufrecht
vent opening Auslassöffnung
tightly capped fest mit einem Verschluss versehen
fume Abgas
passenger compartment Fahrgastkabine
device Gerät/Vorrichtung
luggage compartment Kofferraum
advice Rat

9. Garden

The broken starter

The friends filled the lawn mower but it still didn't work.

Anna: It still won't start! The starter rope is really hard to pull. And I was so happy to be able to plant and lay out the garden.

Hakan: Yes, me too. Let me check the engine, Anna. If the starter rope is hard to pull then the **rewind spring** or **spring anchor points** are usually broken. Ah ja! Here we go, the rewind spring is broken. So, we have to **disassemble** the starter. Have you got a **manual** in which we can read about which starter we need?

Justin: Yes, I saw it in the shed.

Hakan: So, we need a new starter. That should be easy to get at any garden centre.

4. **What problem do the friends have? Describe it.**

5. **Here are three more engine problems and steps to take to check the engine.**

Problem	Steps to check the mower
oil leak near the base of the engine	Very often the fill tube o-ring is **loose**: loosen the **dipstick** and push it down and **tighten** it. Make sure, that there is no leak of any liquids coming out of the engine while working on the machine.
mower does not start/ smell of petrol	Stop trying to start the engine by using the pull rope. Remove the spark plug and watch out for black dust and check if there is any **moisture** on the contacts. Clean the spark plug by using a wire brush, a piece of cloth and some sandpaper. Replace the spark plug, connect it properly to the spark plug wire and start the engine without using the choke.
mower stops/ cutted grass in deck	Remove the spark plug. **Turn** the lawnmower **over** and clean the interior of the deck with a wire brush. The mower can also be cleaned with a jet of water from the garden hose. Make sure that no moisture gets into the engine, especially the air filter.
4-stroke engine exhausts blue dust	Check if you used the right type of petrol. Open the petrol cap and pour out a few drops. Put a drop of this petrol into a glass of water. If the drop spreads out in the colours of the rainbow it might be a 2-stroke oil and petrol mixture. In this case you should empty the whole tank and carburettor and clean it with normal petrol. Fill the tank with normal petrol and start the engine again. After a few minutes the mower should work properly.

Read the three problems.

a) Match the following German translations with the English words found in the text.
Luftfilter – Ölmessstab – Vergaser – Zugseil – Zündkerze

b) Which parts of a lawn mower are mentioned in the texts?

c) Which verbs are used in connection with the parts of the lawn mower? Make a list.

6. **Copy the sentences below and complete them using verbs from exercise 5 c).**

a) If the fill tube o-ring is loose: … (**lockern**) the dipstick and … it … (**herunterdrücken**) firmly then … (**festziehen**) the dipstick.
b) If you want to … (**kontrollieren**) if there is any moisture on the contacts, … (**entfernen**) the spark plug.
c) If you want to … (**säubern**) the spark plug … (**benutzen**) a wire brush.
d) If you … (**verbinden**) the spark plug properly to the spark plug wire, you can perhaps … (**starten**) the engine again.
e) If you want to … (**säubern**) the mower, ….. (**benutzen**) the garden hose.
f) If you want to … (**starten**) the engine, … (**befüllen**) it with normal petrol.

While Hakan is exchanging the starter, he tells Anna how to clean a lawn mower.

Anna, if you're the one cleaning the lawnmower, first empty the tank and **disconnect** the spark plug so that the lawnmower cannot start **by mistake** when you have your fingers near the blades.
Turn the lawnmower on its side and use the garden hose to clean the underside of the **housing**. Make sure the water spray is **at full blast**. This will loosen dirt and **grass clippings**. Use a brush to **scrub off** the rest of the dirt. Use **soapy** water if it is very dirty. Rinse it well with clear water and leave it to dry.

7. **Mediation. Tell your classmates about how to take care of a lawn mower in German.**

8. **Many things need to be remembered for the maintenance of a lawn mower. Make a list using the following words.**

Check and change the spark plug.

check change clean cover	empty **grease** sharpen	air filter air pressure in tyres if they are not out of solid rubber engine and chassis motoroil	mower all other mowing parts petrol spark plug tank

VOCAB

rewind spring Rückspule	**to tighten** festziehen	**grass clippings** Rasenschnitt
spring anchor point Federverankerung	**moisture** Feuchtigkeit	**to scrub off** abkratzen
to disassemble ausbauen	**to turn over** umdrehen	**soapy** seifig
manual hier: Anleitung	**to disconnect** (ab)trennen	**to grease** fetten
loose locker	**by mistake** aus Versehen	**blade** Rasenmähermesser
dipstick Ölmessstab	**housing** Gehäuse	**maintenance** Wartung
	at full blast hier: mit hartem Strahl	

9. Garden

9.2

TO DO

- Talk about parts of a tree
- Distinguish between different wood grains and paving materials
- Form nouns

Cleaning the garden

46

Hakan repaired the starter of the lawn mower and Anna was finally able to finish mowing the lawn. She is talking to Justin about how to arrange the garden.

Anna: We should have some small trees, bushes and some flowers in the front area.
Justin: Yes, okay. What about roses, Anna. Do you like roses?
Anna: Oh, Justin, of course I like roses. We should have climbing roses on the wall here with a grid.
Justin: And some more trees? Why don't we have a few trees for shade on the terrace? Let's have an apple tree and a cherry tree.
Anna: Yes, good idea. But we also have to get the other trees in shape again. The walnut has become really big; we have to cut a few branches. And we should also take away the dead conifer over there. I'm sure it'll break away in the next storm.
Justin: Oh! Would you cut down the conifer?
Anna: Yes, and I would also take away the spruce, but this requires permission, which we won't get. So, let's just cut it back a bit.
Justin: All right. Do we have a saw for this?
Anna: Yes, we have a manual one, but not an electrical one. Let's see if we can manage.
Justin: And what about the hazelnut bushes here. Where I live, the local authorities have cut the bushes down to the ground in front of the house.
Anna: Yes, but they are good protection against prying eyes, let's only cut them back a little bit.

While Anne and Justin cut the trees and bushes, Justin explains the structure and characteristics of a tree and the different kinds of woods to Anne.

1. **Match the words with the different parts of a tree. Note down the number and the word.**

6 sapwood

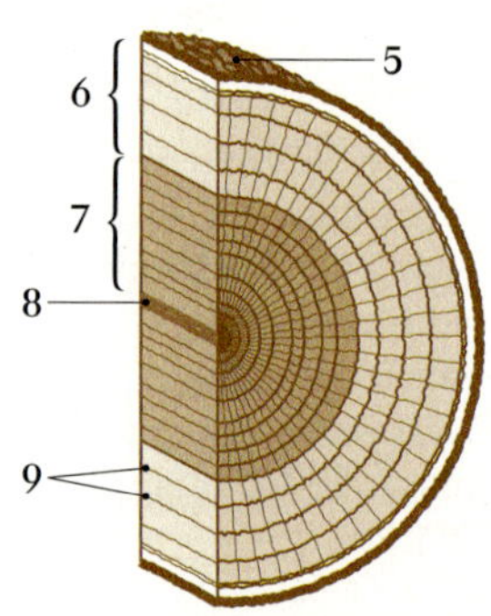

bark
branches
annual rings
heartwood
leaves
pith
roots
sapwood
trunk

2. Copy and complete Justin's explanation with the words below.

Trees grow in _(1)_ from their centre. As the tree _(2)_ and becomes older, the cells closer to the inside of the tree _(3)_ **conducting sap** and _(4)_. The dead cells become the heartwood and the newer cells that still conduct sap, form the _(5)_. In many woods, the sapwood and _(6)_ are clearly **differentiated**, the sapwood is often much _(7)_ in colour.
Growth rings are **concentric** _(8)_. They grow from the centre of the _(9)_, each ring represents one _(10)_ of growth. The term "grain" is the way that growth rings _(11)_ on the surface of a piece of _(12)_. That **appearance** _(13)_ **depending on** how the wood is _(14)_ from the trunk.

appear – changes – cut – die – grows – heartwood – lighter – rings – sapwood – stop – thickness – tree – wood – year

3. Look at the different trees.

a) Match the pictures of the trees with their corresponding furniture pictures.

b) Many things are made of wood. List as many things as you can and the wood they are made of.

VOCAB

to distinguish unterscheiden	**conifer** Konifere	**pith** Mark
grain Maserung	**to cut down** fällen	**sapwood** Splintholz
paving materials Material zum Pflastern	**spruce** Fichte	**trunk** Stamm
noun Substantiv	**to require** hier: verlangen	**to conduct** leiten
to arrange gestalten	**permission** Genehmigung	**sap** Saft
grid Gitter	**manual** hier: manuell	**to differentiate** unterscheiden
shade Schatten	**local authorities** Gemeinde	**concentric** konzentrisch
in shape in Form	**protection against prying eyes** Schutz gegen neugierige Augen	**appearance** Erscheinen
branch Zweig	**heartwood** Kernholz	**to depend on** abhängig sein von

A new path and barbecue area

Anna was quite surprised about Justin's knowledge of the different kinds of wood.

47

Anna: Justin, you know so much about trees and wood. I have the feeling that being a joiner is exactly what you've always wanted to do. Is that right?

Justin: Well, yes. Wood can be used as construction material for houses or for furniture. Being a joiner is cool. It's a creative job, I mean, unless you are only **occupied** with kneeling on a floor and laying it.

Anna: Yes, I can understand that. Justin, I think we did a good job with **pruning** the trees and bushes in our garden, didn't we? So, what's next?

Justin: Well, look at the path to the clubhouse door. It's only a trail. We should pave the way from the **pavement** to the clubhouse. What do you think?

Anna: Oh yes, very good idea, the path is always so **muddy** when it rains. The hall is always so dirty in autumn and winter because everybody has to go through the mud and dirt. I would also like to have a barbeque area in the garden. Don't you think we could lay some **paving stones** there as well?

Justin: Yes, sure, we should pave an area of about 10 m^2 for the barbeque area. Perhaps, we can ask Sebi and the others to help us with it.

4. **Which steps have to be taken to pave a path or an area? Copy the statements below and put them in the right order.**

- Fill the area with sand and **level** it with a wooden board.
- Remove the top **soil** and use it to level off other areas in the garden.
- Fill in the **joints** with fine sand.
- Set the paving stones.
- Measure the area you want to pave and mark it.
- Use a **spirit level** to maintain a **slope** for the water to be able to run off.

Anna is pacing out the length of the path to the clubhouse door and Justin is measuring the width of it with a measuring tape.

Anna: The path is nearly 12 m long and it should be 1.20 m wide.

Justin: Right. And what kind of paving should we have? I think we should make it simple and cheap and take **exposed aggregate concrete**.

Anna: We should also think about paving stones with **permeable surfaces**, for example **grass pavers**.

Justin: Well, yes you are right. But I think that we probably can't **afford** more than normal paving stones. Let's go to our shop for building materials and have a look.

5. page 181

List 8 adjectives or adverbs from the text above. Do you know their corresponding verbs and nouns? Note them down in a table like this.

Adjective	Verb	Noun
surprised	to surprise	surprise
different		

HOW TO … Form nouns

Nouns name persons, places, animals or things, groups of people, ideas and qualities. As a **rule of thumb** we can say that nouns are formed by adding endings to verbs, adjectives or other nouns.
Here are some of the most **common** endings which form nouns:

-ment	≙ forms the noun from verbs	to employ/employ**ment**
-ance, -ence	≙ forms the noun from adjectives and verbs	important/import**ance**, to depend/depend**ence**
-ation, -tion, -ion	≙	to occupy/occup**ation**
-ity	≙ forms the noun from adjectives	normal/normal**ity**
-ness	≙	weak/weak**ness**
-ism	≙	formal/formal**ism**

6. **Which ending do the following words need to become nouns? Note them down.**

careful – clever – cold – communicate – develop – imagine – kind – move – national – patriot – popular

7. **Note down the word with the correct ending and translate this.**

a)	operate	-ion	-ness	-ism	-ity
b)	useful	-ance	-ness	-ity	-ism
c)	invent	-ency	-ness	-tio	-ion
d)	dark	-ion	-ness	-ism	-ity
e)	pave	-ancy	-ment	-ity	-ism
f)	represent	-ation	-ency	-ity	-ism

VOCAB

barbecue area Grillplatz
to be occupied with beschäftigt sein mit
to prune beschneiden
pavement Bürgersteig
muddy matschig
paving stone Pflasterstein/Gehwegplatte
to level ausgleichen
soil Boden
joint Fuge
spirit level Wasserwaage
slope Gefälle
to pace out abschreiten
exposed aggregate concrete Waschbeton
permeable durchlässig
surface Oberfläche
grass paver Rasengitterstein
to afford sich leisten
rule of thumb Faustregel
common gebräuchlich
to employ einstellen
to develop entwickeln

9.3

TO DO

- Describe different paving materials and their uses
- Describe how to build a fish pond

At the building material supplier

The shop assistant at the shop for building materials was really kind and helpful to the friends. He explained the advantages and disadvantages of many different kinds of stones so that Anna and Justin had a good overview of the materials.

1. **Look at the different kinds of materials presented to Anna and Justin. Match the numbers for the stones with the words …**

a) … for their colour (multicoloured, uncoloured, **monochrome**).

b) … for their forms (quadratic, wavy, **rectangular**, bishops hat, hexagonal).

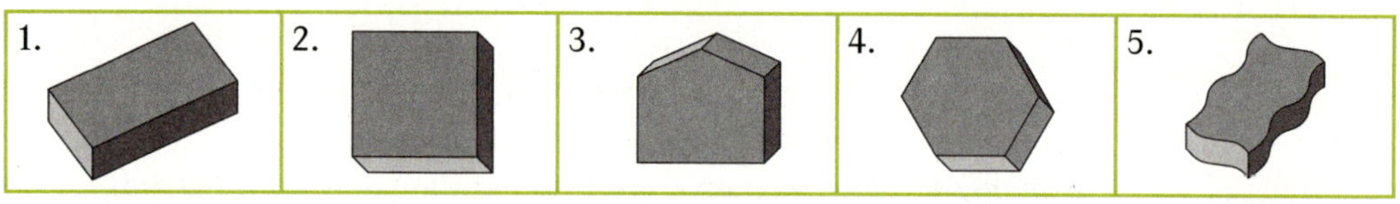

c) … for their material (basalt, concrete, exposed aggregate concrete, granite, **slate**).

d) … for their permeablility: (concrete, pavement with joints for grass, grass paver).

Different kinds of paving materials

The shop assistant explained to the friends for which areas the different kinds of paving materials are usually used.

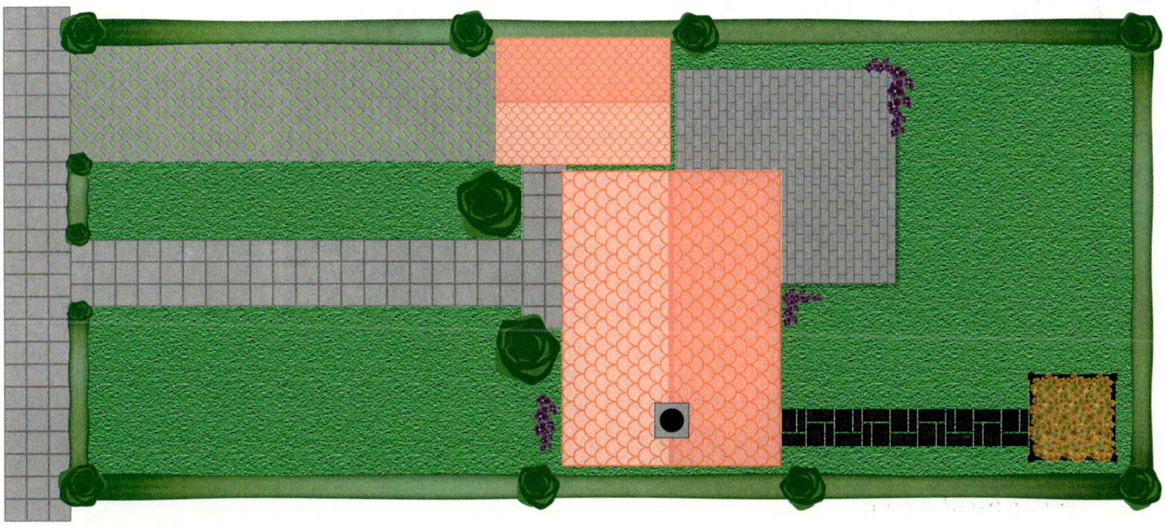

2. **Match the German words with the English translation.**

Auffahrt – Bürgersteig – Terrasse – Weg

driveway – path – pavement – terrace

3. **Look at the picture above.**

a) Read the following sentences. Which paving material is meant?
This paving material is used because …
1. … it's not **impervious**, grass and water can go through it, but also a heavy car can stand on it.
2. … it is not so **slippery**.
3. … it is decorative.
4. … it doesn't have to carry heavy vehicles.
5. … many people go along here therefore it has to be robust.

b) Which paving material is usually used for which area?

VOCAB

fish pond Fischteich	**rectangular** rechteckig	**impervious** undurchlässig
monochrome einfarbig	**slate** Schiefer	**slippery** rutschig

Fish pond?

When Anna, Justin and the friends wanted to start the paving projects, the weather was too bad to do it. It was raining heavily and they had to stay inside the clubhouse.

4.

Listen to the friends' conversation in the clubhouse and answer the following questions.

a) What problem do the friends have?
b) What does Lucy want?
c) Besides the paving, what else do the friends want to do in the garden?
d) The friends nearly get into a **fight**. Why?
e) At the end of the conversation what are the friends going to do?

A fish pond is a good **improvement** to the garden. Fish ponds **attract** different kinds of birds, frogs and insects. It's a peaceful place to sit and relax. The sound of running water and the noises of the wildlife is **soothing** and relaxing.

How to build a pond

First of all you have to find a good place for it. The **suitable** place for a fish pond needs four to six hours of sunlight per day. Don't build it directly next to trees, as the leaves and needles fall into the fish pond and it is difficult to keep it clean.
Mark out the shape of the pond on the area and then **dig** it out. Be sure to **remove** all sharp objects, roots, stones etc. An **additional** area of 30 cms in depth should also be dug around the **perimeter**. This shelf area should be about 30–40 cms wide.
Line the area of the fish pond with the correct **underlay** (sand or if the underground is very stony pond fleece underlay). A **pond liner** is laid over this. Be sure to minimize any **folds** and allow an overhang of at least 15 cms.
Now you can fill the pond. Once again **ease out** wrinkles as the water runs into the pond. Place **coping stones** around the pond on the prepared shelf area. Make sure the liner is above the water surface. **Shallow-water plants** can be used to decorate the **edge** of the pond.

5.

Use a dictionary and explain in keywords what the following mean:

a) A fish pond attracts wildlife.
b) The sound of running water is soothing.
c) Find a good place for the fish pond.
d) Dig a shelf area.
e) Remove sharp objects.
f) Build an underlay.
g) Ease folds out of the pond liner.
h) Arrange coping stones around the edge.

6. **The following verbs are taken from the text. Use a dictionary and find …**

a) … the appropriate antonym.

to attract	to find	to allow	to minimize	to fill
to forbid	to repel	to empty	to lose	to maximize

b) … the appropriate synonym.

to dig	to line	to place	to fall	to remove
to drop	to set	to take away	to excavate	to cover

7. page 184 **The following verbs are irregular verbs. Copy the table and complete it with the correct forms.**

infinitive	build	dig	fall	keep	lay
simple past					
past participle (third form)					

The friends couldn't decide whether or not they wanted to build a fish pond and when Mr Mende heard about the idea he was also not very enthusiastic about it.

Nein, meine Lieben, wir verzetteln uns. Wir haben noch einiges zu tun. Ihr habt zwar die Bäume und Sträucher zurückgeschnitten, aber es müssen noch der Weg und der Grillplatz gepflastert werden. Und Eure Party soll nun auch bald stattfinden. Weiterhin möchte ich doch darauf hinweisen, dass die Arbeit für einen Fischteich oft unterschätzt wird. Wer kontrolliert beispielsweise regelmäßig, und das bedeutet fast täglich, die Filteranlage? Wer füttert die Fische? Ihr könnt eine Vogeltränke aufstellen, aber sonst nichts. Erstmal jedenfalls.

8. **Mr Mende's speech was too quick for Lucy. She asked Anna to tell her what Mr Mende said. Help her and make a list of the most important points in English.**

VOCAB

fight Streit
improvement Verbesserung
to attract anziehen
soothing beruhigend
suitable passend
to mark out markieren

to dig ausheben
to remove entfernen
additional zusätzlich
perimeter Umfang
to line auslegen
underlay Unterlage
pond liner Teichfolie

fold Falte
to ease out hier: ausgleichen
coping stone Abdeckstein
shallow-water plants Pflanzen für die Uferzone
edge Rand

9. Garden

9.4

TO DO

- Describe how to lift heavy objects safely
- Become a member in a fitness club
- Train at a fitness club

Lifting heavy objects safely

The friends decided to take the exposed aggregate concrete for the path to the clubhouse door and pavement with joints for grass for the barbecue area. Although it made the project a bit more expensive, it felt good. Sebi and Patrick helped Anna and Justin with their project.

1. **Listen to the following conversation between the four friends and say if the statements a)–e) are true or false. Give reasons for your decision.**

49

a) Anna can carry a lot of stones.
b) Anna goes to a fitness studio.
c) You can only carry heavy objects when you have a lot of muscles.
d) Patrick thinks that Anna is a really strong woman
e) Sebi thinks that it is important to care about his back.

2. **Anna explains how to carry heavy objects safely.**

a) Match Anna's explanations with the appropriate picture.

- As you are using your knees and hips to take the weight and not your back, keep your knees and toes in line, in order to avoid any knee strain. By keeping your knees firmly in line your body stays aligned while lifting the object.
- Stand up straight. Imagine a rod in your back from your head to the tip of your spine. Keep your back straight and your arms close to your body. This makes lifting easier and avoids strain on the arms, shoulders and back.
- In order to lift a heavy object safely, you need to get as close to the object as possible. In fact the object should be between your legs. Stand with feet wider apart than the width of your shoulders. Anchor your weight firmly into the ground.
- Bend your knees and pick the object up from underneath. In this way you use your leg and hip muscles. Be careful not to bend at your waist as this could cause back strain or even an injury to a disk.

b) Make a list of hints on how to lift and carry things correctly and let a classmate make the movements.
c) What could happen to a person who doesn't follow your advice?

Fitness

Although Justin moved his body as Anna told him, he sweated a lot and didn't really feel fit. Anna and especially also Patrick seemed to be more able to carry the stones and do the paving. Sebi, however, also had his problems.

Justin: Anna, how can you do that? I'm sweating as if I'm not used to carrying things at all. I feel so unfit and out of energy.
Anna: Slow down, Justin, don't overdo it. I'm trained, you know, I do **strength training** at the gym at least twice a week.
Patrick: Yeah, as I told you, she's superwoman.
Anna: No, I'm not, Patrick. Stop saying that.
Justin: Where is your fitness club, Anna?
Anna: It's the Be Fit Training Centre, Schwarzer Weg. Olga, Patrick and Hakan are also members there. It's not so expensive, only 18.95 € a month. Why don't you come with us some time?
Justin: Oh, yes, good idea. Do they offer a **trial practice** or something like that?
Anna: Yes, you can first have a look and make an **appointment** with one of the trainers. Then you can do a trial practice and if you like it there you can become a member and start training.
Justin: Mmmm, that sounds really good.
Patrick: And what about you Sebi, don't you want to **join** us?
Sebi: Oh, no, thank you! Training at a fitness club is not my thing at all. I go dancing once a week.
Anna: **What a pity.** I'm sure it would have been fun for you guys to train together.
Patrick: OK, can you please talk about that later? Let's finish the paving.

3. Read the conversation above and answer the following questions.

a) What's the situation the friends are in?
b) What's the matter with Justin?
c) Anna does strength training. How does it help her?
d) How can Justin become a member in Anna's fitness club?
e) What about Sebi?

VOCAB

member Mitglied	**spine** Rückgrat	**disk** Bandscheibe
to care sich kümmern	**to avoid** vermeiden	**strength training** Krafttraining
appropriate passend	**firmly** fest	**trial practice** Probetraining
apart auseinander	**aligned** ausgerichtet	**appointment** Termin
to anchor verankern	**to bend** beugen	**to join** sich anschließen
rod Stange	**underneath** unter	**What a pity.** Wie schade.
tip Spitze	**injury** Verletzung	

At the fitness centre

A few days later Justin got up the energy and went to the fitness centre together with Patrick and Hakan to make an appointment for a trial practice. He was allowed to look around and watch his friends train on the fitness machines. Hakan and Patrick were especially interested in training their arm muscles.

4. **Look at the pictures and Hakan's explanations of their arm muscle exercise.**

a) Make a list of the words that express movement, **i.e.** a change in position.

b) Mediation: Imagine your classmates should **execute** the arm muscle exercise. Tell one of your classmates Hakan's explanation in German.

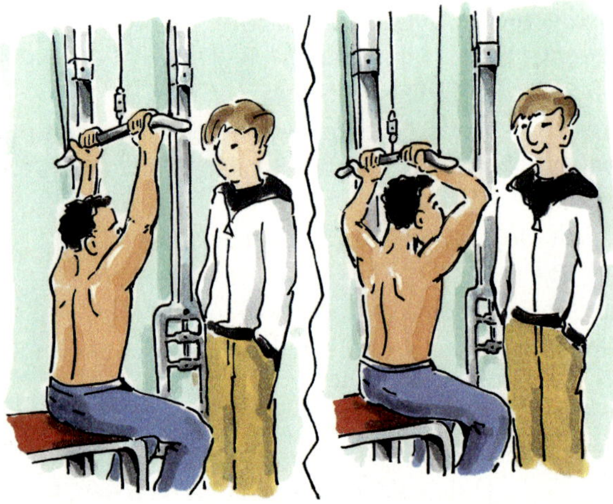

This is the so called seated high pulley overhead curl to train your upper arms. First of all, you have to sit erect on the **bench**; then **grasp** the **bar** with an **underhand grip**. **Raise** your upper arms so your elbows are **at eye level**, arms straight. **Lock** your upper arms in place and sit up straight.
You have to bend your elbows slowly, to pull the bar down and behind your head while keeping your upper arms **steady**. When your elbows **roughly** form a **90-degree angle**, **reverse** the move and slowly come back to the start.
If you want to have good results, it's important not to lean forward or backward when moving. If you move forward or backward the **momentum** makes the move easier but less efficient.

PHRASES	Expressing movement
to **move** up/down/forward/backward	sich nach oben/unten/vorn/hinten **bewegen**
to **press/push** a button	einen Knopf **drücken**
to **pull** a rope to start an engine	an einer Schnur **ziehen**, um einen Motor zu starten
to **lift** a heavy object	einen schweren Gegenstand **heben**
to **crank up** an adjustable desk	einen verstellbaren Tisch **hochdrehen**
to **bend** wood to form a part of a chair	Holz **biegen**, um einen Teil eines Stuhls zu formen
to **turn** a screw	eine Schraube **drehen**
to **stretch** a cable across	ein Kabel **spannen**
to **wind** wool into a ball	Wolle zu einem Ball **aufwickeln**
to **tilt** a barrel to empty it	ein Fass **kippen**, um es zu leeren

5. **Which movements do you make in your job?**
Make a list of sentences of typical movements using the list above and a dictionary.

I lift plants from the ground.

An: Chris@yahoo.ca
Cc:
Betreff: fitness club

Hi Chris,
What's up man? I'm in a fitness club now. Can't wait to start training. Had a trial practice last Friday. The trainer showed me around the gym and how to use the fitness machines. It was quite full so that people had to wait at a machine or took turns in using the machines. Patrick and Hakan said that they don't often go on Friday nights because then it's very **crowded** and people **show off** a little bit. Hakan said that there are always some idiots who come especially on Friday nights just to pump up their muscles again before they go out to a disco or so.
It's really interesting there. They have a lot of training machines on three floors, and they have their own magazine, they publish on a monthly basis. Everybody seems to be very friendly. The trainers all nearly look like Arnold Schwarzenegger, **amazing**! One of the trainers said that you have to be very disciplined in your training and lifestyle (no alcohol, no smoking, eat healthy and **nutritious** food, etc.) to get in that shape. And that it takes years of training to get that muscular.

Take care,
Justin

6. **Read Justin's email to Chris and write a reply to him. Tell him that you are doing very well without sport and that you think working out in a fitness studio is boring and stupid.**

VOCAB

i.e. = that is das heißt	**at eye level** auf Augenhöhe	**momentum** Schwung
to execute ausführen	**to lock** hier: fixieren	**crowded** voll
bench Bank	**steady** stabil	**to show off** angeben
to grasp greifen	**roughly** grob	**to release** herausgeben
bar Stange	**90-degree angle** 90-Grad Winkel	**amazing** erstaunlich
underhand grip Unterhandgriff	**to reverse** umkehren	**nutritious** nahrhaft
to raise heben		

10. Big Hall

10.1

TO DO

- Arrive in a foreign city
- Go through immigration/passport control
- Talk about holidays

At the airport

Justin, Lucy and Mr Time have just arrived at the airport. Chris is due to arrive any minute and Justin can't wait to see his friend again.

Justin: Come on you two, hurry up!
Mr Time: Justin, we have plenty of time. We don't need to rush.
Lucy: I bet the plane's late.
Justin: No, it isn't! I checked before we left home.
Mr Time: So which terminal is he arriving at?
Justin: Terminal 1. Arrivals is on the ground floor, I think. Isn't that where we arrived?
Lucy: I can't remember. I was so tired and excited when we arrived that I don't remember much about our arrival.
Mr Time: There's the sign over there: Arrivals.
Justin: I'll go ahead and check the information board to see if his plane has landed yet.
Lucy: Oh, Justin! You really are like a little child.
Mr Time: Let him go, Lucy. He can't wait to see Chris again. You know how close they are. They've been friends since their sandpit days.

1. **Have you ever flown anywhere?**

a) Tell your partner about your experience at an airport.
 - Which airport was it?
 - Why were you there?

b) Do you like airports? If yes, why? If not, why not?

Meanwhile sitting in seat no. 18A is a very excited young man from Canada who cannot wait to see his friend, Justin. The cabin attendant has just made the following announcement:

Ladies and gentlemen, we have **started our descent** in preparation for landing. Please make sure your seat backs and tray tables are in their **full upright position**. Make sure your **seat belt is securely fastened** and all **carry-on luggage** is **stowed underneath the seat** in front of you or in the **overhead bins**. Please turn off all **electronic devices** until we are **safely parked** at the gate. The flight attendants are **currently** passing through the cabin to make **a final check** and pick up any remaining cups and glasses. Thank you.

2. What do the word partnerships in bold print mean?

a) Explain these to your partner in German.
b) Why should these actions be **carried out**?

**Chris is looking out of the window at the city of Hamburg down below.
He has never been abroad before and he is a little nervous about going through immigration as he cannot speak any German.**

3. Justin sent him some phrases to learn so that he has them if he needs them.

50

a) Together with your partner brainstorm all the German **survival phrases** you think a visitor needs to know at the airport when visiting Germany.
Wo ist der nächste Geldautomat?
b) Now listen to the English phrases and compare them with the German phrases you have written down. Did you miss any? Which ones didn't you have?

4. Role play arriving at immigration passport control. Take turns in being the **immigrations officer.**

Immigrations officer:	Your passport, please.
You:	Here you are.
Immigrations officer:	How long are you staying?
You:	....
Immigrations officer:	Where are you staying?
You:	....
Immigrations officer:	What is the **purpose** of your visit?
You:	...

VOCAB

immigration Passkontrolle **to be due** erwartet werden **sandpit** Sandkasten	**to carry out** durchführen **survival phrase** überlebenswichtige Redewendung	**immigrations officer** Zollbeamter **purpose** Grund

Going through Passport Control or Immigration

After you leave the plane and before you enter a foreign country, you need to go through Immigration. There are normally different **queues** of people waiting to go through passport control. When entering Germany

- EU **citizen**
- Non-EU citizen

If you come from a country that is a partner of the "Schengen Agreement" (Belgium, Germany, France, Luxembourg, the Netherlands, Spain, Portugal, Italy, Austria, Greece, Denmark, Iceland, Norway, Finland, Sweden, the Czech republicx, Estonia, Hungary, Lithuania, Latvia, Malta, Poland, Slovakia, Slovenia and Switzerland) then you needn't go through passport control nor customs.

Your **passport** or **ID card** must be valid for at least the **duration** of your stay in the country you are visiting. Some countries **demand** a longer **validity** of your passport.

5. **Choose one of the following and do some research on the topic. Report back to your classmates. You should give a presentation about the topic of your choice:**

- What is the Schengen Agreement ? When and why was it agreed?
- Travelling to Canada or North America: What are the immigration **requirements** for these countries?
- Choose a country you would like to visit and report back on the immigration requirements of the country.

If you travel to Brazil you need a passport which is still valid for six months.
You do not need a visa for Brazil if you are a German national.

After going through immigrations Chris needs to collect his luggage. As the airport signs are all in German and English, he has no problem finding the baggage collection hall.

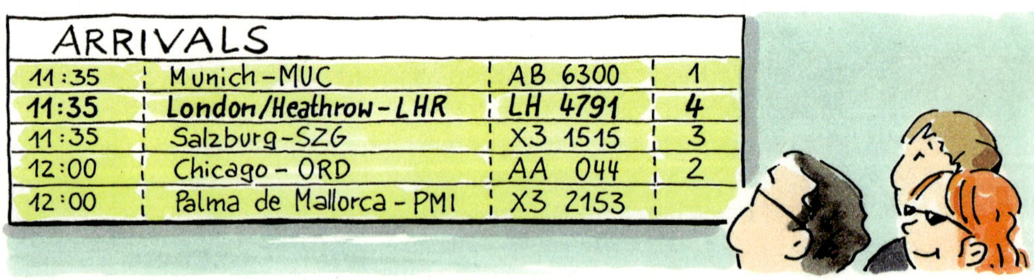

In the baggage claim area, the passengers of flight LH4791 from Heathrow airport have just arrived at carousel no. 4 to collect their luggage.

6. **Look at the arrival board: What do these abbreviations mean? Search the internet for any that you don't know.**

a) MUC, LHR, SZG, ORD, PMI
b) AB, LH, X3, AA

Outside in the arrivals hall Justin is peering through the door each time it opens to try and see Chris inside. Suddenly, he shouts "There he is!" and at that moment, the door opens and Chris walks out to meet his friend again.

In the car Justin tells Chris what he has planned to do with him during his stay in Hamburg. He wants to show him all the sights and landmarks in Hamburg as for example Landungsbrücken, Reeperbahn and places like that.

7. **You have a friend visiting you from another country.**

a) Which places in your city would you take your friend to see?

b) Together with a partner plan a sightseeing tour for your visitor. Explain where you would take the visitor and also why it is important that they go there.
Be prepared to present your tour to the rest of the class.

8. **Together with a partner answer and discuss these questions.**

a) In which cities or countries can you visit these famous buildings, bridges, monuments and towers?
- The Eiffel Tower
- The Colosseum
- The Taj Mahal
- Burj Al Arab
- Big Ben
- Stonehenge
- The Golden Gate Bridge
- The Pyramids

b) Do you know of any other famous landmarks? Tell your partner about them.

VOCAB

queue Schlange	**to demand** fordern, verlangen	**carousel** Laufband
citizen Bürger	**validity** Gültigkeit	**to peer** starren
passport Reisepass	**requirement** Voraussetzung	**menace** Nervensäge
ID card Personalausweis	**baggage** Gepäck	**sight** Sehenswürdigkeit
valid gültig	**baggage claim area** Gepäckausgabe	**landmark** Wahrzeichen
duration Dauer		

10.2

TO DO

- Talk about idols
- Understand general information
- Use the passive
- Use some and any

Stars

At the Time's home Justin, Lucy and Chris have a lot to talk about.

Justin: How are the Edmonton Oilers doing this season?
Chris: They are eighth in the Western Conference now. I hope they'll make the playoffs this season. What about the Hamburg ice hockey team?
Justin: You mean the Hamburg Freezers? They reached the playoffs but lost against Eisbären Berlin in the quarterfinals.
Chris: Do they have a player as famous as Wayne Gretzky?
Justin: No, they don't. Ice hockey is not that popular in Germany. The Germans are more into soccer or football as it is called here in Europe. The most famous player in Hamburg is Uwe Seeler.

Chris: Never heard of him.
Justin: No wonder! He played his last game in 1972.
Chris: In 1972? Why is he still so popular? Did he win the World Championship?
Justin: No never. He started his career in the German national team in 1954 after the German team won their first World Cup and played his last game for the national team in Mexico in 1970. There they came third. After loosing the final against England in 1966, the German team won the revenge in the quarter final in Mexico 3:2. Uwe Seeler **scored** a goal with the back of his head.
Chris: It seems that you have become a real soccer expert. So why is this guy still famous? I guess he won a lot of national championships.
Justin: No, I'm not an expert. At school we had to present a report about famous people. First I wanted to talk about Wayne Gretzky, but my friend Sebastian told me about Uwe Seeler. I had already read his name in a newspaper and I wanted to know more about him and Hamburg so I wrote my report about him. He won the German championship only once, in 1960. I think he is famous because he was born here in Hamburg and only played for the Hamburger SV club. **Despite tempting offers** from Italian and Spanish clubs he **remained** loyal to his club.
Lucy: You boys and your sports stars. A sportsperson could never be my idol.
Chris: Well then, who is your idol?
Lucy: I don't know. My idol is somebody who did something special, somebody who helped to make the world a better place.
Chris: You are talking about Wayne Gretzky.
Lucy: You'll never learn.

1. **Who is your idol. Give reasons.**

Sightseeing

The next morning Lucy, Justin and Chris start their sightseeing tour in Hamburg. First they meet Sebi at the underground station Barmbek. Sebi has brought a tourist guide book.

Sebi: Good morning everybody. Are you ready for our sightseeing tour? Follow me, I'm your guide.

Lucy: So you are an expert for the history of Hamburg?

Sebi: That's right. At least I know how to get all the necessary information. Look, I bought this guide book yesterday. It explains all the interesting things in Hamburg in German and in English.

Justin: That's great. What a splendid idea. Let's get on the underground train.

Lucy: What kind of ticket do we need? I think if we get on and off the train several times it's too expensive to always buy a single ticket. Sebi, do you think we should buy all-day-tickets?

Sebi: It's past 9 o'clock. We should buy a 9 am group ticket, it's **valid** the whole day for up to five people and only costs 8.95 Euros. We can change from the underground to S-Bahn, buses and even harbour ferries.

Chris: Change from the underground? Why do we take the underground for a sightseeingtour, to look at tunnels?

Sebi: No, the U3 is the oldest line in Hamburg and most of it runs overground. It only runs underground in the city centre. Let's get the ticket and start our trip.

When Sebi and his friends leave Landungsbrücken station, Sebi reads from the guide book.

2. **Sum up the main ideas of the following chapter from the guide book in English.**

51

The Landungsbrücken were built from 1907 to 1909. Harbour cruises and ferries to Finkenwerder and Teufelsbrück start here. The ferries can be used with a HVV-ticket. On the right you can see the three-mast Rickmer Rickmers and the white Cap San Diego, a general cargo ship built in 1961. Both are museum ships today. As **global trade** takes place in the harbour of Hamburg, some of the modern container ships that dock there today are already several times bigger than the Cap San Diego. Hamburg port is the largest in Germany and is the leader in the movement of goods to and from China. More than 8.5 million containers are **handled** here yearly.
The Elbphilh armonie, the new architectonical landmark of Hamburg, is being built on the right. Behind the storehouses a complete new quarter, the Hafen-City, is also developing. The cruise terminal is also located there, where the world´s largest passenger liner, Queen Mary II, amongst others, docks. The Hamburg government made a decision in favour of the Hafen-City at the end of the 90s, and 10,000 people should soon be living there. 24,000 people lived here at the end of the 19th century, but they had to move because of the construction of the storehouse quarter.

VOCAB

to score erzielen	**offer** Angebot	**global trade** Welthandel
despite trotz	**to remain** bleiben	**to handle something** etwas umschlagen
tempting verlockend	**valid** gültig	

3. **Read or listen the text about Landungsbrücken once again and answer the questions.**

a) When were the Landungsbrücken built?
b) Which trips can you take from Landungsbrücken?
c) What kind of ticket can be used for the harbour ferries?
d) What kind of museum ships are close to Landungsbrücken?
e) When was the Cap San Diego built?
f) Which ships have replaced the general cargo ships?
g) How many containers are handled in the harbour of Hamburg harbour yearly?
h) Which landmark is being built in front of the storehouses?
i) What are the names of the two quarters close to Landungsbrücken and when were they built?

HOW TO ... **Use the passive**

Active and passive sentences are in the same tense.
For a passive sentence we use **to be** (in the correct tense) + **past participle**

Compare:

Shilbuilders **built** the Cap San Diego in 1961.
The Cap San Diego **was built** in 1961.

Carbuilders **build** cars.
Cars **are built** by carbuilders.

Construction workers **are building** the Elbphilharmonie.
The Elbphilharmonie **is being built** by construction workers.

4. **Use passive instead of active.**

The architect designs the building. The building is designed by the architect.

a) The roofer is putting tiles on the roof.
b) The bricklayer has mixed the cement.
c) The storm blew down five trees.
d) You must wear hard hats on a construction site.
e) A gardener is planting red roses.
f) The plumber has installed three sinks this morning.
g) The painter varnished the windows.
h) A metal worker is fixing the burglar bar.
i) The client pays the bills.
j) An electrician will mend the wiring tomorrow.
k) The trainee replaced the socket.
l) Unskilled workers are sweeping the floor.
m) Carpenters build carports.
n) A tiler is tiling the bathroomfloor.

5. **Sometimes the passive is used for instructions as well. Change the following instruction from active to passive.**

Install a socket

First measure the wall to find out the correct position. Next drill a hole for the socket. Then make a slit for the wire. Fix the wire into the slit and connect it to the socket. Afterwards put the socket in its hole and tighten the screws. Fill the slit with plaster. Finally attach the **faceplate** on the socket.

Start like this: First the wall is measured to find out the correct position. Next ...

A coffee break

Sebi, Justin, Lucy and Chris are walking back to the underground.

Lucy: That was great. But now my feet are hurting. I need somewhere to sit.
Sebi: Look! Over there at the bar is a free table.
Sebi: Would you like something to drink or would you prefer an ice-cream?
Lucy: I'd like a diet-coke. Chris what about you?
Chris: I'll have a shandy. What is it called in German?
Sebi: It's called Alsterwasser, some people call it Radler. I'll have one as well.
Justin: I'd prefer a cup of coffee. I haven't had any breakfast yet and I wonder if they have anything to eat?
Sebi: I'm afraid they won't offer breakfast in the afternoon but you might get some cake.
Justin: That's fine. What about you?
Lucy: No, thanks, nothing fatty for me. I'd prefer a salad or some strawberries.
Chris: Look at the menu. I must try a typical German meal, some sausages for example.
Sebi: You won't get any sausages in a café. If you'd like to have sausages we have to go somewhere else.
Chris: Would anybody else like to have sausages as well?
All: No, thanks.

PHRASES — Using some/any/...body/...one/...thing/...where

Some or **any** with **uncountable** nouns mean '*etwas*', not any means '*kein*'.
Some or **any** with **countable** nouns mean '*einige*', not any means '*keine*'.

We use **some** in **positive statements**:
There's some water in the bucket.
There are some bottles of water on the table.

We use **any** in **questions** and when we **use 'not'**:
Are there any glasses in the cupboard?
There aren't any glasses in the cupboard.

But we use **some** (not any) when we **offer** something or **ask** for things:
Would you like some coffee?
Can you lend me some money?

We use **somebody/someone/anybody/anyone** for people we don't know:
There's somebody at the door.
Does anybody mind if I open the door?

We use **something/anything** for a thing we don't know:
He has got something in his eye.
I wasn't thirsty, so I didn't drink anything.

We use **somewhere/anywhere** for a place:
He lives somewhere in Ireland.
Justin is standing because there isn't anywhere to sit.

Instead of 'not anybody' we can use 'nobody', 'not anything' = 'nothing', 'not anywhere' = nowhere'

6. **Give examples for positive statements, negative statements and questions. Use some/any/-body/-thing/-where. Don't forget offers and requests.**

VOCAB

to look after aufpassen	**faceplate** Abdeckung
socket Steckdose	**request** Bitte

10.3

➔ TO DO

- Give an opinion
- Agree and disagree

Alcohol

In the evening Lucy, Justin and Sebastian take Chris to the Reeperbahn. They have just left St. Pauli underground station and are walking across Spielbudenplatz. After a few minutes they see this sign.

Chris: What about this sign? I saw it already at the underground station. Although most of the symbols are quite clear, what does the symbol below the knife mean? And the bottle? Is drinking not allowed here? I thought the Reeperbahn is the entertainment district of Hamburg. What do the words below the symbols mean?

1. **Answer Chris' questions and explain the symbols and words of the sign to him.**

52

Chris: Does that mean you are allowed to drink alcohol in public on weekdays? In Canada and the USA it's forbidden to drink alcohol on the streets, in parks, in public buildings, on public transport and in vehicles. In some states you're allowed to put bottles into bags and to drink out of the **bag**.

Sebi: We can drink beer on the streets. Let's go to a kiosk or corner shop to get one.

Chris: Don't you have to go to a **liquor store**?

Sebi: No, we don't have to. In Germany you can also get spirits in supermarkets and at petrol stations.

Chris: Probably you don't have to be 21, as in Canada, to get alcohol.

Sebi: That's true. You can buy beer and wine when you're 16, but you must be 18 to buy spirits.

Chris: What about drinking and driving?

Sebi: The legal blood alcohol limit in Germany is 0.5 mg per mil, that's **equivalent** to one small beer. If you're involved in an accident the blood alcohol limit is 0.3 per mil.

Chris: At home in Canada it's a crime for any driver to drive with a BAC (blood alcohol content - concentration) of 0.08 % and above. When you drink you don't drive and the other way round.

Sebi: Look at this. There's another sign with "Flaschenverbot". What does it mean?

2. **Answer Chris' question and explain the sign.**

PHRASES	Expressing opinions
Giving your opinion In my opinion, ... From my point of view ... As far as I know ... I think/believe/suppose ... I am sure/certain/**convinced** that ... I am not sure/certain, but ... In my experience ... As far as I understand/can see, ...	**Outlining facts** The fact/point is that ... This proves that ... It is obvious/certain/clear that ... There is no **doubt** that ...
Agreement There are many reasons for ... I simply must agree with that. I am of the same opinion. I completely/absolutely agree with ...	**Disagreement** I very much doubt whether ... What is even worse, ... I am of a different opinion because ... I cannot **share** this view. I cannot agree with this idea.

3. **What do you think of the alcohol regulations and laws in Germany and the USA/ Canada? Discuss in class.**
Use the expressions above to give your opinion and to agree or disagree.

Think of:
- drinking in public
- drinking and driving
- sale of alcohol (place)
- **purchase** of alcohol (age)

4. **Think about these statements and discuss in class.**
Use the expressions above to give your opinion and to agree or disagree.

a) Bayern München is the best football team in Germany.
b) Men should earn more money than women.
c) Nuclear power is safe and clean.
d) Everybody should be entitled to vote. Parents vote for children under 16.
e) Cigarettes are too cheap.
f) Everybody should do two hours of community service a week.
g) Religion is the **opium** of the people.
h) A **minimum wage** of 10 Euros should be set for every job.
i) DSDS is the best TV show ever.
j) There is too much sport on TV.
k) The EURO is safe.
l) The length of training should depend on the graduation from school.
m) Job centres should choose and **assign** jobs and trainings.
n) Students should get more homework.

VOCAB

bag Tüte **liquor store** Spirituosengeschäft **equivalent** entsprechend **convinced** überzeugt	**doubt** Zweifel **to share** teilen **purchase** Kauf	**opium** Opium **minimum wage** Mindestlohn **to assign** zuweisen

Ban of weapons

The next day Justin and Chris search the internet for the ban of bottles on the Reeperbahn. This is what they found.

Since 11 December 2007 weapons have been banned from the Reeperbahn area in Hamburg. This resulted in an increase in the use of broken glass bottles in fights (128 times in 2008).
From Friday evening to Monday morning between 10pm and 6am nobody is allowed to walk along the Reeperbahn with a bottle in his hand any longer. This refers to all kinds of glass bottles, even bottles for milk or juice. However, it is allowed to carry bottles in bags or backpacks. Pubs and restaurants are allowed to serve bottles at their outside tables. **Violation** of this law can be **fined** with up to 60 Euros, in the event of a **recurrence** a 5,000 Euro fine is possible. The sale of bottles is punished with a fine of 5,000 Euros.

5. Think about these regulations: Can violence be stopped by banning glass bottles?

a) Work in groups and make notes with pros and cons.
b) Discuss in class using the phrases of express an opinion and agreeing or disagreeing.

While searching the internet Justin found the following text about youth violence in Great Britain.

Every day youth violence in Great Britain is in the news. The streets of Great Britain seem to be full of violent teenagers. **Stabbings**, fights and anti-social behaviour seem to be everywhere. In Great Britain, 16 % of the children say they've been beaten or kicked on the streets – and 7 % report they've been attacked with a weapon. 60 % say they've witnessed violence between young people. Knife murders of teenagers by other teenagers have become common place on the streets of some cities. In London 26 teenagers were killed through stabbings in 2008.
Sociologists say the British youth spend far less of their free time with their families than other European teenagers. They also spend most of their evenings with their friends rather than being at home. Other European young people spend far more time under **supervision**. Alcoholism is also a big problem. Kids are starting to drink earlier and they drink more frequently. Drinking gives them an excuse to behave in ways that they normally wouldn't if they were **sober**.

6. Violence seems to be a problem in Great Britain and other countries as well. Work in groups and make notes to prepare a discussion in class.

a) Why is there all this violence among the youth of today?
b) Do you think a ban of weapons and bottles will reduce or stop violence?
c) What can be done to reduce violence?

Next weekend there is going to be a clubhouse party. The young people want to celebrate the end of the renovation and the reopening of the big hall. To avoid trouble with authorities and to prevent injuries to visitors and damage to the renovated rooms, Sebastian and Justin want to discuss safety rules for the party.

Sebi: The other day I was with Lucy, Justin and Chris on the Reeperbahn. Guns, knives, baseball bats, tear gas and glass bottles aren't allowed there.

Anna: Oh! Can't I bring my tear gas with me?

Hakan: What for? Do you want to use it during the party? Everybody will have to leave the room if you use it inside the big hall.

Anna: No, of course not. I carry it for self-defence just in case I **am molested** on my way home.

Victor: Well, I'm not sure about that. What about glass bottles? Don't we sell beer, water, coke and juice in bottles?

Olga: We can sell drinks in plastic mugs. If someone drops a mug, there won't be pieces of glass all over the floor.

Justin: I prefer to drink beer out of a glass bottle or a glass mug. We haven't talked about smoking yet.

Patrick: Everybody can go outside to smoke a cigarette.

Lucy: I don't like it when the room is full of smoke. It makes my eyes **sting**. Otherwise it will spoil the party if lots of visitors are permanently outside just to smoke.

Sebi: Is our youth club a private or a public place? If it is public we don't need to discuss this anymore.

Chris: Is there an age limit for admission?

Mr Mende: We have to **distinguish** between teens under sixteen and under eighteen.

Chris: There is an age limit for drinking alcohol as well, isn't there?

Mr Mende: Yes, that's true. Although most rules and regulations are quite clear, we should have an information placard at the entrances to make the clubhouse rules clear and visible.

7. **Work in groups of three or four. Design an information placard for the youth club. Use signs and words. You should use *must/mustn't/need*. Give statements about the words in red in the text above.**

Code of behaviour	
	You mustn't bring guns.
	You must smoke outside.

VOCAB

violation Zuwiderhandlung	**to punish** bestrafen	**to be molest** belästigt werden
to fine mit einer Geldstrafe belegen	**stabbing** Messerstecherei	**to sting** brennen
recurrence Wiederholung	**supervision** Aufsicht	**to distinguish** unterscheiden
	sober nüchtern	**code of behaviour** Verhaltensregeln

10.4

TO DO

- Plan a party
- Talk about music
- Discuss own past and future

The night of the party

The clubhouse party is underway and everything seems to be running smoothly. Obviously, the friends have thought of everything that is important to have a great party.

1. Now it's over to you: You have been asked to organize a school party. Together with a partner brainstorm what is needed to have a great party. Draw a concept map with party as your key word. Some headings you could use are: food, security, lighting, music, safety, etc.
Also think about the theme of your party. Do you have a special theme as for example, karaoke, Halloween, carneval etc.

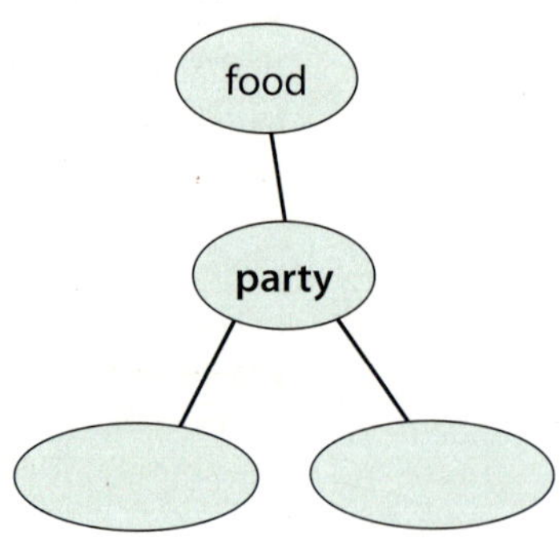

The friends enter the room and Chris looks across at the stage and shouts:

Chris: Hey Justin, look there's a karaoke machine. Are you having a karaoke competition tonight?

Justin: Yes, we thought it would be great to get the party going. We sometimes go to the Karaoke Bar over on the Kietz as it's a lot of fun.

Lucy: Yeah! Justin is the best singer we've heard in a long time.

Chris: Of course, you also play the guitar. I had forgotten about that.

Sebi: Come on, Justin. Why don't you announce that the karaoke competition is starting.

Justin: Okay. I think we should start it now. There are so many people here and I'm sure that there will be enough **volunteers**.

Justin gets up on the stage and taps on the mike and says:
"Good evening **guys** and **dolls**. All of us here at 'ESCAPE' thank you for coming to our party and we hope you'll have a great time. As you can see, we have a karaoke machine here and we are looking for volunteers to come up on stage and show us what a star you are. Who would like to start?"

In the background the friends, who worked so hard for the party, start to chant:
Justin! Justin! Justin! Let's hear what you can do!

Did you know that karaoke originates from Japan? The Japanese enjoy parties and these always become livelier when people start singing. It doesn't matter whether the person can sing well or not. The main thing is to sing and have fun. Karaoke is also a popular form of entertainment for Japanese business men. After work they drop into a bar, have a drink with their colleagues and sing popular songs. A Japanese 'after work party' kind of entertainment.
Karaoke was **invented** about 20 years ago and is now firmly established in many countries throughout the world.

2. **Discuss in class.**

a) What is a karaoke machine?
b) Which country does it come from?
c) What so you think of karakoke? Give reasons.

VOCAB

spread Auswahl	**concept map** Übersichtsplan	**mike** Mikrophon
do oneself proud stolz auf sich sein	**volunteer** Freiwilliger	**guy** Kerl
Put a cork in it! Halt die Klappe!	**habit** Gewohnheit	**doll** Puppe,
underway im Gange	**Singstar** Name eines Karaokespiels	**to chant** rhythmisch rufen
obviously offensichtlich	**to tap** klopfen	**to invent** erfinden

10. Big Hall

It's 10.30 in the evening and the party is going full swing when all of a sudden the lights go out!

Suddenly the lights go on again and there in the middle of the dance floor is Hakan and a group of his friends all dressed the same. Everybody is surprised when the music begins and Hakan and his team start to dance. Hakan, dancing?!
Wow! What a show they put on. Hip hop, break, funk, street, locking, R&B, krump, you name it and they danced it. The audience applauded and cheered them on wanting more and more. Hakan was the star of the show.

3.

53

Listen to Hakan telling his clubhouse friends about his dancing.
Draw a timeline and fill in the important stages of his dancing career so far.
You can draw the line horizontally or vertically whichever way you prefer.
Write the dates and the event next to each point.

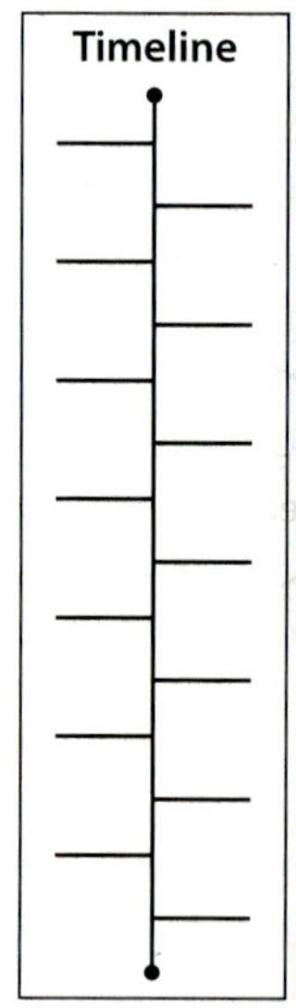

4.

What about you?

a) Are you a good dancer, singer, footballer, or anything else? Draw a timeline of your life from your birth date until today and then add another 5 years.
b) Write the dates and events in your life that you don't mind talking about. Write keywords next to the dates and then exchange your timeline with a partner and ask each other questions about the dates and events marked on your timelines.
How long have you lived in Germany?
When did you come to Germany?
What did you do in 1990?

It's way past midnight and the friends and Mr Mende are busy packing up for the night. The party was a huge success. Everybody enjoyed it tremendously. All safety and security precautions worked well. There was no fight – everybody behaved. The Karaoke was a winner and Justin was the hit, especially for Laura, who would now surely become a regular visitor to The Clubhouse and to the Time's home. Chris thinks that Justin and Lucy are very lucky to have found such good friends in their new hometown. Mr Mende is also really satisfied with all the clubhouse members. Patrick is looking forward to his stay in Manchester and his friends are already planning their visit to him.
The leave the clubhouse, Mr Mende switches off the lights and they all go home. There is only one more job they have to do – clean the clubhouse tomorrow.

5. **Read the above text once more and together with a partner identify and write down all the different tenses used in the paragraph and explain why the tenses are used.**
The first sentence has been done for you.

- is = The simple present is used to tell the time.
  What's the time, please? It is half past two. I must go home.
- are packing up = The present continuous is used because it is happening at the time of speaking, now, at this moment.

It's very late when Justin, Lucy and Chris get home.

Justin: I'm so pleased you're here, Chris and I don't have to write you an email. I'm just so tired.
Chris: Yeah, so am I but perhaps we can write my blog tomorrow for my family to tell them all about the party.
Justin: Good idea! Tomorrow is a good idea!

6. **Write an entry for your own blog about your last party:**
What was it like? What did you eat? What music was played there? …

VOCAB

go full swing voll im Gange sein	**to encourage** ermutigen	**tremendous** gewaltig, riesengroß
all of a sudden plötzlich	**to perform** auftreten	**precaution** Vorsichtsmaßnahme
audience Zuschauer	**don't mind** nichts ausmachen	**to behave** sich benehmen
to cheer jubeln, anfeuern	**to pack up** zusammenpacken	**satisfied** zufrieden
		to be pleased erfreut, zufrieden sein

Grammar

Grammar Time with Lucy and Justin

Lucy and Justin want to help their friends at the clubhouse learn the English grammar rules. Join them and find out all about English grammar. It really is easy.

Grammar

1.	Simple present	166	7.	Word order	176
2.	Simple past	168	8.	Prepositions of time	177
3.	Present continuous	170	9.	Prepositions of place and directions	179
4.	Future	172	10.	Adjectives and adverbs	181
5.	Present perfect	174	11.	Modal verbs	183
6.	Asking questions	176	12.	Conditional clauses (if-clauses)	183

Justin, do you remember the rhyme we learnt at school about time?

Sure do! It went like this:

The past is history
The future is mystery
Now is a gift and that's why

It's called the present

That's right and the different times are different colours:

The past is red.
The present is blue.
The future is green.

This was helpful to remember how to use the different tenses correctly.

1. Simple present

Let's begin with the **simple present** because it is used to talk about facts, habits and routines.
Here is an example:
My name is Justin Time and I live in Hamburg. I am an apprentice joiner. I go to school twice a week, every Tuesday and Friday. I go to work and school by bus. My hobbies are ice hockey, music and hanging out with my friends at our clubhouse.
I have a sister, Lucy, who is a pest. My father works in Hamburg but my mother doesn't work. She is a housewife. We don't have any pets. My best friend, Chris, lives in Canada.

These are all facts about my family and me. They are true at the time of talking. This is called the simple present.

That's right! But we must remember that he, she and it must add an '**s**' to the verb.

- Patrick plays soccer and reads Harry Potter books.
- Olga works in the garden and she loves it.
- The cat catches mice.

Simple present	
I play	We play
You play	You play
He She plays It	They play

We use the simple present to talk about:
General truths:
It snows in Germany in winter.
Timetables:
My train **always** leaves at 6.30 in the morning.
Habits and routines (things we do again and again): I go to work by train. I **don't** smoke.

Remember: We use the verb 'do' to form the negative and for questions.

Negations	
I don't play soccer	We don't play soccer
You don't play soccer	You don't play soccer
He She doesn't play soccer It	They don't play soccer

Questions

Do you play soccer?
Does he play soccer?
Do they play soccer?

Do you live in Paris?
No, I **don't**. I live in Hamburg.

Does Sebi play tennis?
No, he **doesn't**.

One more thing:
When we add 's' to the verb we have to be careful. So watch out!

If the verb ends in **s**, **z**, **ch** or **sh** always add 'es'.
kiss – kisses, wash – washes, touch – touches

If the verb ends in a **consonant** + **y**, the **y** changes to **i**.
dry – dries, cry – cries

2. Simple past

It's Wednesday evening and Lucy, Sebi and Justin are watching a talent show on TV.

This is a laugh, isn't it? They can't sing but think they can.

That guy *has been* on the show last year.

You mean 'That guy **was** on the show last year.' Sebi.

Do I? Why?

Because you're talking about the past. When we use words like yesterday, last week, last year we need to use the simple past tense.

Yeah, I've got problems using the past tense in German because in German you say:
Ich habe ihn gestern gesehen.
Shouldn't it be:
Ich sah ihn gestern, Sebi?

No, we don't really use that form anymore.

So that's why a lot of Germans don't use the simple past tense correctly. They think it's the same as in German.

Yeah, and in English there is a special past tense form for some verbs and these are called **irregular verbs.**
An example is **see** – **saw**.

The other verbs are called **regular verbs.**
They all form the past tense by adding – **ed**.
An example of this is **walk** – **walked**.

But how do I know which are regular and irregular verbs?

I'm afraid you have to learn them, Sebi. No way around that!

We always use the simple past to talk about events that were completed in the past. The simple past is a bit like a photograph album. You look at the photos and remember:
On my 18th birthday we threw a fantastic party. I celebrated together with Chris and we invited fifty friends. We hired a hall near our house and we decorated it.
We chose the theme of *American Pie*. It was hilarious because our friends came dressed as the characters in the movies and we danced to the soundtracks of the movies. We chose that theme because we always watched the movies together.

Remember: We use the verb **did** to form the negative and for questions. Like this:
Did you enjoy the party?
Yes, I did.

Did Chris go with you to the airport?
No, he didn't.

Why didn't he go with you to the airport?
He didn't go with me because he had to work.

Keywords used to indicate the past:
yesterday I went to the building site yesterday.
last week/month/year Last year we lived in Canada.
a week/two days ago I saw the movie Avatar two days ago.

Regular verbs		**Irregular verbs**	
celebrate	celebrate + d	be	was/were
dance	dance + d	break	broke
decorate	decorate + d	choose	chose
enjoy	enjoy + ed	come	came
hire	hire + d	drink	drunk
invite	invite + d	eat	ate
try	tri + ed*	go	went
watch	watch + ed	throw	threw

*If a word ends in a consonant + 'y
then the 'y' changes to an **i + ed**.
try – tried, dry – dried
(See page 184 for a list of irregular verbs.)

3. Present continuous

Justin: Hey Lucy, that was Sebi. I'm off to see a building site with him.

Lucy: Oh, I thought you were giving him a grammar lesson.

Justin: Oh, that's because he always mixes up the present simple and the present continuous.

Lucy: Yeah, I know. So does Olga. I wonder why?

Justin: I found that when I speak German, I have to use the word 'gerade' to indicate that I'm doing something 'at the moment' or 'now'.

Lucy: It's so much easier in English, isn't it? I mean, we're discussing it and we don't have to use the word 'now'. When we use the 'ing' form it's clear.

Justin: Yeah, we're renovating the clubhouse and everybody's doing their share of the work. Mr Mende is organizing all the orders.

Lucy: That's right, but we are not doing it right at this very moment and I think that some of our friends find that a bit difficult to understand. How can we explain it to them?

Justin: Well, I'm reading the book, *The Absolutely True Diary of a Part-Time-Indian*, at the moment. But Lucy, can you see the book in my hand?

Lucy: No.

Justin: So that means we use the present continuous tense to talk about something that we are doing at the moment, which started in the past and ends in the near future. It is only a **limited period of time.**

Lucy: Yeah, like our clubhouse! We started renovating two months ago and it'll be finished for the party in July. So that's why we say: We are renovating the clubhouse. If it were our job to renovate clubhouses, then we would say: We renovate clubhouses because it is routine, right?

Justin: That's it! That's how we have to explain it to the others. I'll practise on Sebi at the building site, but I must rush now as he is waiting for me.

Lucy: That's right. Sebi's waiting for you. Well done Justin! Good use of the present continuous.

At the building site Justin and Sebi are talking to the site manager. Justin has a lot of questions which Sebi has to answer.

Justin: Why are they removing the roof tiles?
Why are they painting the house green?
How many roofers are working on the roof?
What is the site manager doing in the cellar?
Why is that plasterer not helping his colleague?
Why are you looking at me like that?

Sebi: Why are you asking me so many questions?

Justin: Well done, Sebi. You did it!

Sebi: What?

Justin: You used the present continuous tense correctly. Now I'll treat you to a coke.

Be careful: These verbs are not used in the continuous form:

- Verbs of state (= Zustand), ownership (= Besitz), belonging (= Zugehörigkeit): be, have (got), belong to, need, cost, own
- agree, imagine, know, promise, realize, wonder, remember, believe, understand, think (meinen, nicht denken)
- like, love, prefer, hate, want, wish
- see, hear, feel, smell, taste

I ~~am understanding~~ you. X
I understand you. √

Attention!
Sometimes these verbs can have another meaning, then it is possible to use the present continuous form.
Justin is seeing Laura at the party. Here "seeing" means "meeting".

You are stupid. That's how you are.
You are being stupid. That's how you're behaving.

4. Future

Later in the day ...

Justin: Thanks Sebi. That was an interesting afternoon. Where are we meeting this evening?

Sebi: What? Why do you say: Where are we meeting this evening? Justin, you're confusing me!

Justin: No sweat, Sebi. We also use this tense to talk about the planned future. It's okay to use it as long as you add a future word to it like, tomorrow, this evening, next week/month/year and so on.

Sebi: That's cool. So I just add on a future word and it becomes the future tense. That's easy: We're having a clubhouse warming party in July. Chris is coming to the party from Canada.
Thanks Justin. You're a great teacher. Wish you were our English teacher at school.

Remember these key words:
Present continuous: now, at the moment
Planned future: tomorrow, this afternoon/evening, next year

When Mr Time helped Patrick, they talked about Patrick's plans for the future. Patrick also had some questions for Mr Time.

Patrick: Mr Time, why don't you always use 'going to' when you speak about future plans?

Mr Time: Patrick, that's because we English speakers have different ways of talking about our future plans and intentions.
For example: You are flying to Manchester in July. Is that correct?

Patrick: Yes, I will fly to Manchester in July.

Mr Time: Good. We have used two forms of the future tense: are flying + in July
Here we use the present continuous to talk about your future arrangements and these are fixed by dates or appointments in the future. They are fixed plans. You already have your ticket and you know you are flying with Ryanair.

Patrick: So does that mean I can't say: I will fly to Manchester in July?

Mr Time: We usually use 'will' if it's a spontaneous decision.

Patrick: What do you mean by spontaneous?

Mr Time: You don't plan it, you simply decide at the time of speaking. Do you have a credit card, Patrick?

Patrick: No, I don't.

Mr Time: I suggest you get one. It's good to have access to money if you need it.

Patrick: Good idea. I'll go to the bank tomorrow. Hey! I just used 'will'.

Mr Time: Good. Did you plan to go to the bank tomorrow?

Patrick: No!

Mr Time: When did you decide to go to the bank tomorrow?

Patrick: Right now.

Mr Time: Spontaneous decision. Well done, Patrick. And what are you going to do at the bank?

Patrick: Apply for a credit card?

Mr Time: Correct! And that is your intention and we use 'going to' to talk about our intentions.

Patrick: Okay! So when I'm in Manchester I'm going to practise my English every day. I'm going to go to a Manu game. I'm going to work hard. I'm going to enjoy every minute I'm there.

This is how we talk about the future:
We use 'going to'
- to talk about things we want to do in the future, our intentions.
  I'm going to work hard.
- to predict something based on physical evidence.
  It's going to rain.

We use 'will'
- when it's a spontaneous decision.
  I'll go to the bank tomorrow.
- when we talk about our opinions using words like: think, hope, perhaps, maybe, possibly, probably.
  I think it'll rain, so I'll take my umbrella with me.

We use am/is/are … ing
- to talk about fixed arrangements.
  I'm flying to Manchester in July.

We use simple present
- when we talk about timetables.
  The plane leaves at 15.30. (It always leaves at that time; it is a fixed timetable.)

4. Present perfect

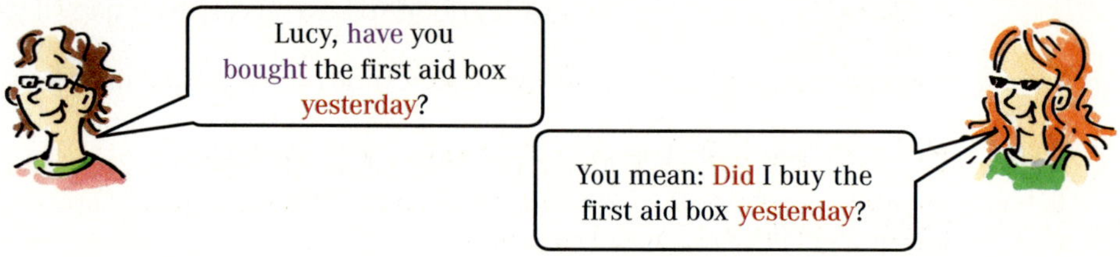

Olga: Do I? I don't understand. In German we say: Hast Du den Erste-Hilfe-Kasten gestern gekauft?

Lucy: I know, Olga. In German there's no difference between "Ich habe gekauft." and "Ich kaufte." but in English we use this tense, the present perfect, to link a situation in the past to the present.

Olga: Sorry, I don't understand.

Lucy: Well, when I say: Did you buy the first aid kit yesterday. Then the action is completed and finished. Yesterday is over and you use the past tense.

Olga: Okay, but if it wasn't yesterday?

Lucy: If you don't use yesterday, then you can say: Have you bought the first aid kit? You are really only interested in the fact and not the time. It means: Have you bought it up to now.
Remember, yesterday is a key word to use the simple past tense.

Olga: Hmmm. Not sure I understand.

Lucy: Let's take another example: Have you seen Viktor today?

Olga: No.

Lucy: Okay, what time is it?

Olga: It's half past three.

Lucy: Right, that means today is not over yet, correct?

Olga: Correct.

Lucy: That means that you still have a chance to see him before you go to sleep tonight.

Olga: Yes.

Lucy: Look, there's Viktor. Hi, Viktor!

Olga: Hi Viktor.

Lucy: Have you seen Viktor today, Olga?

Olga: Yes, I have. But why can't I say "I saw Viktor today."?

Lucy: Because today is not over yet and you might still see him again before you go home.

Olga: But I could say: I saw Viktor a few moments ago.

Lucy: Correct! That moment has past and won't come again. As you know we cannot go back in time.
The present perfect is very useful because we can also use it in another way.
We stress the result of an action and its impact on the present. For example, look at the pictures of Hakan's accident on page 128.

We see Hakan sitting on the floor holding his leg. What has happened?
Here we use the present perfect because the action has just happened and we are interested in the result of the action.

He tripped over the car battery and injured his knee.
Here we simply give facts about what happened.
The actions are completed and are not important at the moment. They are facts in the past.

Hakan has had an accident! Poor Hakan! We must help him.
The action (accident) is more important than when (the time) the action happened.
The result of the action is important for the present and has an impact on the present.

Remember:

I/you/we/they	+	have	+	past participle
he/she/it	+	has	+	past participle
Hakan	+	has	+	hurt his knee.

Key words for the present perfect:

- **already, just, so far, till now, up to now**
  Have you **already** bandaged Hakan's knee?
  Mr Mende has **just** bandaged it.

- **ever** (schon)
  Have you **ever** injured your knee?
  Have you **ever** played football?

- **not yet** (noch nicht)
  I have**n't** seen Hakan's knee **yet**.

- **since** (a point of time), **for** (a period of time)

  I have been an apprentice **since** the 1 August.
  since = der Zeitpunkt, an dem die/der Auszubildende angefangen hat.

  I have been an apprentice **for** 6 months.
  for = der Zeitraum, in dem er/sie schon Auszubildende/r ist.

6. Asking questions

When I came to Hamburg I had to ask a lot of questions because everything was new to me. I was surprised that sometimes the people I spoke to mixed-up the question words '**who**' and '**where**'.
Later I understood the reason. In German we have the word '**wo**', which means '**where**', but seems to be like 'who' which means '**wer**'.
In English we have six question words and here is a quote to help you remember them:

I keep six honest serving-men
(They taught me all I knew);
*Their names are **What** and **Why** and **When***
*And **How** and **Where** and **Who**. …*

what = was	why = warum
when = wann	how = wie
where = wo	who = wer

So typical questions that I asked were:
What's the teacher saying? I don't understand!
Why has the lesson been cancelled? I got up early to be here at 7.45!
When does the lesson end? It's so boring!
How much time is left? I haven't finished my test yet.
Where is the office? I have to hand in my application form.
Who is our teacher? I hope he understands English.

7. Word order

The word order in English is also fairly simple. I think German word order is more difficult. In English the word order always remains the same, even when we ask questions. We simple add some words.

This is how I explained it to Anna the other day:
At school you learnt: Subject + predicate + object + rest of the sentence.

Let's try it a different way:

who/what	+ action	+ what	+ where	+ when
Anna	mows	the lawn	at the clubhouse	on Fridays.

If we want to ask a question in the simple tense then we need our helping verb do/does:

question word	auxiliary verb	who what	action verb	what	where	when
		Anna	mows	the lawn	at the clubhouse	on Fridays.
Where	does	Anna	mow	the lawn		on Fridays?
Answer: at the clubhouse						
When	does	Anna	mow	the lawn	at the clubhouse?	
Answer: on Fridays.						

Here are some more examples:

question word	auxiliary verb	what, who ('wer')	action verb	what, who ('wem')	where	when
What	are	the friends	planning		at the clubhouse	this evening?
Answer: They are planning their party.						
Who	wants to		visit	Justin	in Hamburg	in the summer?
Answer: Chris wants to visit Justin in the summer.						
Who	has	Justin	written	an email to?		
Answer: Justin has written an email to Chris.						

As you can see the word order stays the same, we simply put the question word at the beginning of the sentence.

8. Prepositions of time

Lucy: Have you noticed that our friends sometimes confuse by and until Justin?

Justin: Yeah. I think it's because they both mean the same in German 'bis'.

Lucy: I don't know about that. But how can we help them to see the difference?

Justin: Well, if I have the time from now till 2 o'clock, that means that I have all that time to do something.

Lucy: That's right. Yesterday, our maths teacher told us that we have **until** Friday to do our homework. Today is Tuesday. That means I have Tuesday, Wednesday and Thursday to do my homework.

Justin: Correct!

Lucy: And that means that the deadline is at 8 o'clock on Friday morning. That's when we have maths and that's when our teacher wants the homework. If we give it to him after Friday then we'll get a six.

Justin: Correct. You have to give it to him **by** Friday. That is the latest point of time that you can do your homework. That's the deadline!

now —— **until** ——→ **by (Friday 8 a.m.)**

Lucy: Oh, what a pain. I hate maths!

Justin: Here is some more help with the prepositions of time.

Grammar

Time to look at time

this morning/afternoon/evening — tonight — in the night

two hours/one hour/a few minutes ago — **Now** — in a minute/an hour/two hours

In the Past

last year/month/week evening — the day before yesterday — yesterday morning/afternoon/ four days ago — **Now**

a year ago — a month ago — a week ago — last night

In the future

Now — tomorrow morning/afternoon/ evening/night — the day after tomorrow — next week/month/year

in two days — in a week — in a month — in a year

Time for more time

at 9 o'clock	at 5 o'clock	at twenty-five past five	at twenty to six	time on the clock
at midnight	at Easter	at Halloween	at Christmas	a special time
on my birthday	on Wednesday	on holiday	on 15 August	a day or date
in July	in summer	in 2011		a month/season/year
From 2009 to 2011 I did my apprenticeship.				from time to time
Between 7.30 and 14.30 I will be at school.				between time and time
Mr Mende needs the list by 6 o'clock.		It must be there by Monday.		give a deadline
You can work in the office until five p.m.		We can use it until Sunday.		up to a deadline

Remember:
"**in** the morning/afternoon/evening" BUT "**at** night"

We use "**at** Christmas" if we mean the time around Christmas.
That means the dates 24, 25 and 26 December.
We say "**on** Christmas Day" because it is a special day, only one day.

We use "**at** New Year" when we talk about the days around New Year (31 December and 1 January).
When we say "**on** New Year's Day", then it is the 1 January.

9. Prepositions of place and direction

Here are some explanations to help you describe where something is or how to get somewhere.

above	higher than something else	They hung the picture **above** the armchair.
across	from one side to the other side	The Köhlbrand bridge goes across the Elbe River.
after	one follows the other	Mr Mende ran after the friends to give them some money.
along	from one point to another	They walked along the Elbe River.
among	in a group	Lucy likes being among her friends at the clubhouse.
around	in a circular way	The friends are sitting around the table discussing the party.
behind	at the back of something/someone	Our house is **behind** the clubhouse.
below	lower than something but not directly under it	The batteries are on the shelf below the CDs.
beside	next to	The DIY shop is **beside** the supermarket.
between	something or somebody on each side	The restaurant is **between** the supermarket and the DIY shop.
down	from high to low	Walk **down** the hill to the supermarket.
from	the place where something/someone starts	Justin and Lucy come **from** Canada.
inside	opposite of outside	Mr Mende is **inside** the clubhouse in his office.
into	enter somthing	Let's go **into** the clubhouse for a coke.
near	close to	Our house is **near** the clubhouse.
next to	beside	The supermarket is **next to** the DIY shop.
off	away from something	Lucy took the batteries **off** the shelf.
onto	moving to a place	Lucy put the billard queues **onto** the billard table.
opposite	on the other side	Sebi lives **opposite** Justin and Lucy.
out of	leaving something	The friends walked **out of** the DIY shop into the sunshine.
outside	opposite of inside	The friends are **outside** working in the garden.
over	covering something	They plastered **over** the cracks in the wall.
past	going near something/someone	Go **past** the DIY shop.
round	in a circle	We're sitting **round** the barbecue.
through	going from A to B with things on all sides	Girls shouldn't walk **through** the city alone at night.
to	towards somthing/someone	Laura is going **to** the party.
towards	in the direction of something	Justin ran **towards** arrivals to meet Chris.
under	hidden/covered by something	Your pen is **under** the newspaper.
up	from low to high	The friends walked **up** the hill.

Telling the way

Hakan told Justin about Mr Mende's conversation with the lorry driver. Justin has made some drawings to help Hakan learn how to give directions.

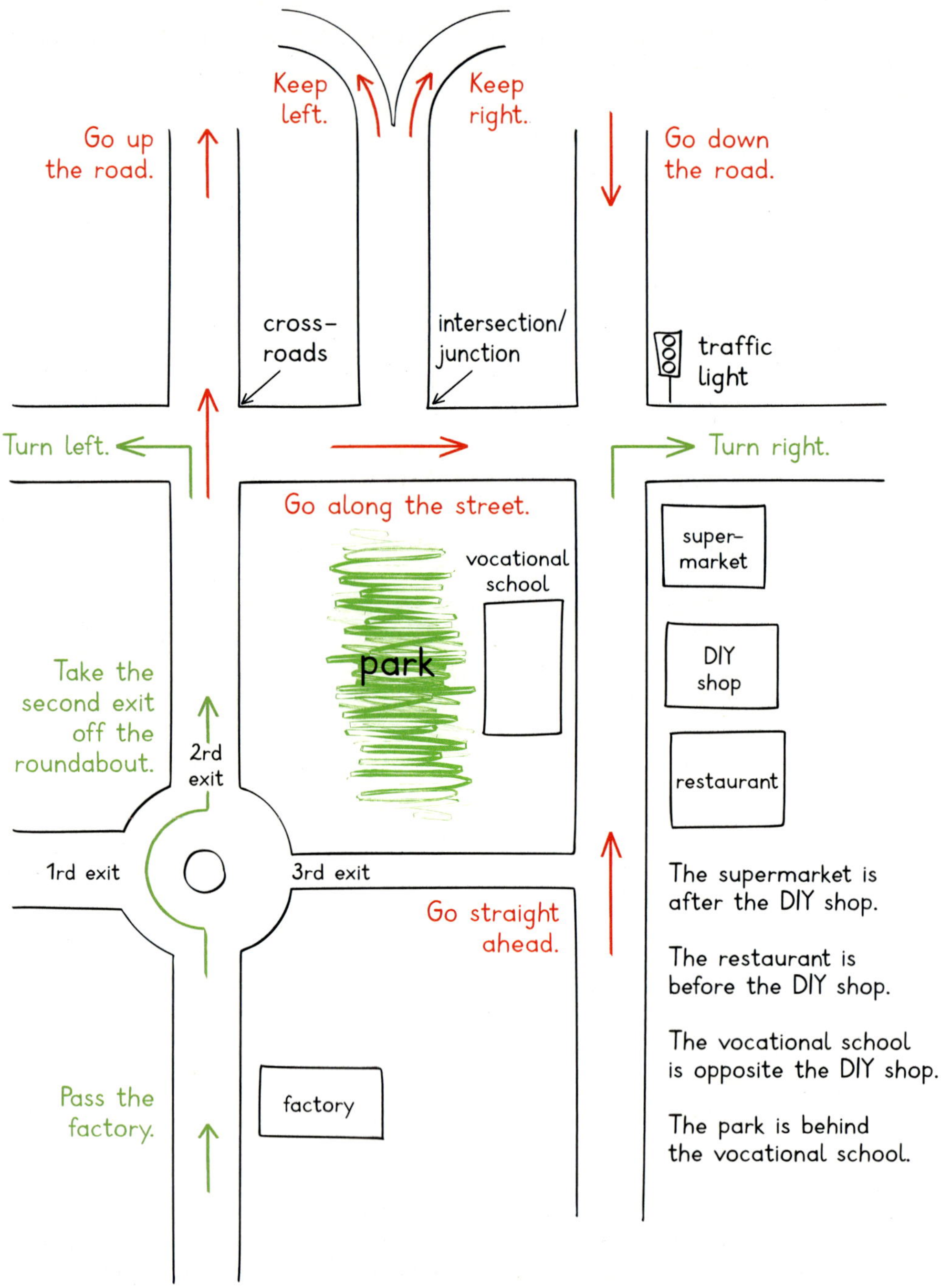

10. Adjectives and adverbs

Lucy, the other day, we were discussing different types of wood in class and Sebi was asking me about adjectives and adverbs. I know how to use them, but I was unsure if I explained them to Sebi correctly. Can you remember all the rules?

Well, an adjective gives you more information about a noun. It modifies a noun. It changes it in some way.

We painted the **room**.
Room is a noun.

We painted the small room.
Small is an adjective because it answers the question '**Which**?'
and gives you more information about the room.

The tough teacher told us our results.
Tough is an adjective because it answers the question '**What kind**?'.

Three apprentices passed the test.
Three is an adjective because it answers the question '**How many**?'.

So you see if you ask these three questions you can always find out which is the adjective.

Adverbs are a little different. They usually end in -ly, don't they?
I speak English fluently but I speak German badly.
Adverbs describe how something is done, they describe a verb.
I work carefully and I'm a careful worker.

Yes, but remember that there are some exceptions!

I work hard = I'm not lazy, I really work.
As you can see hard doesn't end in -ly.
Hardly means not very much (= kaum).
So if I hardly work then I don't do much work. So we have to be careful!

Patrick is a good driver. He drives well.
Hakan is a fast driver. He drives fast.

Remember:
Sometimes adjectives can also end in -ly.
Look at these two sentences:
1. Sebi goes for his **daily** jog at 6 o'clock in the evening.
2. Sebi runs through the park **daily**.

In number 1 **daily** is an adjective because it answers the question '**Which jog**?'.
In number 2 **daily** is an adverb of time because it tells us **when** he runs.

Grammar

Comparing adjectives and adverbs

It is also possible to compare adjectives and adverbs.
Justin is a **good** English speaker but I'm **better** than him.
In fact, I'm the **best** English speaker in our class.

How do we compare?
I'm **tall** but Justin is taller than me and Patrick is the **tallest**.
Mr Mende is **friendly**. Olga is **friendlier** than Mr Mende, but Hakan is the **friendliest** of us all.

We can add **-er** and **-est** to words of

- one syllable (fat, long, short, big etc.)
  long longer the longest

- two syllables that end in -y (**the y changes to i**)
  (silly, funny, easy, lazy etc.)
  silly sillier the silliest

- two syllable words which end in -er (clever), -le (gentle), -ow (narrow)
  clever cleverer the cleverest
  gentle gentler the gentlest

We use 'more' and 'the most' for words of several syllables
expensive more expensive the most expensive
beautiful more beautiful the most beautiful

Remember:

good	better	best
bad	worse	worst
little	less	least
much many some	more	most

11. Modal verbs

Sometimes, I get really angry when people tell me I **must** do something. Don't they know you need to be careful about using this word? How can a friend tell me I **must** clean the kitchen? I'm not the cleaning lady! They can't order me about!
Justin told me not to get so angry, because they usually mean should when they say must. They don't realize that when we use the word **must** in English, we are giving orders. The German word 'müssen' is not like the English word **must**.
They could say: Lucy, you **should** tidy up the kitchen after you have used it. I know that I'm rather messy and don't always clean up after I have used something, but they can still be polite, can't they? I have made a table to show them how to use these different words. I hope it helps them.

% of obligation										
0	10	20	30	40	50	60	70	80	90	100
	might	may	could	can	should/ ought to	would	need to	want to	have to	must (urgent)

12. Conditional clauses (if-clauses)

We use if-clauses to say that something will happen only if another action happens.
For example: I want to watch football this evening.
It is now 7.50 p.m. and I am at the clubhouse. The football match starts at 8.15 p.m. It takes me 20 minutes to cycle home. That means I should get home by ten past eight. I still have to put my bicycle in the garage and that takes a few minutes. So I have to hurry up in order to be on time for the match.

So there are two possibilities:
- If I hurry up ≙ I will see the beginning of the football match.
- If I take my time ≙ I won't see the beginning of the football match.

So the condition is hurry.
We use this conditional to talk about our plans or predictions in the future.

Conditional 1

if + simple present + will/going to

The modal verbs can also be used in this if-clause:
If I have enough money, I **might** buy a new dress for the party.
If Chris stays longer, we **could** go to Denmark for a week.
If it doesn't rain tonight, we **can** have a barbecue in the clubhouse garden.
If you burn your hand, you **should** cool it immediately.
If you want to drive a car, you **must** know the rules of the road.

Important irregular verbs

infinitive	simple past	past participle	German
awake	awoke	awoken	aufwachen, aufwecken
be	was/were	been	sein
beat	beat	beaten	schlagen
become	became	become	werden (false friend!)
begin	began	begun	beginnen, anfangen
bet*	bet	bet	wetten
bite	bit	bitten	beißen
blow	blew	blown	blasen
break	broke	broken	zerbrechen
bring	brought	brought	herbringen
build	built	built	bauen
burn*	burnt	burnt	brennen
burst	burst	burst	zerplatzen
buy	bought	bought	kaufen
catch	caught	caught	fangen
choose	chose	chosen	wählen
come	came	come	kommen
cost	cost	cost	kosten
cut	cut	cut	schneiden
deal	dealt	dealt	verhandeln, verteilen
dig	dug	dug	graben
do	did	done	tun, machen
draw	drew	drawn	zeichnen
dream*	dreamt	dreamt	träumen
drink	drank	drunk	trinken
drive	drove	driven	ein Fahrzeug führen
eat	ate	eaten	essen
fall	fell	fallen	fallen
feed	fed	fed	füttern
feel	felt	felt	fühlen
fight	fought	fought	kämpfen
find	found	found	finden
fly	flew	flown	fliegen
forget	forgot	forgotten	vergessen
freeze	froze	frozen	frieren
get	got	got, gotten (AE)	bekommen
give	gave	given	geben
go	went	gone	gehen
grow	grew	grown	wachsen
hang	hung	hung	hängen, aufhängen
have	had	had	haben
hear	heard	heard	hören
hide	hid	hidden	verstecken
hit	hit	hit	schlagen, treffen
hold	held	held	halten
hurt	hurt	hurt	verletzen
keep	kept	kept	behalten
know	knew	known	wissen, kennen
lay	laid	laid	legen
lead	led	led	führen, leiten
learn*	learnt	learnt	lernen
leave	left	left	verlassen
lend	lent	lent	verleihen
let	let	let	lassen
lie	lay	lain	liegen

infinitive	simple past	past participle	German
light*	lit	lit	anzünden
lose	lost	lost	verlieren
make	made	made	machen (herstellen)
mean	meant	meant	bedeuten
meet	met	met	treffen
pay	paid	paid	bezahlen
put	put	put	setzen, stellen, legen
read	read	read	lesen (Aussprache!)
ride	rode	ridden	reiten
ring	rang	rung	klingeln, läuten
rise	rose	risen	aufgehen, ansteigen
run	ran	run	rennen
say	said	said	sagen
see	saw	seen	sehen
sell	sold	sold	verkaufen
send	sent	sent	schicken
set	set	set	setzen, stellen, legen
shake	shook	shaken	schütteln
steal	stole	stolen	stehlen
shine	shone	shone	scheinen
shoot	shot	shot	schießen
show*	showed	shown	zeigen
shut	shut	shut	schließen
sing	sang	sung	singen
sink	sank	sunk	sinken, untergehen
sit	sat	sat	sitzen
sleep	slept	slept	schlafen
slide	slid	slid	ausrutschen
speak	spoke	spoken	sprechen
spell*	spelt	spelt	buchstabieren
spend	spent	spent	Geld ausgeben, Zeit verbringen
stand	stood	stood	stehen
stick	stuck	stuck	steckenbleiben
stink	stank	stunk	stinken
swear	swore	sworn	schwören
sweep	swept	swept	kehren
swim	swam	swum	schwimmen
swing	swung	swung	schwingen
take	took	taken	nehmen, (weg)bringen, dauern
teach	taught	taught	lehren, unterrichten
tear	tore	torn	zerreißen
tell	told	told	erzählen, berichten
think	thought	thought	denken
throw	threw	thrown	werfen
understand	understood	understood	verstehen
wake	woke	woken	aufwecken
wear	wore	worn	anhaben, tragen (Kleidung)
weave	wove	woven	weben
win	won	won	gewinnen
write	wrote	written	schreiben

* Diese Verben bilden auch eine regelmäßige Form (mit Endung -ed).

Der Trend zur Standardisierung der unregelmäßigen Verben ist nicht nur im Amerikanischen Englisch, sondern auch im Britischen Englisch üblich.

Appendix

	Kardinalzahlen	cardinal numbers
1	eins	one
2	zwei	two
3	drei	three
4	vier	four
5	fünf	five
6	sechs	six
7	sieben	seven
8	acht	eight
9	neun	nine
10	zehn	ten
11	elf	eleven
12	zwölf	twelve
13	dreizehn	thirteen
14	vierzehn	fourteen
15	fünfzehn	fifteen
16	sechzehn	sixteen
17	siebzehn	seventeen
18	achtzehn	eighteen
19	neunzehn	nineteen
20	zwanzig	twenty
21	einundzwanzig	twenty-one
22	zweiundzwanzig	twenty-two
23	dreiundzwanzig	twenty-three
24	vierundzwanzig	twenty-four
25	fünfundzwanzig	twenty-five
26	sechsundzwanzig	twenty-six
27	siebenundzwanzig	twenty-seven
28	achtundzwanzig	twenty-eight
29	neunundzwanzig	twenty-nine
30	dreißig	thirty
31	einunddreißig	thirty-one
40	vierzig	forty
41	einundvierzig	forty-one
50	fünfzig	fifty
60	sechzig	sixty
70	siebzig	seventy
80	achtzig	eighty
90	neunzig	ninety
100	hundert	one hundred
101	hundert(und)eins	one hundred and one
200	zweihundert	two hundred

	Kardinalzahlen	cardinal numbers
1.000 1,000	eintausend	one thousand
2.000 2,000	zweitausend	two thousand
10.000 10,000	zehntausend	ten thousand
100.000 100,000	hunderttausend	one hundred thousand
1.000.000 1,000,000	Million	one million
1.000.000.000 1,000,000,000	Milliarde	one billion

	Ordinalzahlen	ordinal numbers
1./1st	erste	first
2./2nd	zweite	second
3./3rd	dritte	third
4./4th	vierte	fourth
5./5th	fünfte	fifth
6./6th	sechste	sixth
7./7th	siebente	seventh
8./8th	achte	eighth
9./9th	neunte	ninth
10./10th	zehnte	tenth
11./11th	elfte	eleventh
12./12th	zwölfte	twelfth
13./13th	dreizehnte	thirteenth
14./14th	vierzehnte	fourteenth
15./15th	fünfzehnte	fifteenth
16./16th	sechzehnte	sixteenth
17./17th	siebzehnte	seventeenth
18./18th	achtzehnte	eighteenth
19./19th	neunzehnte	nineteenth
20./20th	zwanzigste	twentieth
21./21st	einundzwanzigste	twenty-first
22./22nd	zweiundzwanzigste	twenty-second
30./30th	dreißigste	thirtieth
31./31st	einunddreißigste	thirty-first
40./40th	vierzigste	fortieth
50./50th	fünzigste	fiftieth
60./60th	sechzigste	sixtieth
70./70th	siebzigste	seventieth
80./80th	achtzigste	eightieth
90./90th	neunzigste	ninetieth
100./100th	hundertste	one hundredth

Appendix

	Währung	currency
1 EUR (€) ≙ 1,3/1.3 USD ($)	Ein Euro entspricht etwa eins Komma vier US Dollar.	One Euro is equivalent to one point four US dollars.
1 USD ($) ≙ 0,8/0.8 EUR	Ein US Dollar entspricht etwa null Komma sieben Euro.	One US dollar is equivalent to nought point seven of a Euro.
1 EUR ≙ 0,8/0.8 GBP (£)	Ein Euro entspricht etwa null Komma neun britisches Pfund.	One Euro is equivalent to nought point nine of a British pound.
1 GBP (£) ≙ 1,2/1.2 EUR	Ein britisches Pfund entspricht etwa eins Komma eins Euro.	One British pound is equivalent to one point one Euros.
1 EUR ≙ 1,4/1.4 CAD (C$)	Ein Euro entspricht etwa eins Komma vier kanadische Dollar.	One Euro is equivalent to one point four Canadian dollars.
1 CAD (C$) ≙ 0,7/0.7 EUR	Ein kanadischer Dollar entspricht etwa null Komma sieben Euro.	One Canadian dollar is equivalent to nought point seven of a Euro.
1 EUR ≙ 1,4/1.4 AUD (A$)	Ein Euro entspricht etwa eins Komma fünf australische Dollar.	One Euro is equivalent to one point five Australian dollars.
1 AUD (A$) ≙ 0,7/0.7 EUR	Ein australischer Dollar entspricht etwa null Komma sieben Euro.	One Australian dollar is equivalent to nought point seven of a Euro.

(Stand August 2010)

	Dezimalzahlen	decimals
0,5/0.5	null Komma fünf	nought point five; zero point five
0,012/0.012	null Komma null eins zwei	nought point nought one two; zero point zero one two
2,67/2.67	zwei Komma sechs sieben	two point six seven

Beispiel/example	Mathematische Ausdrücke	mathematical terms
+	plus	plus
-	minus	minus
x	mal	multiplied by/times
:	durch	divided by
=	ist gleich	is equal to/equals
≠	ist nicht gleich	is not equal to/does not equal
≅	ist ungefähr gleich	is approximately equal to
<	ist kleiner als	is less than
>	ist größer als	is more/greater than
≤	ist kleiner oder gleich	is less than or equals
≥	ist größer oder gleich	is more/greater than or equals
%	Prozent	per cent
‰	Promille	per thousand

	Rechenanweisungen	arithmetical instructions
x + y	x plus y	x plus y
5 + 7 = 12	fünf plus sieben ist gleich zwölf	five plus seven is equal to (equals) twelve
x – y	x minus y	x minus y
12 – 7 = 5	zwölf minus sieben ist gleich fünf	twelve minus seven is equal to (equals) five
x x y	x mal y	x multiplied by y; x times y
2 x 4 = 8	zwei mal vier ist gleich acht	two multiplied by four is equal to (equals) eight two times four is equal to (equals)eight twice four is equal to (equals) eight
x/y	x durch y	x divided by y; x over y; x by y
30 : 6 = 5	dreißig geteilt durch sechs ist gleich fünf	thirty divided by six is equal to (equals) five thirty over six is equal to (equals) five thirty by six is equal to (equals)five
3 < 5	drei ist kleiner als fünf	three is less than five
½ > ¼	einhalb ist größer als ein Viertel	one/a half is more/greater than one/a quarter
x ≠ y	x ist nicht gleich y	x is not equal to/does not equal y
π ≅ 3,14/3,14	ist ungefähr gleich drei Komma eins vier	is approximately equal to three point one four

	Brüche	fractions
½	ein halb	one half; a half
1 ½	eineinhalb; anderthalb	one and a half
1/3	ein Drittel	one third; a third
¼	ein Viertel	one fourth; a fourth; a quarter
¾	drei Viertel	three fourths; three quarters
1/8	ein Achtel	one eighth; an eighth
3/8	drei Achtel	three eighths
3 ¼	dreieinviertel	three and a quarter
	Mehrfache	multiples
	einmal	once
	zweimal	twice; two times
	zweimal so viel	twice as much
	zweimal so viele	twice as many
	dreimal	three times
	einfach	single
	zweifach	double
	dreifach	triple; threefold
	vierfach	quadruple; fourfold
	fünffach	fivefold
	sechsfach	sixfold
	mehrfach	multiple
∞	unendlich	infinite

Appendix

	Potenzen	powers
x^2	x Quadrat; x hoch 2	x squared; x to the power of 2; x to the power of two
x^3	x hoch drei	x cubed; x to the third; x to the power of three
x^4	x hoch vier	x to the fourth; x to the power of four
x^n	x hoch n	x to the nth; x to the power of n
x^{-n}	x hoch -n	x to the power of minus n
$1/x$	Kehrwert von x	reciprocal value of x
$(x+y)^2$	x plus y in Klammern zum Quadrat	x plus y in parentheses squared; x plus y all squared

	Wurzeln	roots
$\sqrt{}$	Wurzel; Quadratwurzel zweite Wurzel	root square root
$\sqrt{10}$	Wurzel aus zehn	root of 10
$\sqrt[2]{10}$	Quadratwurzel aus zehn zweite Wurzel aus zehn	square root of 10
$\sqrt[3]{10}$	dritte Wurzel aus zehn	cube root of ten; cubic root of ten
$\sqrt[4]{10}$	vierte Wurzel aus zehn	fourth root of ten

	Logarithmen	logarithms
$\log_n$	Logarithmus zur Basis n	logarithm to the basis n
$\log_{10}$; lg	Logarithmus zur Basis zehn; Zehnerlogarithmus; dekadischer Logarithmus	common logarithm
$\log_e$; ln	Logarithmus zur Basis e; natürlicher Logarithmus	natural logarithm
$\log_2$; lb	Logarithmus zur Basis zwei; binärer Logarithmus	logarithm to the basis 2
$4! = 24$	vier Fakultät ist gleich vierundzwanzig	four factorial is equal to (equals) twenty four

	Formeln	formulas
$P = \frac{F \cdot s}{t}$	P gleich F mal s durch t	(capital) P equals (capital) F times (small) s, all over (small) t
$c = \sqrt{a^2 + b^2}$	c gleich Wurzel aus a-Quadrat plus b-Quadrat	(small) c equals square root of (small) a squared plus (small) b squared
$v_c = \frac{d \cdot \pi \cdot n}{1000}$	v c gleich d mal Pi mal n durch 1000	(small) v sub c equals (small) d times pi times (small) n, all over 1000

	Maßstäbe	scales
	maßstabsgerecht	to scale
	Verkleinerung	reduction
	Vergrößerung	enlargement
	nicht maßstäblich	not to scale (NTS)
	ohne Maßstab	no scale
1:1	eins zu eins	full size
1:2	eins zu zwei	half size
1:4	eins zu vier	quarter size
1:5	eins zu fünf	five size
1:10	eins zu zehn	ten size
2:1	zwei zu eins	double size
5:1	fünf zu eins	five times size
10:1	zehn zu eins	ten times size

	Länge	length
1″	2,54 cm	1 inch (1 in)
1′	30,48 cm	1 foot (1 ft)
	91,44 cm	1 yard (1 yd)
	1 km	0.62 miles
	1,609 km	1 mile

	Flächen	square measures
	6,452 cm^2	1 square inch (1 sq in)
	929,03 cm^2	1 square foot (1 sq ft)
	0,836 m^2	1 square yard
	0,405 Hektar	1 acre
	2,59 km^2	1 square mile

	Gewichte	weights
	28,35 g	1 ounce (1 oz)
	454 g	1 pound (1 lb)
	1016,06 kg	1 long ton (1 tn.l.)

	Mechanik	mechanics
	Masse (Tonne, Kilogramm, Gramm)	mass (ton, kilogram, gram)
	Dichte (Gramm je Kubikzentimeter, Kilogramm je Kubikdezimeter)	density (gram per cubic centrimetre, kilogram per cubic decimetre)
	Kraft (Newton)	force (Newton)
	Drehmoment (Newtonmeter)	torque (Newtonmetre)
	Druck (Pascal, Bar)	pressure (Pascal, Bar)
	Energie (Joule)	energy (Joule)
	Leistung (Watt)	power (Watt)

Appendix

	Volumen	measure of capacity (english)
	0,568 l	1 pint (1 pt)
	4,55 l	1 gallon (1 gal)
	159,11 l (für Öl), 163,66 l (für Bier)	1 barrel (1 bl) = (35 gallons)

temperature (Kelvin)	Temperatur (Celsius,°C)	temperature (Fahrenheit, °F)
0	– 273	– 460
255	– 17,8	0
273	0	32
283	10	50
293	20	68
303	30	86
311	37,8	100
373	100	212

	Zeit	time
	Sekunde	second
	Minute	minute
	Stunde	hour
	Tag	day
	Woche	week
	Jahr	year

	Geschwindigkeit (Kilometer pro Stunde, km/h)	speed (miles per hour, mph)
	1 km/h	0.62 mph
	1,61 km/h	1 mph
	Frequenz	frequency
	Beschleunigung	acceleration

Abk./abbr.	Tage	days
Mo/Mon	Montag	Monday
Di/Tues	Dienstag	Tuesday
Mi/Weds	Mittwoch	Wednesday
Do/Thurs	Donnerstag	Thursday
Fr/Fri	Freitag	Friday
Sa/Sat	Samstag; Sonnabend	Saturday
So/Sun	Sonntag	Sunday

Abk./abbr.	Monate	months
Jan/Jan	Januar	January
Feb/Feb	Februar	February
Mar/Mar	März	March
Apr/Apr	April	April
– / –	Mai	May
Jun/ –	Juni	June
Jul/ –	Juli	July
Aug/Aug	August	August
Sep/Sept	September	September
Okt/Oct	Oktober	October
Nov/Nov	November	November
Dez/Dec	Dezember	December

	Datum	date
6. Oktober 20010 (D) 6 October 2010 (GB) October 6, 2010 (USA)	sechster Oktober zweitausendundzehn	the sixth of October two thousand and ten October the sixth two thousand and ten
04.08.2011 (D) 4/8/2011 (GB) 4-8-2011 (GB)	vierter achter zweitausendundelf	the fourth of August, two thousand and eleven the fourth of August, two thousand and eleven
04.08.2012 (D) 8/4/2012 (USA) 8-4-2012 (USA)	vierter achter zweitausendundzwölf	August the fourth two thousand and twelve August the fourth two thousand and twelve

Buchstabiertabelle		Britisch English phonetic alphabet
A Anton	Alfa	Alfred
B Berta	Bravo	Benjamin
C Cäsar	Charlie	Charles
D Dora	Delta	David
E Emil	Echo	Edward
F Friedrich	Foxtrot	Frederick
G Gustav	Golf	George
H Heinrich	Hotel	Harry
I Ida	India	Isaac
J Julius	Juliett	Jack
K Kaufmann	Kilo	King
L Ludwig	Lima	London
M Martha	Mike	Mary
N Nordpol	November	Nellie
O Otto	Oscar	Oliver
P Paula	Papa	Peter
Q Quelle	Quebec	Queen
R Richard	Romeo	Robert
S Samuel	Sierra	Samuel
T Theodor	Tango	Tommy
U Ulrich	Uniform	Uncle
V Viktor	Victor	Victor
W Wilhelm	Whisky	William
X Xantippe	X-Ray	X-ray
Y Ypsilon	Yankee	Yellow
Z Zacharias	Zulu	Zebra

Wordlist English/German

A

4-stroke engine Vier-Takt-Motor
abbreviation Abkürzung
ability Fähigkeit
abroad im Ausland
access Zugang
accident Unfall
accidentally zufällig, versehentlich
according to entsprechend
accordingly dementsprechend
acre Morgen (Flächenmaß)
actor/actress Schauspieler/in
actually tatsächlich, eigentlich
ad(vertisement) Anzeige
to adapt angleichen
to add hinzufügen
additional zusätzlich
adhesive klebend, Klebstoff
to administer first aid Erste Hilfe leisten
adult Erwachsener
advantage Vorteil
advertising campaign Werbekampagne
advice Rat
to afford sich leisten
agree zustimmen
agreement Zustimmung
ahead vorwärts
ailment Leiden
aisle Gang
aligned ausgerichtet
alignment Ausrichtung
almond Mandel
alongside neben
already schon, bereits
although obwohl
amazing erstaunlich
among unter
to anchor verankern
angle Winkel
ankle Knöchel
annual ring Jahresring
anxiety Angst, Sorge
apart auseinander
appearance Erscheinen
appendix Anhang
applicant Bewerber/in
to apply auftragen
to apply for sich bewerben um
appointment Termin
apprentice Auszubildende/r
apprenticeship Ausbildung
appropriate passend
approval Zustimmung
apron Schürze
armpit Achselhöhle
to arrange gestalten, vereinbaren
to assemble zusammenbauen
to assign zuweisen
assistance Unterstützung
to assume annehmen
to attach befestigen, anhängen
attempt Versuch
attitude Einstellung
to attract anziehen
audience Publikum, Zuschauer
auxiliary verb Hilfsverb
available verfügbar
to avoid vermeiden
awkward hier: ungünstig

B

to back rückwärts fahren
back Rücken
bacon Schinkenspeck
bag Tasche, Tüte
baggage Gepäck
baggage claim area Gepäckausgabe
to bake backen
bar Stange
barbecue area Grillplatz
bargain Schnäppchen
bark Borke
barrel Fass
baseboard Fußleiste
basket Korb
beam Träger
beef Rindfleisch
to behave sich benehmen
behaviour Verhalten
bell Glocke
belly (US) Bauch
belt Gürtel
bench Bank
to bend biegen, beugen
benefit Vorteil
berry Beere
bicycle tube Fahrradschlauch
birch Birke
birth Geburt
black comedy schwarzer Humor
blade Rasenmähermesser, Sägeblatt
to block verstopfen
board Brett
to boil kochen
bold fett
bolt Schraube
bookshelf Bücherregal
boot 1. Kofferraum 2. Stiefel
to borrow leihen
bottom Hintern
bow saw Bogensäge
bracket hier: Befestigungsarm
brake Bremse
brake test rig Bremsenprüfstand
branch 1. Ast, Zweig 2. Geschäftszweig
bricklayer Maurer/in
brief knapp
bright hell
to brighten aufhellen
broccoli Brokkoli
broomstick Besenstiel
brush Pinsel, Bürste
to brush bürsten
bucket Eimer
to buckle up anschnallen
to buff aufrauen
to build in einbauen
building site Baustelle
building under construction Neubau
bulb Glühlampe
bumper Stoßstange
burglar Einbrecher
burglar bars Fenstergitter
burglar-proofing Einbruchsicherung
burglary Einbruch
burial chamber Grabkammer
burl wood Wurzelholz
busy beschäftigt

C

to calculate berechnen
calculation Berechnung
to calm down sich beruhigen
can Dose
capital (city) Hauptstadt
capital (letter) Großbuchstabe
capped verschlossen, abgedeckt
to capture einfangen
car hoist/lift Hebebühne
car jack Wagenheber
car mechanic Kfz-Mechatroniker/in
carburettor Vergaser
cardboard Pappe
to care sich kümmern
caretaker Hausmeister/in
carousel Laufband
carpenter Zimmerer/in
carpet Teppich
to carry tragen
to carry out durchführen
carton Karton
cash machine Geldautomat
casters Laufrollen
to cause verursachen
caustic ätzend
ceiling (Zimmer-) Decke

to celebrate feiern
central heating Zentralheizung
certain bestimmt, sicher
certainly sicherlich
chain saw Kettensäge
to challenge herausfordern
change Veränderung
to chant hier: rhythmisch rufen
cheek Wange
to cheer jubeln
cheerful fröhlich
cherry Kirsche
chest Brust
chicken Huhn, Hähnchen
chimney Schornstein
chin Kinn
chives Schnittlauch
choice Wahl
to chop zerhacken
to chop down fällen
citizen Bürger/in
civil engineer Bauingenieur/in
clamp Schelle
to clean up aufräumen
clear übersichtlich
client hier: Bauherr/in
cloth Tuch
clue Hinweis
clutch Kupplung
collar Kragen
colleague Kollege/Kollegin
colloquial umgangssprachlich
to colour färben
to comb kämmen
combination pliers Kombizange
combustion engine Verbrennungsmotor
to come a cropper Schiffbruch erleiden
comfortable bequem
commitment Engagement
common gebräuchlich
community service Zivildienst
competition Wettbewerb
to complete something etwas vervollständigen
complimentary close Grußformel
concentric konzentrisch
concept map Übersichtsplan
conclusion Abschluss, Schlussfolgerung
concrete Beton
to conduct leiten
conductive leitend
confident selbstsicher
confused verwirrt
conifer Konifere
conracting authority öffentliche/r Auftraggeber/in
constitution Verfassung
construction work Bauleistung
to contain enthalten
container Behälter
contamination Verunreinigung
content Inhalt
to contribute beitragen
convince überzeugen
convinced überzeugt
cooker Herd
coping stone Abdeckstein
copper Kupfer
core Kern
corner Ecke
corresponding zugehörig
cotton Baumwolle
to cough husten
cough mixture Hustensaft
countable zählbar
counter Tresen
couple Paar
coupling sleeve Schiebemuffe
courtyard Hof
covering letter Bewerbungsschreiben
coward Feigling
to crack knacken
crate Kiste
to creak knarren
to crease verknittern
to crop up passieren
crowded voll
crumb Krümel
to crumble bröckeln
cucumber Gurke
curb Bordstein
curiosity Neugier
current aktuell
curriculum vitae Lebenslauf
curtain Vorhang
curved hier: gebogen
customer Kunde/Kundin
to cut down fällen, zurückschneiden
cut resistant schnittfest
cut retardant schnitthemmend
cutter knife Cuttermesser
CV Lebenslauf

D

damp feucht
dashboard Armaturenbrett
to deal with umgehen mit
debris Bauschutt
to deburr entgraten
decayed verfault
to deduct abziehen
deep tief
delicious lecker
to deliver liefern
delivery Lieferung
to demand verlangen
dent Beule, Delle
department Abteilung
to depend on abhängen von
depth Tiefe
to describe beschreiben
desk Schreibtisch
despite trotz
dessert Nachtisch
detached alleinstehend
to develop entwickeln
device Gerät, Vorrichtung
diet Ernährung
to differ unterscheiden
to differentiate unterscheiden
difficult schwierig
to dig ausheben
dilapidated heruntergekommen
dimension Dimension
to dip tauchen
dipstick Ölmessstab
to disassemble ausbauen
disaster Katastrophe
to disconnect abtrennen
discount Preisnachlass
disgusted angeekelt
dishwasher Geschirrspülmaschine
disk Bandscheibe
to dispatch abschicken
disposal Beseitigung, Entsorgung
to distinguish unterscheiden
to divide teilen
doll Puppe
dot Punkt
doubt Zweifel
drain Abfluss, Rohr
draughtsperson Bauzeichner
to draw to scale maßstabsgerecht zeichnen
to dredge ausbaggern
to drive in einschlagen
driveway Auffahrt
driving licence Führerschein
due fällig
duration Dauer
during während
duty Pflicht
to be on duty Dienst haben

Wordlist English/German

E

ear Ohr
to ease out hier: ausgleichen
edge Rand
educational bildend
elbow Ellenbogen
embarrassed verlegen
emergency Notfall
to employ einstellen
employer Arbeitgeber/in
enclosed anliegend
enclosure Anlage
to encourage ermutigen
engaged besetzt (Telefon)
engine analyser Motortester
to enquire sich erkundigen
enquiry Anfrage, Auskunft
to enslave versklaven
to ensure sicherstellen
enthusiastically mit Begeisterung
entire ganz
entrance Eingang
environment Umwelt
equipment Ausstattung
equivalent entsprechend
escape hier: Zuflucht
to escape flüchten
escape route Fluchtweg
especially besonders
event Ereignis
evidence Hinweis, Spur
example Beispiel
excess Überschuss
to execute ausführen
exhaust Auspuff
exhausting anstrengend
to experience erfahren
experience Erfahrung
to explain erklären
exposed aggregate concrete Waschbeton
expression Ausdruck
to extend erweitern
extension 1. Anbau 2. Durchwahl (Telefon)
extension pole Teleskopstange
eye level Augenhöhe
eyebrow Augenbraue
eyelash Wimper

F

faceplate Abdeckung
to faint ohnmächtig werden
yours faithfully hochachtungsvoll
false falsch
fashion magazine Modezeitschrift
fatality Todesopfer
fault Fehler
favourite Lieblings …
to fell fällen
felt pads Filzscheiben
to fetch holen
fight Kampf, Streit
file Feile
filler spout Einfüllöffnung
filling knife Spachtel
finally schließlich
fine Geldstrafe
fire fighter Feuerwehrmann/-frau
fire-brigade Feuerwehr
firmly fest
first aid kit Erste-Hilfe-Kasten
fish pond Fischteich
to fit together anpassen
to fix befestigen, reparieren
fixture Armatur
flu Grippe
to be flush bündig sein
to fold falten
fold Falte
folding rule Gliedermaßstab
to be fond of mögen
force Kraft
forearm Unterarm
forehead Stirn
foreman Vorarbeiter/in
form Formular
former ehemalig
formular Formel
freight forwarder Spediteur/in
frequently häufig
fridge freezer Kühlschrank mit Gefrierfach
fright Schreck
front door Eingangstür
to frown runzeln
to fry braten
fuel Treibstoff
fume Abgas
furniture Möbel

G

gap Lücke
gap year ein Jahr Auszeit
garage Garage
garbage Abfall
gardener Gärtner/in
to gargle gurgeln
garlic Knoblauch
gate Tor
gauge Messgerät
gazebo Pavillion
German Unity Day Tag der deutschen Einheit
to get stuck steckenbleiben
gherkin Gewürzgurke
ginger Ingwer
girl guide Pfadfinderin
global trade Welthandel
glossy glänzend
goal Ziel
government agency Regierungsbehörde
to grab greifen
grain Maserung
granite Granit
to grasp greifen
grass clippings Rasenschnitt
grass paver Rasengitterstein
grated gerieben
grease Gleitmittel
to grease fetten
grid Gitterrost
griddle pan Grillpfanne
to grieve trauern
to grip greifen
to guess vermuten
guilty schuldig
gutter Dachrinne
guy Kerl
gym Sporthalle

H

habit Gewohnheit
half-round file Halbrundfeile
hallway Flur
to halt blockieren
to handle something hier: etwas umschlagen
harness Gurt
hassle Auseinandersetzung
hatch Luke
hazard Gefährdung
head 1. Leiter/-in 2. Kopf
heading Überschrift
headmaster Schulleiter/in
health care organisation Gesundheitsorganisation
healthy gesund
heartwood Kernholz
hedge Hecke
height Höhe
herbs Kräuter
herring Hering
hip Hüfte
to hire einstellen
honest ehrlich
honour Ehre

hoody Kapuzenpullover
hose Schlauch
housing Gehäuse
to hug umarmen
Human Resources Department Personalabteilung
to hunt jagen
hyphen Bindestrich

I

ID card Personalausweis
illiterate Analphabet, ungebildet
illness Krankheit
image Bild
to imagine something sich etwas vorstellen
immediately sofort
immigration Passkontrolle
immigrations officer Zollbeamte/r
impact-resistance Schlagfestigkeit
impervious undurchlässig
impolite unhöflich
impressive beeinduckend
to improve verbessern
improvement Verbesserung
incident Ereignis
to include einschließen
to indicate anzeigen
infinitive Grundform
ingredients Zutaten
injury Verletzung
to inoculate impfen
inquiry Anfrage, Auskunft
to insert einfügen, einschrauben
to install installieren
instead stattdessen
intention Absicht
intercom system Gegensprechanlage
interior features Innenausstattung
to interrupt unterbrechen
to introduce (a person) vorstellen (eine Person)
introduction Einführung, Vorstellung
intrusion hier: Einbruch
to invent erfinden
to be involved in hier: verwickelt sein
iron Eisen
irregular unregelmäßig
irritable reizbar
item Gegenstand

J

jar Glas
job application Bewerbung
job interview Vorstellungsgespräch
join Naht, Verbindungsstelle
to join sich anschließen
to join together zusammensetzen
joiner Tischler/in
joint Fuge
to jumble up durcheinanderbringen
junk food minderwertige Kost

K

key phrases Schlüsselsätze
kickback Rückschlag
kindness Freundlichkeit
kitchen Küche
knee Knie
knocking-off time Feierabend

L

label Hinweisschild
ladder Leiter
landmark Wahrzeichen
lawn Rasen
lawn mower Rasenmäher
to lay out anlegen
lead Blei
league Liga
to leak lecken
at least mindestens
to leave verlassen
leaf Blatt
leg Bein
lettuce Kopfsalat
level eben, Ebene
to level ausgleichen
lifejacket Rettungsweste
limbs Gliedmaßen
to line auslegen
to link verbinden
lips Lippen
liquor store Spirituosengeschäft
literally buchstäblich
load Ladung
load lifter Lastenheber
local authorities Gemeinde
to lock schließen
lock Schloss
to look after aufpassen
loose locker
lorry Lastkraftwagen
lounge hier: Aufenthaltsraum
loyalty Treue
luggage compartment Kofferraum
lunch Mittagessen
luxurious luxuriös

M

mahogany Mahagoni
main contractor Generalunternehmer/in
to maintain pflegen
maintenance Wartung
mandatory vorgeschrieben
manual 1. Anleitung 2. manuell
maple Ahorn
marble Marmor
marine propeller Schiffsschraube
mark Zensur
to mark (out) markieren
masking tape Abdeckklebeband
meaning Bedeutung
to measure messen
measurement Maß
measuring tape Maßband
medical insurance Krankenversicherung
medium mittlere(r/s)
to meet treffen
member Mitglied
menace Nervensäge
to mend reparieren
to mention erwähnen
message Nachricht
messy unordentlich
metal worker Metallbauer/in
microwave Mikrowelle
mike Mikrophon
to mill mahlen
minimum wage Mindestlohn
mistake Fehler
by mistake versehentlich
mnemonic Eselsbrücke
moisture Feuchtigkeit
to be molested belästigt werden
momentum Schwung
monochrome einfarbig
mood Stimmung
to mop wischen
mouldy schimmlig
mouth Mund
movement Bewegung
to mow mähen
mud Schlamm
muddy matschig
mug Becher
multi-purpose Mehrzweck ...
mustard Senf

N

national Staatsangehörige/r
nauseous übel
navel Nabel

Wordlist English/German

nearly fast
neat ordentlich
neck Hals
neglected vernachlässigt
night shift Nachtschicht
nipple Brustwarze
noble edel
to nod nicken
noun Substantiv
nozzle Zapfventil
nut (Gewinde-)Mutter
nutritious nahrhaft

O

oak Eiche
to obtain erhalten
obviously offensichtlich
to be occupied with beschäftigt sein mit
to occur auftreten
offer Angebot
office Büro
office management assistant Bürokauffrau/-mann
ointment Salbe
onion Zwiebel
opening hours Öffnungszeiten
operator Telefonist/in
opium Opium
opinion Meinung
to order bestellen
to overhaul überholen
to oversleep verschlafen

P

to pace out abschreiten
to pack up zusammenpacken
painful schmerzhaft
painkiller Schmerzmittel
paint roller Farbenroller
painter Maler und Lackierer/in
parquet Parkett
parsley Petersilie
to pass vorbeigehen, -fahren
to pass a test einen Test bestehen
to pass something etwas reichen
passenger compartment Fahrgastkabine
passport Reisepass
paste Kleister
paste table Tapeziertisch
pasting brush Kleisterbürste
patch Flicken
path Weg
patio Terrasse
pattern Muster
pavement Bürgersteig
paving Straßenpflaster
paving stone Pflasterstein
to peel abblättern, schälen
to peer starren
Pentecost Pfingsten
pepper Paprika, Pfeffer
to perform hier: funktionieren
to perform auftreten
perimeter Umfang
permeable durchlässig
permission Genehmigung
petrol can Benzinkanister
phrase Redewendung
to pickle einlegen
pincers Kneifzange
pine Kiefer
pineapple Ananas
pipe Leitung, Rohr
pit Grube
pith Mark
plaice Scholle
plane Hobel
to plane hobeln
plank Brett
to plaster verputzen
pleased zufrieden
plumb lotrecht
plumb bob Senklot
plumber Anlagenmechaniker/in
plywood Sperrholz
to polish den letzten Schliff geben
polite höflich
pollack Seelachs
pond liner Teichfolie
popular beliebt
porch Veranda
pork Schweinefleisch
possible möglich
post 1. Post 2. Pfosten
power tool elektrisches Werkzeug
powerdrill Bohrmaschine
to practise üben
to praise loben
precaution Vorsichtsmaßnahme
precise genau
to prefer bevorzugen
preference Vorliebe
to prepare vorbereiten
pre-processed vorbehandelt
pressure Druck
to prevent verhindern
to process verarbeiten
processing Bearbeitung
procrastination Aufschiebung
prohibited verboten
prohibition Verbot
to promise versprechen
proper passend
properly ordentlich, richtig
property Grundstück
prospective voraussichtlich
protection Schutz
protective clothing Sicherheitskleidung
to protrude überstehen
proud stolz
to prove beweisen
to prune beschneiden
public holiday Feiertag
pumpkin Kürbis
to punish bestrafen
purchase Kauf
purpose Grund
to push drängen, stoßen
putty knife Kittspachtel

Q

quantity Menge
quantity surveyor Kostenplaner
questionnaire Fragebogen
queue Schlange
quick-release mechanism Schnelllösemechanismus
quite ziemlich
quotation marks Anführungsstriche

R

railing Geländer
to raise heben
rash Ausschlag
rather eher
rawl plugs Dübel
ray Strahl
reach erreichen
real estate agency Immobilienmakler/in
to realize merken
to rebound zurückschnellen
to receive erhalten
recently kürzlich
to record aufnehmen
rectangular rechteckig
recurrence Wiederholung
to redecorate renovieren
to refer to sich beziehen auf
reference Empfehlung
to refuse ablehnen
to reject ablehnen
relationship Beziehung
to release herausgeben, lösen

to remain bleiben
remedy Arzneimittel
to remove entfernen, herausschrauben
to replace ersetzen
replacement Ersatz
to request anfordern
request Bitte
to require benötigen, verlangen
requirement 1. Erfordernis
2. Voraussetzung
research Forschung, Recherche
residence Wohnhaus
responsibilty Verantwortung
to restore restaurieren
résumé (US) Lebenslauf
resuscitation Wiederbelebung
return flight Rückflug
reverse umkehren
rewind spring Rückspule
rim Felge
to rinse ausspülen
to roast rösten
rocket Rakete
rod Stange
roll Brötchen
roller tray Farbwanne
to roll over überschlagen
roof Dach
roofer Dachdecker/in
root Wurzel
rotten verfallen
to roughen aufrauen
roughly grob
to rub reiben
rubber Gummi
rubbish Abfall
rule Regel, Vorschrift
rule of thumb Faustregel
run-down heruntergekommen

S

safety engineer
Sicherheitsingenieur/in
salutation Begrüßung
to sand something down
etwas abschmirgeln
sandpaper Schleifpapier
sandpit Sandkasten
sap Saft
sapwood Splintholz
satisfactory befriedigend
satisfied befriedigt
sausage Würstchen
to saw off absägen
to saw up zersägen
scaffolder Gerüstbauer/in
scaffolding Baugerüst
scared ängstlich
on schedule pünktlich, termingerecht
scientifically wissenschaftlich
scientist Wissenschaftler/in
scissors Schere
to score erzielen
to scratch kratzen
screen definition Bildschirmauflösung
screwdriver Schraubendreher
to scrub off abkratzen
seagull Möwe
to seal abdichten
seam Falz
seam roller Nahtroller
search Suche
to seat platzieren
to seep sickern
self-contained abgeschlossen
sense of humour Humor
shabby schäbig
shade Schatten
shallow seicht
shape Form
to share teilen
to sharpen schärfen
shed Schuppen
sheet metal Blech
shipment Transport
shipshape tipptopp
short knapp
short cut Abkürzung
shoulder Schulter
shovel Schaufel
to show off angeben
to shrug zucken
siblings Geschwister
sidewalk Bürgersteig
sight Blick, Sehenswürdigkeit
sign Zeichen
signature Unterschrift
similar ähnlich
sink Spülbecken, Waschbecken
site manager Bauleiter/in
size Größe
skill Können
to skin enthäuten
to skip forward weiterschalten
to slam zuschlagen
slate Schiefer
slippery rutschig
slope Gefälle
to smear schmieren
smoke detectors Rauchmelder
smooth glatt
to sneeze niesen
snug-fitting festsitzend
soapy seifig
sober nüchtern
soccer (US) Fußball
social science Sozialwissenschaften
social studies Gemeinschaftskunde
socket Steckdose
soft weich
soil Boden
solvent Lösemittel
soothing beruhigend
sore throat Halsschmerzen
source Quelle
spade Spaten
spanner Schraubenschlüssel
spare parts Ersatzteile
spare wheel Ersatzrad
spark plug Zündkerze
sparkling sprudelnd
speciality Besonderheit
specification Beschreibung
to specify genau angeben
to spell buchstabieren
spice Gewürz
spicy gewürzt
spine Rückgrat
spiral staircase Wendeltreppe
spirit level Wasserwaage
splinter Splitter
to split spalten
sponge Schwamm
spooky gruselig
spot Fleck
spread Auswahl
spring anchor point Federverankerung
spruce Fichte
to squeak quietschen
to squirt spritzen
stabbing Messerstecherei
stack Stapel
to stack stapeln
to state angeben
state-of-the-art modern
steady stabil
steel toe cap Stahlkappe
step Stufe
step ladder Trittleiter
stereotype Klischee
to sting brennen, stechen
to stir rühren
stomach Bauch
storey Stock
straight gerade
straight on geradeaus
strain Belastung
stranger Fremde/r
strength Stärke
strength training Krafttraining